CAN ETHICS PROVIDE ANSWERS?

Studies in Social, Political, and Legal Philosophy

General Editor: James P. Sterba, University of Notre Dame

This series analyzes and evaluates critically the major political, social, and legal ideals, institutions, and practices of our time. The analysis may be historical or problem-centered; the evaluation may focus on theoretical underpinnings or practical implications. Among the recent titles in the series are:

Moral Rights and Political Freedom
  by Tara Smith, University of Texas at Austin
Democracy and Social Injustice
  by Thomas Simon, Illinois State University
Morality and Social Justice: Point/Counterpoint
  by James P. Sterba, University of Notre Dame; Tibor Machan, Auburn University; Alison Jaggar, University of Colorado, Boulder; William Galston, White House Domestic Policy Council; Carol C. Gould, Stevens Institute of Technology; Milton Fisk, Indiana University; and Robert C. Solomon, University of Texas
Faces of Environmental Racism: Confronting Issues of Global Justice
  edited by Laura Westra, University of Windsor, and Peter S. Wenz, Sangamon State University
Plato Rediscovered: Human Value and Social Order
  by T. K. Seung, University of Texas at Austin
Punishment as Societal-Defense
  by Phillip Montague, Western Washington University
Liberty for the Twenty-First Century: Contemporary Libertarian Thought
  edited by Tibor R. Machan, Auburn University, and Douglas B. Rasmussen, St. John's University
Capitalism with a Human Face: The Quest for a Middle Road in Russian Politics
  by William Gay, University of North Carolina at Charlotte, and T. A. Alekseeva, Institute of Philosophy and Moscow State University
In the Company of Others: Perspectives on Community, Family, and Culture
  edited by Nancy E. Snow, Marquette University
Perfect Equality: John Stuart Mill on Well-Constituted Communities
  by Maria H. Morales, Florida State University
Citizenship in a Fragile World
  by Bernard P. Dauenhauer, University of Georgia
Critical Moral Liberalism: Theory and Practice
  by Jeffrey Reiman, American University
Nature as Subject: Human Obligation and Natural Community
  by Eric Katz, New Jersey Institute of Technology
Can Ethics Provide Answers? And Other Essays in Moral Philosophy
  by James Rachels, University of Alabama at Birmingham

CAN ETHICS PROVIDE ANSWERS?

And Other Essays in Moral Philosophy

James Rachels

ROWMAN & LITTLEFIELD PUBLISHERS, INC.
Lanham • Boulder • New York • London

ROWMAN & LITTLEFIELD PUBLISHERS, INC.

Published in the United States of America
by Rowman & Littlefield Publishers, Inc.
4720 Boston Way, Lanham, Maryland 20706

3 Henrietta Street
London WC2E 8LU, England

British Cataloging in Publication Information Available

Library of Congress Cataloging-in-Publication Data

Rachels, James, 1941–
Can ethics provide answers? : and other essays in moral philosophy
/ James Rachels.
p.   cm. — (Studies in social, political, and legal philosophy)
Includes bibliographical references and index.
1. Ethics.   2. Social ethics.   I. Title.   II. Series.
BJ1012.R289   1997   170—dc20   96–29130   CIP

ISBN 0–8476–8347–8 (cloth : alk. paper)
ISBN 0–8476–8348–6 (pbk. : alk. paper)

Printed in the United States of America

Contents

Preface

"Philosophy recovers itself," said John Dewey, "when it ceases to be a device for dealing with the problems of philosophers and becomes a method, cultivated by philosophers, for dealing with the problems of men."[1] By this standard, moral philosophy made a remarkable recovery starting around 1970. In the mid-1960s, when I was a graduate student, philosophy was understood by its practitioners to be a technical subject that dealt with questions of logical analysis. Moral philosophers discussed such matters as the meaning of ethical language and whether evaluative conclusions could be derived from factual premises, but they studiously avoided questions about how people should live. "Philosophers are not priests or guidance counselors," it was said. Despite Dewey's admonition, delivered in 1917, this was the prevailing orthodoxy for most of the twentieth century.

Looking back on this period, many commentators pronounce it a sterile and unproductive time for philosophical ethics. I do not share that view. Useful advances were made on many fronts, and some issues, such as the relation between moral judgment and the emotions, came to be understood better than ever before. Nonetheless, "the problems of men," as Dewey put it, were notably absent from most philosophical writing. Then, around 1970, a number of things happened, seemingly all at once: Daniel Callahan founded the Hastings Center, which was to become the preeminent think tank for issues in biomedical ethics; the journal *Philosophy and Public Affairs* was launched, with its inaugural issue featuring papers on abortion, war, draft resistance, and social class; and John Rawls's *A Theory of Justice* appeared, a book that would provide a new model for how moral philosophy could be pursued. The field was transformed, and philosophers began to write about virtually every controversial issue of the day. Celebrating the change, it was commonly said that philosophy had "returned to its historic mission" of providing guidance for life. But this comment understated the novelty of what was happening. The new literature in "applied ethics" had no real precedent. One could, of course, find discussions of practical issues in the writings of the great philosophers. But those discussions were mostly scattered and brief, sidelights to more important business. By contrast, in the 1970s philosophers began to produce a torrent of work on such issues. Never had such detailed attention been paid to the philosophical aspects of so many moral problems.[2]

The essays in this book were written starting in 1970, and they deal with a variety of practical matters. But unlike some who work in this area, I do not believe that "applied ethics" can profitably be pursued apart from the concerns of ethical theory. The relation between applied ethics and ethical theory is not that one "applies" the theory to the practical issue. Rather, it is that in dealing with practical problems, one encounters all sorts of theoretical issues that must be addressed before one can make progress. Richard Hare has said that it was his desire to solve practical problems that first got him interested in philosophy; for me it was the reverse—I was attracted to the study of practical issues because they involve such intriguing philosophical questions. The controversy over euthanasia, for example, involves such theoretical questions as: What is a human life, and why does it have such value? Does a person's life have any objective value, apart from the value it has for us? How far should a person's autonomy extend? Is there an important moral difference between acts and omissions? Is a person's intention relevant to assessing the rightness of an action? And thinking about the controversy over animal rights requires us to examine perhaps the deepest assumption in all of ethics—that promoting *human* interests is the point of the whole moral scheme.

But there is a larger subject that each of these essays addresses in its own way, namely, the nature of ethics and ethical reasoning. We want to know, most fundamentally, what ethics is and whether ethical questions can be answered by rational methods; and if so, what those methods are. Here it is especially important to consider theoretical and practical issues side by side. The practical discussions provide data about how ethical reasoning actually works. It is no good to say, in your theoretical discussion, that ethical reasoning has such-and-such character, if in your practical discussions you engage in reasoning that isn't like that at all. Thus the essays include a large number of practical examples that are of interest not only for their own sakes but also for what they reveal about the nature of ethical thinking.

I did not, in the beginning, set out to champion any large-scale ethical theory. I believed, instead, that each issue could be addressed on its own terms, using whatever intellectual resources were handy. But over the years, I noticed that my conclusions always seemed congenial to utilitarianism. When I wrote about famine relief, I concluded that we have an extensive duty to use our resources to help those in need; when I wrote about euthanasia, I concluded that it is justified to put an end to suffering; and when I wrote about animals, I ended up agreeing with Bentham that their suffering counts equally with our own. I even defended one of util-itariansm's most scandalous implications, that our duty to our own chil-dren is not fundamentally different from our duty to all children. In the meantime, however, my considered opinion about utilitarianism was that it is false because it cannot account for our duty to treat people according to their individual deserts.

Why balk at this, you might ask, after having swallowed so much else? Now I believe I was probably wrong to insist on an independent princi-ple of desert. While I was revising chapter 12 for this collection, I was especially concerned to get clear *why* it is important to treat people as they deserve. I had always believed the answer would be nonutilitarian in character. But as it turned out, the answer—to simplify matters greatly— is that people are better off under a system of norms that acknowledges desert than they would be under a system that does not. The justification for acknowledging deserts, like so many other moral justifications, turns out to be just the sort we would expect utilitarianism to provide. So per-haps I should stop correcting people who remark that these essays are the work of a utilitarian. Instead, perhaps I should say that they record my progress toward that view. Utilitarianism is the position I seem to have ended up with, as the result of thinking about a lot of different issues, even though I never aimed at any such destination.

Notes

1. John Dewey, "The Need for a Recovery of Philosophy," in *John Dewey: The Middle Works, 1899–1924*, vol. 10, ed. Jo Ann Boydston (Carbondale and Edwardsville: Southern Illinois University Press, 1980), 46.

2. In 1969 I set out to edit a book (*Moral Problems* [New York: Harper & Row, 1971]) that would bring together previously published essays by contemporary philosophers on practical issues. Although I collected everything I could find, it wasn't enough to fill the book, and I had to include some essays that were only marginally concerned with practical issues and some by nonphilosophers. On abortion, for example, philosophers had written almost nothing. (Two topics were exceptions: there was a lot of writing about criminal punishment, because it was a test case for utilitarianism; and a number of articles about civil disobedience had been inspired by the civil rights movement. But I couldn't fill the book with essays about just those topics.) Happily, Sara Ruddick helped by writing a splendid new piece for the book, in the process becoming one of the first philosophers to write about sex. By the mid-1970s there were many books like *Moral Problems*, and edi-tors could choose from among hundreds of suitable essays. Such books have been staples of undergraduate ethics instruction ever since.

Acknowledgments

The essays in this collection appeared in earlier forms in various books and journals. None of them is reprinted in precisely its original form. Every writer, looking back at previously published work, sees things he wishes he could change. I have happily made some of those changes.

1. "Moral Philosophy as a Subversive Activity" first appeared in *Applied Ethics: A Reader*, edited by Earl Winkler and Jerrold R. Coombs (Oxford: Blackwell, 1993), 110–30. Reprinted by permission.

2. "Can Ethics Provide Answers?" is a substantially revised version of a paper that appeared in the *Hastings Center Report* (June 1980): 32–40. Reproduced by permission. © The Hastings Center.

3. "John Dewey and the Truth about Ethics" is from *New Studies in the Philosophy of John Dewey*, edited by Steven M. Cahn (Hanover, N.H.: University Press of New England, 1977), 149–71. Reprinted by permission.

4. "Active and Passive Euthanasia" was originally published in the *New England Journal of Medicine* 292 (1975), 78–80. © 1975 Massachusetts Medical Society. Reprinted by permission.

5. "Killing, Letting Die, and the Value of Life" appeared, in Italian translation, in *Bioethica: Revista Interdisciplinare* 2 (1993): 271–83. Reprinted by permission.

6. "Do Animals Have Rights?" incorporates parts of two previously published papers: "Do Animals Have a Right to Liberty?" in *Animal Rights and Human Obligations*, edited by Peter Singer and Tom Regan (Englewood Cliffs, N.J.: Prentice-Hall, 1976), 205–23; and "Do Animals Have a Right to Life?" in *Ethics and Animals*, edited by Harlan B. Miller and William H. Williams (Clifton, N.J.: Humana Press, 1983) 275–84. Reprinted by permission.

7. "The Moral Argument for Vegetarianism" incorporates parts of "Vegetarianism and 'The Other Weight Problem,'" in *World Hunger and Moral Obligation*, edited by William Aiken and Hugh LaFollette (Englewood Cliffs, N.J.: Prentice-Hall, 1977) 180–93; and "Do Animals Have a Right to Life?" Reprinted by permission.

8. "God and Moral Autonomy" appeared under the title "God and Human Attitudes" in *Religious Studies* 7 (1971): 325–37. Reprinted with the permission of Cambridge University Press.

9. "Lying and the Ethics of Absolute Rules" is a revised version of "On Moral Absolutism," *Australasian Journal of Philosophy* 48 (1970): 338–53. Reprinted by permission.

10. "Why Privacy Is Important" appeared in *Philosophy and Public Affairs* 4 (1975): 323–33. Reprinted by permission.

11. "Reflections on the Idea of Equality" is from *On the Track of Reason: Essays in Honor of Kai Nielsen*, edited by Rodger Beehler, David Copp, and Bela Szabados (Boulder, Colo.: Westview Press, 1991), 1–18. Reprinted by permission.

12. "What People Deserve" first appeared in *Justice and Economic Distribution*, edited by John Arthur and William H. Shaw (Englewood Cliffs, N.J.: Prentice-Hall, 1978), 150–63. Reprinted by permission. However, the version that appears here has been so extensively revised and expanded that it is virtually a new paper.

13. "Coping with Prejudice" is an expanded version of an argument from "Prejudice and Equal Treatment," in *Ethical Issues in Contemporary Society*, edited by John Howie and George Schedler (Carbondale: Southern Illinois University Press, 1995), 54–77. Reprinted by permission.

14. "Morality, Parents, and Children" is from *Person to Person*, edited by George Graham and Hugh LaFollette (Philadelphia: Temple University Press, 1989), 46–62. Reprinted by permission.

15. "When Philosophers Shoot from the Hip" appeared in *Bioethics* 5 (1991): 67–71, but it was originally the concluding section of "Moral Philosophy as a Subversive Activity."

1

Moral Philosophy as a Subversive Activity

Pyrrho, an uncommonly adventurous philosopher of the third century B.C., accompanied the army of Alexander the Great to India, where he and his teacher Anaxarchus became the first Western thinkers to encounter the philosophers of the East. We are told by Diogenes that Pyrrho met with the Indian Gymnosophists (literally, the "naked sophists") and from them he learned "a most noble philosophy," taking the form of agnosticism not only about the gods but about all matters whatsoever. Pyrrho soon came to believe that we cannot know anything at all. In ethics, he said, we cannot know anything because there is nothing to know. He held that "Nothing was honorable or dishonorable, just or unjust. And so, universally, he held that there is nothing really existent, but custom and convention govern human action; for no single thing is any more this than that."[1]

If this is indeed what Pyrrho learned from the Gymnosophists, it fit well with ideas that were already flourishing in Athens, where skeptical teachers in the Academy that had been founded by Plato were advancing the very un-Platonic doctrine that no proposition can ever be known for certain. Anaxarchus, in fact, was one of those who accepted this view. Diogenes tells us that Anaxarchus "used to declare that he knew nothing, not even the fact that he knew nothing."[2] Later skeptics were to transform this into the doctrine that for every argument that can be given in favor of any assertion, an equally good argument can be given for its opposite. Therefore, they concluded, the wise man will suspend judgment about everything and believe nothing. Pyrrho was to become so closely identified with this view that it would be known to later generations simply as "Pyrrhonism."

Such a philosophy has its charms, but it also seems to have preposterous implications. Can it be taken seriously? Suppose you are standing in the highway and there appears to be a truck coming in your direction. Your first impulse might be to run. But if Pyrrhonism is true, you can never have any better reason to believe there is a truck coming than to believe there is no truck coming. Moreover, you can have no good reason to believe it is better to go on living than to die. So why should you move? Why not just stand there and see what happens?

Surely, one might think, Pyrrho could not have meant *that*. That sounds like the sort of unfair parody that has always been used to discredit radical thinkers. But according to Diogenes, it is exactly what Pyrrho intended: "Pyrrho led a life consistent with his Skepticism, going out of his way for nothing, taking no precaution, but facing all risks as they came, whether carts, precipices, dogs or what not, and generally, leaving nothing to the judgment of the senses. But he was kept out of harm's way by his friends who used to follow close after him."[3] One story is that Pyrrho came upon Anaxarchus stuck in a ditch. Unable to think of any good reason to rescue him, Pyrrho did not. Another passerby pulled the old man from the ditch and castigated Pyrrho for his heartlessness. The teacher, however, commended the student for having learned his lesson well.

Pyrrho's skepticism was epistemological; it was a view about the limits of what we can know. The primary recommendation of his philosophy, however, was ethical. The suspension of judgment about matters of truth and falsity, about good and evil, was said to lead to a state of tranquility that is the only secure path to happiness. Pyrrho seems to have been absolutely serious about this, no matter how much one might doubt that leaving old people in ditches and not avoiding carts and precipices lead to happiness.

We do not know whether these stories about Pyrrho's personal behavior are true. They are hard to believe, and in keeping with Pyrrho's own teaching, we might well be skeptical about them. Diogenes records that some ancient authorities also doubted them: "Aenesidemus says that it was only his philosophy that was based upon suspension of judgment, and that [Pyrrho] did not lack foresight in his everyday acts."[4] The truth probably lies somewhere between the two extremes. Pyrrho taught that one should always strive to maintain an attitude of indifference; it would be surprising, however, if anyone, Pyrrho included, could always succeed. "When a cur rushed at him and terrified him," says Diogenes, "he answered his critic that it was not easy to strip oneself of human weakness."[5] This story, more than the others, has the ring of truth.

It is clear, however, that Pyrrho took philosophy seriously in a way that it is not always taken seriously today. He did not believe that one's philosophical thinking should be insulated from one's everyday beliefs and practice. For him, philosophical ideas were not merely notions to be entertained during a theoretical discussion and then forgotten. They were guides to life.

There is something undeniably attractive about this attitude. After all, if philosophy is not to be taken seriously, why bother with it? Pyrrho's seriousness becomes problematic only when it is combined with his skepticism. He thought that even the simplest beliefs of common sense will have to be revised if reasons are found for doubting them—and, he added, there frequently are good reasons to doubt what "common sense" decrees. He even went so far as to declare that there are good philosophical reasons for doubting the reality of space and time; so he concluded that we should not be so sure that we are here now, since "here" and "now" refer to space and time. This in turn meant that we should not act as though we know such things. Hence his reported indifference to carts, dogs, and precipices.

Pyrrho's assumption that what we think and what we do go hand in hand was shared by most thinkers throughout Western history. In the twentieth century, however, we have become accustomed to a different way of understanding philosophical ideas. Today, if a philosopher doubts the reality of space and time, or the legitimacy of our usual ways of talking about space and time, this is taken to be no reason at all for him or her not to apply for a sabbatical next year. Somewhere along the way, we learned to insulate our philosophical thinking from our first-order beliefs, and we even developed theories about the nature of our inquiry to justify this. When did this happen? Who invented insulation? Myles Burnyeat has written a splendid paper about this question in which he argues that Kant did it.[6] But that is not what I want to discuss here. Here I want to discuss insulation as a continuing practice in philosophical thinking about ethics.

Moorean Insulation

Skepticism about the reality of space and time has never attained the status of orthodoxy among philosophers, but it has been a perennial philosophic theme. Its last great advocates were the nineteenth-century idealists. Figures such as G. W. F. Hegel in Germany and F. H. Bradley in England rejected "common sense" about space and time no less emphatically than had Pyrrho. But common sense is not easily dismissed, and when G. E. Moore came to its defense at the beginning of the twentieth century, his arguments soon carried the day.

Moore's argument is familiar to all students of the history of philosophical thought. Faced with skeptical doubts about the reality of time, Moore responded simply: today I had breakfast before I had lunch; therefore, time is real.[7] In its day, this was regarded as a powerful riposte. For a while, to deny common sense came to seem not merely wrong but disreputable. It became fashionable for philosophers to say that simple facts such as this one are far more certain than any convoluted arguments that might be marshaled against them. Today this is no longer so fashionable. Instead, it is commonly said that Moore was naïve to think that the skeptical arguments could be refuted so easily. The philosopher's claims about time, it is now said, are different from the sorts of claims that ordinary people make about breakfast coming before lunch. Therefore, nothing follows from the ordinary judgments about the philosophical issues.

Burnyeat comments that any philosopher who thinks he is not an insulator should consider his reaction to Moore. Moore was not an insulator, for he thought that philosophical claims do have straightforward implications for first-order judgments, and vice versa. Those who consider Moore's argument to be naïve apparently disagree. But Moore was an insulator of a more limited kind. Let me explain by making a distinction between doing philosophy *safely* and doing philosophy *with risk*.[8] Those who do philosophy safely proceed in such a way that their first-order beliefs are never called into doubt. They begin with the assumption that they know a great many (first-order) things to be true, and for them, philosophical thinking involves (only?) a search for principles and theories that would justify and explain what they already know. Those who do philosophy with risk, on the other hand, expose their first-order beliefs to the perils of thought. Everything is up for grabs. Any belief may have to be rejected if reasons are found against it; and one cannot say, in advance, what reasons might turn up for doubting what beliefs.

Those who do philosophy safely are insulators, but for them insulation works in only one direction. Their philosophical views will be tailored to accommodate their first-order beliefs, but the first-order beliefs are themselves held sacrosanct. They are not placed at risk. Moore was an insulator of this qualified sort. An ordinary belief might discredit a theory, but not the other way around. In his honor, if it is an honor, we might call this Moorean Insulation.

Moorean Insulation, when applied to the traditional issues of metaphysics—to questions about space and time, about physical objects, and so forth—is an appealing doctrine. It does seem right to say that we know breakfast comes before lunch; and it is tempting to conclude straightaway, as Moore did, that any philosophical doctrine that says otherwise must be false. But when we turn to moral philosophy, Moorean Insulation loses much of its appeal, because moral "common sense" is less trustworthy. The moral beliefs that are common in our society, and that philosophers perforce share (or at least that they begin by sharing), may be in part the result of sensible thinking. But they may also be the products of historical and psychological processes that have involved superstition, selfishness, false religion, bad science, and bad metaphysics. Moorean Insulation would protect these beliefs from revision. It is, therefore, a profoundly conservative approach, bent on justifying whatever moral views we already happen to have.

Paradoxically, however, it is in moral philosophy that Moorean Insulation continues to be practiced. Metaphysicians, to whose subject it seems most agreeable, have largely rejected it. But in thinking about ethics, where it seems more dubious, it persists.

Moorean Insulation has been associated, throughout twentieth-century moral philosophy, with a certain style of argument—the familiar method of argument by counterexample. A thesis about morality will be advanced, together with arguments in its favor, and this will be met by the claim that the thesis cannot be true because it is contrary to a commonly held moral belief. Act-utilitarianism has been "refuted" a thousand times by this method. "Act-utilitarianism says that we should do whatever will produce the best results. But it might sometimes produce the best results to secure the judicial execution of an innocent person. This is never right. Therefore, act-utilitarianism must be rejected." In philosophical debate one still hears this sort of argument, although the examples given have changed over the years. More recently, examples involving what Bernard Williams calls "personal integrity" have been popular weapons against utilitarianism.[9] Now, however, many philosophers, including Williams, regard this style of reasoning as overly crude and recognize that it must at least be supplemented by a persuasive explanation of why it is always wrong to secure the judicial execution of the innocent, or why personal integrity is so important, or why whatever other example is being used has the significance it allegedly has. Happily, counterexamples alone are no longer considered so decisive as they once were.

Yet the eclipse of this style of argument has not meant the disappearance of Moorean Insulation. Moorean Insulation is also revealed by the extent to which, in constructing one's moral theory, one takes conformity to prereflective belief as a guiding consideration. One of the great virtues of John Rawls's work is that this methodological issue is out in the open.[10] Rawls explicitly endorses the idea of using one's moral intuitions as checkpoints for testing the acceptability of theory. Moral theory, he has said, is like linguistics. Just as a linguistic theory should reflect the competent speaker's sense of grammaticalness, a moral theory should reflect the competent moral judge's sense of rightness. In some places, Rawls backs off from this strong statement and substitutes the idea that one's considered moral judgments should be brought into a "reflective equilibrium" with one's theoretical pronouncements. But the individual judgments still play an important regulative role, and the extent to which cherished moral beliefs are really placed at risk is left somewhat murky.

In Rawls's work this issue is out in the open; elsewhere, however, the issue may not be in the open, and Moorean Insulation may do its work unnoticed. One might, for example, reject utilitarianism and prefer a different sort of theory (one that emphasizes "the virtues," for example) because the latter sort of theory "does a better job of explaining" what is presumed to be our actual moral situation. The underlying conception of our actual moral situation may not be placed at risk. Instead, it may simply be presented in an attractive way that appeals to our prereflective sense of what moral life is like. Then the theorizing proceeds apace, and the developed theory is finally displayed as "explaining" why we should live in just the way we thought all along.

Or, to take a different sort of example, recently there has been a good bit of philosophical writing about the nature of personal relationships, taking it as a datum that we have special responsibilities and obligations to our parents, children, and friends. These are said to be responsibilities and obligations that we do not have to just everybody, but only to specific people in virtue of our specific type of relationship with them. A common move is to take this "fact" as a reason for rejecting any moral theory that seems to imply otherwise and to look instead for a theory that will give these relationships, and the responsibilities they involve, a central place. Frequently it is said that, even if we do not yet have such a theory, this is a necessary condition that any acceptable theory must meet.[11]

This is troubling, and not merely because it involves Moorean Insulation. Like everyone else, I have a deep feeling, which I can't shake, that my responsibilities to my own children are special. If I have to choose between feeding my own children and giving the food to starving orphans, I am going to feed my own. (More than that: faced with a choice between sending my own children to an expensive college and using the money to help feed starving orphans, I send my own to college.) It would be reassuring simply to assume that I am right to feel this way; and as a philosopher I could cast my vote in favor of a moral theory that makes my behavior come out right.

But there are disturbing arguments on the other side. After all, my children were merely lucky to have been born into a relatively affluent family, while the orphans, who have the same needs and are equally deserving, were unlucky to have gotten stuck with their situation. Why should the just distribution of life's goods, right down to food itself, be determined in this way? Why should it be counted as a virtue for a moral theory to allow so much to depend on mere luck? But taking such an argument seriously means placing at risk the prereflective belief in the special importance of family relations. A Moorean Insulationist could, of course, take this argument seriously in a certain sense: it could be taken as something to be seriously refuted. But if one approaches the argument with anything like an open mind, allowing the possibility that there may be something to it, then the prereflective belief—even so fundamental a belief as the belief about the specialness of one's duties to one's own children—is suddenly in jeopardy.[12]

Can Moral Philosophy Be Subversive?

The alternative to Moorean Insulation is an approach that sees moral philosophy as a subversive activity that could, at least potentially, undermine even the most deep-seated assumptions of ordinary morality. The advantages of such an approach are evident. It makes no sense to conduct a search for the truth by assuming from the outset that we already know what the truth is. Moreover, only by rejecting insulation can we avoid incorporating into our theory the prejudices and other irrational elements that infect our prereflective judgments. However, matters are not so simple. Although it is appealing to say that we should abjure Moorean Insulation, getting rid of it may be hard to do.

One reason it might be hard to shake off Moorean Insulation is connected with the idea that in any inquiry we must have some starting point from which our reasoning proceeds. As Hume pointed out, every argument leads back to some first principle that is itself unjustified. If we ask for a justification of that principle, one can perhaps be given, but only by appealing to still another unjustified assumption. We can never justify all our assumptions, not even "in principle." This is a feature not merely of moral reasoning but of reasoning in general. In moral philosophy, though, it means that we must ultimately begin with some conception of what is morally important, which is itself taken for granted. A utilitarian might assume that what is important is maximizing welfare. Someone with a different cast of mind might make a different assumption. But no one can escape reliance on some starting point, which is insulated from challenge by its very place in the scheme of reasoning.

Thus it might seem that we have only two options: either we accept one or more moral principles (our "axioms") as self-evident and derive particular moral judgments from them; or we begin with the set of particular judgments that we find most plausible and work back to the general principles that explain and justify them. If these are our options, then the latter—which is nothing more than Moorean Insulation laid bare—might well be the more appealing.

But the first alternative has had its advocates. Peter Singer, among others, has argued in its favor. Speaking of those who, like Rawls, assume that our considered moral judgments are largely correct, he says:

> Why should we not rather make the opposite assumption, that all the particular moral judgments we intuitively make are likely to derive from discarded religious systems, from warped views of sex and bodily functions, or from customs necessary for the survival of the group in social and economic circumstances that now lie in the distant past? In which case, it would be best to forget all about our particular moral judgments, and start again from as near as we can get to self-evident moral axioms.[13]

This is about as radical a proposal as one could imagine. We are to start with self-evident axioms and then accept the particular judgments that follow from them, no matter how far from ordinary morality those judgments turn out to be. There are a number of fairly obvious objections that might be raised against this.

First, it is no obvious improvement to switch one's allegiance from self-evident judgments to self-evident axioms. Either way, our starting point is taken on faith. Furthermore, what is to prevent our choice of axioms from being influenced by the same irrational forces that warp our particular judgments?

Second, it may be observed that philosophers who have tried to do this have always failed. The utilitarians have come closest to succeeding. Taking the principle of utility as their self-evident starting point, utilitarians have been notably critical of ordinary morality. However, we might ask exactly what is supposed to be so self-evident about the principle of utility. The classic formulation of the principle—that we should act so as to maximize happiness and minimize suffering for all sentient beings—might fairly be described as self-evident. But it has never been self-evident that this is our *only* duty. Moreover, few utilitarians have stuck to the classic principle when confronted with objections. They have instead reformulated their principle in terms of such technical notions as "expected utility" or "overall preference satisfaction," and they have worried about whether it is average or total happiness that should be pursued.

The result is a set of contending principles that may be more philosophically defensible but that are a lot less self-evident. And furthermore, the utilitarianians have revised their basic principle precisely to avoid unwanted implications at the level of particular judgments—so intuitions about particular cases are still playing at least some regulative role.

Third, and finally, Singer's suggestion seems unreasonable on its face. Moral principles tend to be vague and abstract; we hardly know what they mean until we see exactly what particular judgments follow from them. Suppose, for example, we start with an "axiom" that seems self-evident, but then, upon investigating its consequences, we discover that it leads to the conclusion that murder is permissible. If this seems far-fetched, consider the following familiar point. It seems self-evident that we should do whatever will decrease the amount of unhappiness in the world. But we might help to accomplish this by quietly murdering a few chronically unhappy people. Should we then conclude that these murders are justified? Remember that the recommendation is that we accept the consequences of self-evident starting points no matter how contrary to accepted morality those consequences might be—after all, as Singer points out, our prereflective judgments are tainted by all sorts of irrational influences. Plainly, though, when confronted with such implications, reasonable people will conclude that their axioms need to be revised, no matter how attractive those axioms might have seemed before the implications were exposed.

Faced with all this, the conclusion seems unavoidable: if we must begin with principles that are not themselves justified, why not choose those principles that will yield the first-order judgments that we find most plausible? This seems eminently sensible. So embracing Moorean Insulation seems to be the wisest course. We seem to be stuck, then, with the depressing realization that moral philosophy is, in the end, just an elaborate rationalization of what we already want to believe.

Morality and the Web of Belief

Happily, there is a way to avoid this conclusion. The familiar chain of reasoning that I have just recounted depends on assuming that our moral principles and beliefs form an axiomatic system. But we do not have to make that assumption. There is an alternative way of conceiving the subject.

What, exactly, is the relation between our particular moral judgments and the theoretical ideas to which philosophers appeal in discussing them? The higher-order considerations typically invoked form a large and varied group. These include moral "principles" in the usual sense, but they also include other sorts of theoretical ideas. Here is a small sample:

- that pain, frustration, and ignorance are bad

- that friendship, knowledge, and self-esteem are good

- that human life has a special value and importance

- that human interests have a fundamental importance that the interests of other animals do not have

- that people should always to be treated as ends in themselves and never as mere means

- that personal autonomy—the freedom of each individual to control his or her own life—is especially important

- that we have special obligations and responsibilities to our own family and friends

- that there is an important moral difference between causing harm and merely allowing it to happen

- that there is a difference in stringency between our strict duties and other duties that are matters of "mere" charity or generosity

- that a person's intention in performing a given action is relevant to determining whether the action is right

We could think of these as axioms from which conclusions about particular actions are derived. But we need not think of them in that way. Instead we may think of them, together with the multitude of particular judgments we make, as forming part of a network of beliefs that are connected with one another in various ways. Rather than thinking of morality as a deductive system with axioms at the top and particular judgments at the bottom, we may think of it as forming part of what W. V. Quine calls "the web of belief."

The Center of the Web and Its Fringes

Quine originally conceived of this metaphor as a way of expressing his view about the relation between empirical observations, scientific theories, and the laws of logic. He held that none of these, including the laws of logic, are immune from criticism; as new evidence is discovered and new considerations come to light, no element of the web is protected from the possibility that it might have to be revised or even rejected. He realized, of course, that we may be more reluctant to abandon some of our beliefs than others. Let us say that these are near the center of the web, while the beliefs that we hold with less confidence are closer to its outer fringes.[14]

If we think of our moral system as forming part of the web of belief, it is clear that there is no firm correlation between a belief's position on the web—whether it is near the center or on the fringes—on the one hand and its status as a particular moral belief or a general moral principle on the other hand. Some of our moral judgments about particular cases are near the center of the web. We would be extremely reluctant ever to abandon the belief that the murder of Anne Frank was wrong. And some of our general principles are also near the center: for example, that causing pain is wrong.

But there are also both general principles and particular judgments that are nearer the fringes—for example, the particular judgment that Reagan's people should not have swapped arms for hostages is not nearly so certain as the judgment that the Nazis acted wrongly; and the theoretical idea that there is a difference between causing harm and allowing it to happen is not so certain as the principle that causing pain is wrong. It is an important feature of this approach, however, that no belief, theoretical or practical, is absolutely insulated from revision, whatever its position in the web may be at any given time.

How Beliefs Get Moved around in the Web, and How They Are Even Expelled from It

A moral belief or principle can be moved from the center of the web to its fringes, or even be abandoned altogether. Let me mention one moral idea that used to be near the center of our common web but that I think has now been shown to be untenable. For centuries it was part of the orthodoxy of Western thought that mere animals have no moral claim on us. A few isolated thinkers did not share this view, but they were so few that they could be ignored. So throughout history animals have been used as food, as experimental subjects, as sources of leather and wool, and in general have been treated as resources for human use and enjoyment without regard for their own interests. Indeed, to justify these practices, it was sometimes even argued that mere animals have no interests that could be figured into our moral calculations. Within the past two decades, however, this belief has been challenged so effectively by philosophers such as Peter Singer and Tom Regan that it has been rendered virtually untenable.[15] At the very least, one can no longer simply assume, as philosophers did for centuries, that the interests of nonhumans can be ignored.

It is not merely philosophical argument in the narrow sense that has brought about this change. Our moral views are connected, in our overall web of belief, with all sorts of nonmoral considerations. Charles Darwin did as much to bring this particular part of moral orthodoxy into doubt as anyone, by showing that human beings share a common origin, and common characteristics, with the members of other species. A short time ago the presumed "difference" between human life and interests and those of other animals might have been cited as one of those central moral "facts" that could be used to test the acceptability of moral theory, but that is no longer true. Even if this idea still occupies a place in one's web of belief, it has surely been moved much farther toward the periphery, if one has been paying attention to the progress of thought.

Connections between Beliefs in the Web

Some elements in our system of beliefs are connected by logical entailment. Thus we may believe that murder is wrong and that in killing Anne Frank the Nazis committed murder; and so we also believe that what they did was wrong. This much is simple. The relation of logical entailment has been studied closely and is reasonably well understood. Other elements in the system, however, may be connected by logical relations other than strict entailment, and these are less well understood.

In our example—murder is wrong; the Nazis committed murder; so what they did was wrong—the third belief is entailed by the other two. But what about the first belief, that murder is wrong? It may be connected, more generally, with the belief that there is something morally special about human life, so that human life is especially precious and deserving of protection. This belief may be connected in turn with religious beliefs about human origins, but the precise nature of that connection, familiar as it is, may be murky. Or, the belief in human specialness may be connected with nonreligious beliefs about our nature. Humans are rational and possess language, and in general they have psychological capacities superior to those of the members of other species. This somehow sets them apart from other animals and puts them in a privileged moral category. But once again, it may not be so clear exactly how this puts them in a privileged moral category.

Thus, when we look beyond the simple deductive argument about Anne Frank, we find a whole network of beliefs, some moral, some "factual," some religious, and some hard to classify. The logical relations between all these beliefs are puzzling, to say the least.

Philosophers have often assumed that the relation between all such beliefs must really be one of entailment. It is a common strategy in philosophical discussion to invent principles that would fill in logical gaps and to imply that people must be relying on those principles, even if unconsciously. This procedure has the advantage of keeping things logically simple and manageable. There is, however, another possible view of the matter. Perhaps some of the elements in the web of belief are connected by relations other than entailment. Perhaps, for example, the belief that humans are morally special and the belief that humans have psychological capacities not found in other species are related in this way: the two beliefs fit together, and indeed fit neatly with other elements of the web as well, so that the total system of beliefs forms a consistent and satisfying whole. The relation of "fitting together" might be interestingly different from the relation of strict entailment. It might have more in common with such notions as *providing evidence for a belief* or *being a reason for holding* a *belief.* These notions are not so well understood as logical entailment, and it is not obvious that they are reducible to logical entailment.

There is a connection between this point and the point about the moral status of animals mentioned earlier. It seems to many people that, after Darwin, it is much harder to believe in the moral specialness of human beings—after all, we now know that we are but modified apes. Hasn't Darwin shown that humans are just another species that exists only by evolutionary accident and that humans and other animals have much more in common than we previously supposed? To this the standard reply is that nothing in Darwin's theory entails any moral conclusions. As Stephen Jay Gould puts it, "Science can no more answer the questions of how we ought to live than religion can decree the age of the earth."[16]

This may be so, but there is something hollow about the reassurance. Moral beliefs are connected in all sorts of ways with other beliefs, especially beliefs about the nature of the world and our place in it. The moral belief in human specialness might "fit" much more comfortably with a pre-Darwinian view of the world than with a Darwinian view. If what I have suggested about the web of belief is correct, it is easier to see how a theory such as Darwin's might undermine confidence in the moral specialness of human beings, not by entailing that the moral view is false, but by taking away some of its support.[17]

How an "Ultimate Principle" May Be Supported by Other Beliefs without Being Entailed by Them

Hume, as we have seen, pointed out that moral reasoning always refers back to some initial principle that is taken for granted. If we ask for a justification of that principle, one may be given, but only by appealing to some further principle that is unjustified. It seems to be a limitation of reason itself that we can never discharge all our assumptions. We always end up taking something for granted, no matter how much we might wish to avoid it.

One of the perennial pursuits of moral philosophy has been the attempt to identify the ultimate moral principle—the one standard of conduct from which all the others derive. Familiar candidates include the principle of self-interest, Kant's categorical imperative, and the principle of utility. Each has had its champions. But the Humean point about moral reasoning has a discouraging implication for this project. It would seem that no matter what ultimate principle is chosen, it will be in a certain sense arbitrary. Standing as it does at the beginning of the chain of justifications, it cannot itself be justified.

Utilitarians, who have generally been no-nonsense philosophers with an eye for logical niceties, have frequently noticed this problem and commented on it. The principle of utility, they say, is the standard by which moral judgments are justified. But what justifies it? If the principle is justified in terms of some other principle, then that other principle, and not the principle of utility, becomes the ultimate standard. Plainly this would be self-defeating. Thus one might naturally conclude that nothing much of interest can be said.

But despite the apparent impossibility of finding anything useful to say, utilitarian philosophers have said quite a lot. They have argued, variously, that utilitarianism should be accepted by people of a benevolent temperament,[18] that it is consonant with a properly "scientific" way of viewing the world,[19] that it is the ethic toward which common sense is striving,[20] that it is the only moral view that fits the logic of moral language,[21] that it is a natural ethic for a species formed by Darwinian evolution,[22] and that alleged "duties" contrary to utility may be explained away as the products of superstition and false religion.[23] Notoriously, even if all this were true, none of it would be a proof in the sense of deducing the principle of utility from higher-order moral principles. So what is to be made of such arguments?

What is going on, I suggest, is that connections are being found between the principle of utility and other beliefs in those philosophers' total webs. The connections are weaker than logical entailment, but they are nonetheless important. These various considerations support the ultimate principle without strictly entailing it. The arguments being offered have more to do with showing that the total set of beliefs forms a consistent and satisfying whole than with trying to "prove" that the principle of utility is true.

John Stuart Mill said something very much like this. "Questions of ultimate ends," he said, "are not amenable to direct proof," at least not "in the ordinary and popular meaning of the term." He continues:

> We are not, however, to infer that acceptance or rejection [of the principle of utility] must depend on blind impulse or arbitrary choice. There is a larger meaning of "proof," in which this question is as amenable to it as any other of the disputed questions of philosophy. The subject is within the cognizance of the rational faculty; and neither does that faculty deal with it solely in the way of intuition. Considerations may be presented capable of determining the intellect either to give or withhold its assent to the doctrine; and this is equivalent to proof.[24]

And what, exactly, are the decisive considerations to which Mill adverts? It is the fact that, according to his analysis, happiness is the only thing that people seek as an end in itself. (If people appear to seek other ends, he says, it is only because those other ends constitute "part of" their happiness.) Given that people seek only happiness, Mill thinks it only reasonable to accept the principle of utility—which directs us to increase happiness—as the ultimate standard for judging conduct. This, he says, is the only sort of "proof" of which the principle of utility is susceptible.

It is possible to read Mill as advancing a deductive argument here. The argument might be formulated thus: We ought to do whatever will promote that which all people seek; all people seek one thing and one thing only, happiness; therefore, we ought to do whatever will promote happiness. But plainly this would be a "proof in the ordinary and popular meaning of the term," which Mill explicitly says he does not mean to be offering.

There is a different reading, consistent with Mill's stated intention. Rather than attempting to derive the principle of utility from a conception of "what men seek," we may take Mill to be suggesting that utilitarianism fits comfortably with that conception in a way that no other principle could. Mill takes it to be a fact that people seek happiness and only happiness. Therefore, if one accepts the principle of utility, there will be a pleasing theoretical fit between the facts about ultimate human ends and one's theory of morals. If one accepts some other moral theory, there will be no such fit, and indeed the two may clash, since one may end up endorsing actions as morally right that frustrate the ends of the people doing those actions. The ideas of what it is right to do and of what it is rational for people to do given their ultimate ends would be pried apart. Perhaps they should be pried apart, but this thought is difficult to defend. This does not prove that the alternative conception of morality is wrong, "in the ordinary and popular meaning of the term." But in Mill's view this plainly counts against it and in favor of his own theory.

Mill's treatment of the nature of happiness may be overly simple, as many philosophers believe. Nevertheless, he is surely right to distinguish proof in the "ordinary and popular meaning" from other, equally important ways in which the rational intellect may be determined. Whether one's total set of beliefs fits together in a reasonable and theoretically satisfying way is no small matter.

The Web of Belief and Moral Theories

Finally, it is necessary to say something about the relation between all this and the traditional philosophical task of theory construction. Some thinkers, such as Thomas Nagel and Bernard Williams, have argued that it is impossible to construct a moral theory in the traditional sense. Morality, they say, has multiple and incommensurable sources that cannot be reconciled in the way that a unified theory would require.[25]

The idea that we should think of morality not as a deductive system but as part of the overall web of belief is neutral with respect to the possibility of developing a theory in the traditional sense. It might or might not be possible, when surveying the web at any given time, to systematize in the traditional way what one finds there. It could turn out, for example, that all the actions one regards as right conform to the principle of utility, in which case utilitarianism would be vindicated. The inference from the totality of one's beliefs to the tenets of utilitarian theory could then be regarded as a type of "inference to the best explanation," with the theoretical apparatus proposed by the philosophers viewed as explaining, in the best theoretical manner available, the various elements of the web and their relations to each other. But if one adopts the strategy I have suggested, one would not have reached this conclusion by taking the principle of utility as a self-evident starting point. Instead, that principle would have been subjected to the same scrutiny as every other element of our moral thinking. It would simply have survived the critical process.

A Modest Pyrrhonism

Pyrrho taught that we should believe nothing, "for no single thing is any more this than that." When he applied this principle to moral judgment, he reached the conclusion that all of morality was, in effect, a sham: "Nothing," he said, "is honorable or dishonorable, just or unjust." This part of his view does not seem right. On the contrary, because some judgments about what is honorable or just may be supported by good reasons, they may rightfully claim the assent of thoughtful people.

But other aspects of Pyrrho's teaching might be more appealing—his attitude toward philosophical argument and his view regarding its connection with moral life, as well as his skeptical attitude toward received wisdom. The way of understanding moral philosophy that I have sketched above is Pyrrhonist in this broad sense. Philosophical argument is to be taken seriously even when it leads to doubt about the truth of commonly held opinions. No moral belief, however firmly it may be established in common practice, is to be regarded as immune from criticism. Any belief in the web may be modified or even rejected altogether if sufficiently good reasons are found against it.

Whether this is an attractive view will depend to a great extent on the confidence one has in commonsense morality. Those who have great confidence in received opinion may not be attracted to such a skeptical approach; for them, Moorean Insulation, with its guarantee of preserving at least the main elements of what they already believe, might be more appealing. Others might, for the reasons we have outlined, believe that insulation of any kind is unjustified. If nothing else, it just seems contrary to the spirit of proper philosophical inquiry to mark off, in advance, any belief as beyond question.

Still, it may seem that the kind of Pyrrhonist attitude I am endorsing does not give ordinary morality enough credit. Ordinary morality, it might be said, is no ordinary thing. It embodies the accumulated wisdom of many generations of people who have struggled to live together and deal with their common problems. The view I have outlined seems to treat the results of all that experience as nothing more than a collection of misguided prejudices, to be lightly cast aside if only some clever arguments against them can be found. It may seem not only ungrateful but more than a little arrogant to dismiss the accumulated experience of one's culture and to assume that merely by giving the matter a little thought, one can do better.

Of course, ordinary morality is both these things. It is, on the one hand, a workable system of precepts, developed over a long period of time, that makes social living possible. Its usefulness is proven. We know that it provides an effective framework for a society at least no worse than the one we have—and this, as conservative thinkers have often observed, is no small recommendation. At the same time, it also seems clear that ordinary morality does incorporate irrational elements. The trick, as always, is to figure out which ones they are.

A compromise, at least at the outset, might therefore be in order, and we might take our cue in this from another philosopher who advocated skepticism about commonly held beliefs. In the seventeenth century Descartes resolved to suspend judgment about all things until he could discover principles in which he could have confidence. Because this was not just an academic exercise for him—like Pyrrho, he took philosophy seriously—he worried about what to do during the interim, when he would have no principles to guide his conduct. In part 3 of the *Discourse on Method* Descartes discusses this problem and solves it to his own satisfaction by adopting a set of rules to be followed until his inquiry was completed. Chief among these was to

> obey the laws and customs of my country, constantly retaining the religion which I judged best, and in which, by God's grace, I had been brought up since childhood, and in all other matters to follow the most moderate and least excessive opinions to be found in the practice of the most judicious part of the community in which I would live.[26]

This seems a reasonable proposal: to think of "the most moderate and least excessive opinions" of "the most judicious part of the community" as providing a guide for life, but only with the proviso that if those opinions should be found wanting in the light of reason, they may have to be replaced. The existing web of belief may therefore be taken as our starting point. But we need not assume that any part of it is acceptable as it stands.

Notes

1. Diogenes Laertius, *Lives of Eminent Philosophers*, vol. 2, in the Loeb Classical Library (Cambridge: Harvard University Press, 1955), 475.

2. Diogenes, *Lives*, 471.

3. Diogenes, *Lives*, 475.

4. Diogenes, *Lives*, 475.

5. Diogenes, *Lives*, 479.

6. M. F. Burnyeat, "The Sceptic in His Place and Time," in *Philosophy in History*, ed. Richard Rorty, J. B. Schneewind, and Quintin Skinner (Cambridge: Cambridge University Press, 1984), 225–54.

7. G. E. Moore, "A Defence of Common Sense," in *Philosphical Papers* (New York: Collier Books, 1962), chap. 2.

8. I owe this terminology to Gareth Matthews.

9. Bernard Williams, "A Critique of Utilitarianism," in *Utilitarianism: For and Against*, ed. J. C. Smart and Bernard Williams (Cambridge: Harvard University Press, 1973), sec. 5.

10. John Rawls, *A Theory of Justice* (Cambridge: Harvard University Press, 1972).

11. See, for example, various essays in George Graham and Hugh LaFollette, eds., *Person to Person* (Philadelphia: Temple University Press, 1989).

12. These matters are discussed at greater length in chap. 14.

13. Peter Singer, "Sidgwick and Reflective Equilibrium," *Monist* 58 (1974): 516.

14. This is different from Quine's way of characterizing what is near the center of the web and what is on its fringes. Quine originally said that beliefs along the edge "impinge on experience," while those in the interior are less directly connected with particular experiences. W. V. Quine, *From a Logical Point of View*, 2d ed. (Cambridge: Harvard University Press, 1961), 42.

15. See Peter Singer, *Animal Liberation*, 2d ed. (New York: New York Review Books, 1990); and Tom Regan, *The Case for Animal Rights* (Berkeley and Los Angeles: University of California Press, 1983).

16. Stephen Jay Gould, "Darwinism Defined: The Difference between Fact and Theory," *Discover*, January 1987, 70.

17. For a full discussion of this point, see James Rachels, *Created from Animals: The Moral Implications of Darwinism* (Oxford: Oxford University Press, 1990).

18. Jeremy Bentham, *An Introduction to the Principles of Morals and Legislation* (Oxford, 1789), chap. 10, sec. 4; John Stuart Mill, *Utilitarianism* (London, 1861), chap. 3.

19. J. J. C. Smart, *Essays: Metaphysical and Moral* (New York: Basil Blackwell, 1987), 1.

20. Henry Sidgwick, *Methods of Ethics*, 1st ed. (London: Macmillan, 1874).

21. R. M. Hare, *Moral Thinking: Its Level, Method, and Point* (Oxford: Clarendon Press, 1981).

22. Peter Singer, *The Expanding Circle: Ethics and Sociobiology* (New York: Farrar Straus & Giroux, 1980). Singer does not mention utilitarianism by name in this book, yet the overall argument of the book is an argument for it.

23. Singer, *Expanding Circle*, chap. 6.

24. Mill, *Utilitarianism*, chap. 1.

25. See, for example, Thomas Nagel, "The Fragmentation of Value," in *Knowledge, Value, and Belief*, ed. H. Tristram Engelhardt Jr. and Daniel Callahan (Hastings-on-Hudson, N.Y.: Hastings Center, 1977), 279–94; and Bernard Williams, *Ethics and the Limits of Philosophy* (Cambridge: Harvard University Press, 1985).

26. René Descartes, *Discourse on Method*, trans. Laurence J. Lafleur, in Descartes, *Philosophical Essays* (Indianapolis: Bobbs-Merrill, 1964), 18. Originally published in 1637.

2

Can Ethics Provide Answers?

I once saw a proposal written by a distinguished professor of business to add a course in "business ethics" to his school's curriculum. It was an enthusiastic document, detailing the virtues and benefits of such an offering. But it concluded with the remark that "since there are no definite answers in ethics, the course should be offered on a pass-fail basis." I don't know why he thought that, lacking definite answers, it would be easier to distinguish passing from failing work than B work from C work, but what was most striking was the casual, offhand manner of the remark—as though it were obvious that no matter how important ethical questions might be, no "definite answers" are possible.

Can ethics provide answers? Philosophers have given a great deal of attention to this question, but the result has been a great deal of disagreement. There are generally two schools of thought. On one side are those who believe that ethics is a subject, like history or physics or mathematics, with its own distinctive problems and its own methods of solving them. The fundamental questions of ethics are questions of conduct—what, in particular cases, should we do?—and the study of ethics provides the answers. On the other side are those who, like the professor of business, deny that ethics is a proper subject. There are ethical questions, to be sure, and they are important; but since those questions have no definite answers, there cannot be a subject whose business it is to provide them. The debate between these two points of view has grown enormously complicated, and we will examine some of those complications at various points in this book. But at the outset it may be useful to consider the main sorts of reasons that lead people to be skeptical about ethics.

The Case against Ethics

It is remarkable that every day people make ethical judgments every day about which they feel strongly—sometimes even becoming angry and indignant with those who disagree—and yet, when they reflect on what they are doing, they profess that their opinions are no more "correct" than the contrary opinions they reject so vehemently. How can this be? What could persuade people to adopt such a peculiar stance?

Ethics and Culture

An appreciation of human diversity seems to many people incompatible with a belief in the reality of right and wrong. Sociologists and anthropologists have impressed upon us that moral standards differ from culture to culture and that what the "natural light of reason" reveals to one people may be radically different from what seems obvious to another. This, of course, has been known for a long time. Herodotus made the point clearly in the fifth century B.C:

> Darius, after he had got the kingdom, called into his presence certain Greeks who were at hand, and asked—"What he should pay them to eat the bodies of their fathers when they died?" To which they answered, that there was no sum that would tempt them to do such a thing. He then sent for certain Indians, of the race called Callatians, men who eat their fathers, and asked them, while the Greeks stood by, and knew by the help of an interpreter all that was said—"What he should give them to burn the bodies of their fathers at their decease?" The Indians exclaimed aloud, and bade him forbear such language. Such is men's wont herein; and Pindar was right, in my judgment, when he said, "Custom is the king o'er all."[1]

Today any educated person could list countless other examples of cultural variations in ethics: the Eskimos allow firstborn daughters to die of exposure; the Muslims practice polygamy; the Jains will not eat meat. In light of such variations, it seems merely naïve to think that our moral views are anything more than one particular cultural product.

In its crudest form, cultural relativism says simply: "Different cultures have different moral codes; therefore there is no objective truth in ethics." This, however, is most certainly mistaken. In the first place, the fact that different societies have different moral codes proves nothing. There is also disagreement from society to society about scientific matters: in some cultures it is believed that the earth is flat and in others that disease is caused by evil spirits. We do not on that account conclude that there is no truth in geography or in medicine. Instead, we conclude that in some cultures people are not well informed. Similarly, disagreement in ethics might signal nothing more than that some people are less enlightened than others. Why should we assume that, if ethical truth exists, everyone must know it?

Moreover, it may be that some values are relative to culture while others are not. Herodotus was probably right to think that the treatment of the dead—whether to eat or to burn them—is not a matter governed by objectively true standards. It may be simply a matter of convention that respect for the dead is shown in one way rather than another; and if so, the Callatians and the Greeks were equally naïve to be horrified by each other's customs. Alternative sexual customs—another favorite example of relativists—might also be equally acceptable. But this does not mean that there are *no* practices that are objectively wrong. Torture and slavery could still be wrong, independent of cultural standards, even if those other types of behavior are not. It is a mistake to think that because some standards are relative to culture, all must be.

We can, in fact, explain *why* some standards are relative to culture and some are not. It is a matter of the availability of reasons. In some cases, no good reason can be given to show that one custom is better than another. Can any good reason can be given to show that burning the dead is better than burying them? Or that clothing that conceals women's knees is preferable to clothing that exposes the knee? If not, the acceptability of these practices is merely culture-relative. On the other hand, in other cases reasons *can* be given to show that some customs are better than others. We can, for example, give reasons to show that slavery is unacceptable, regardless of the conventions of the society in which it is practiced. Thus, the acceptability of this practice is not merely culture-relative.

MacIntyre's Argument

Yet one might easily doubt that reason is such a powerful tool. In his book *Whose Justice? Which Rationality?* Alasdair MacIntyre warns that we should not expect so much from reason. The idea of impartial reason justifying norms of conduct binding on all people is, he says, an illusion fostered by the Enlightenment. In reality there is no such thing. Rationality is possible only within a historical tradition, which sets standards of inquiry for those working within it. But the standards of rational thinking differ from tradition to tradition; and so we cannot speak of "what reason requires" in any universal sense. MacIntyre writes:

What the enlightenment made us for the most part blind to and what we now need to recover is, so I shall argue, a conception of rational enquiry as embodied in a tradition; a conception according to which the standards of rational justification themselves emerge from and are part of a history in which they are vindicated by the way in which they transcend the limitations of and provide remedies for the defects of their predecessors within the history of that same tradition.[2]

Thus, in MacIntyre's view, the reasons that would be adduced by a modern liberal in arguing, say, that slavery is unjust would not necessarily be acceptable to an Aristotelian, whose standards of rationality are different; and the search for standards that transcend the two traditions is a fool's quest. No such tradition-neutral standards exist, except, perhaps, for purely formal principles such as noncontradiction that are far too weak to yield substantive ethical results.

At first hearing, this sounds like a sophisticated version of cultural relativism. But MacIntyre insists he is no relativist—relativism is one of the modern ideas that he rejects. One of the major challenges confronting the reader of *Whose Justice? Which Rationality?* is to figure out how, after embracing this view of rationality, MacIntyre can escape being a relativist. His idea seems to be this: traditions confront one another historically, and one tradition succeeds in establishing its superiority over its rival by demonstrating that it can solve the problems internal to the other tradition while at the same time incorporating within itself everything in the other tradition that survives the dialectical examination.

This, however, only invites an awkward question. MacIntyre represents the confrontation as involving rational debate and not mere institutional power—Augustinian Christianity displaces Aristotelianism, on his view, not merely because of the combined political power of church and state, but because it could be demonstrated to be superior, even to the partisans of the other tradition. But if there are no standards of practical rationality that are neutral between the two traditions, how is this possible?

MacIntyre believes that an abstract answer to this question is not to be found; for an answer one must look to history for examples of how the process has actually taken place. So the bulk of his book is occupied by an examination of four traditions (the Aristotelian, the Augustinian-Christian, the Scottish, and the modern liberal) and the various clashes between them. To meet MacIntyre's argument head on, then, we would have to examine the details of the historical debates and see whether their outcomes did or did not depend on the application of standards of rationality that were not merely tradition bound. That would be a big project, which will probably never be undertaken by anyone—there is only one

Alasdair MacIntyre. Nevertheless, there are several relevant points that might be made.

First, the type of confrontation that MacIntyre pictures as taking place between traditions is possible only because the partisans of the different traditions have a lot in common. If they were not trying to solve the same problems, then it would make no sense to say that one tradition does a better job of solving a problem than does another; and if the traditions had no common content, it would make no sense to talk about one tradition's incorporating within itself the worthy aspects of its rivals. This suggests that what the people in the different traditions have in common might form the basis of a shared rationality that would make possible the development of norms applicable to them all.

Aristotle, who epitomized a tradition that MacIntyre rejects, believed that this is so. Surveying various ancient societies, Aristotle declared, "One can see in one's travels to distant countries the experiences of recognition and affiliation that link every human being to every other human being."[3] He observed that all humans face danger and fear death, and so all have need of courage; that all have bodily appetites that are sometimes difficult to control, and so all have need of ways to manage themselves; that none are self-sufficient, and so all have need of friends. Aristotle thought that such universal elements of human experience provided the basis for an ethic that was not simply local to one culture. He did not, however, expect universal agreement about that ethic. (He did not make the mistake of confusing the question of whether a moral argument of universal validity can be constructed with the different question of whether people can be persuaded to accept that argument.) The fact that people do disagree about norms—the endless disputation that MacIntyre says is typical of modern, rootless humans—was as familiar to Aristotle as it is to us. But as Aristotle realized, there is more than one possible explanation of that disagreement. The disagreement is not necessarily the result of differences in standards of rationality. The best explanation may be that such disagreement stems from a combination of causes, significantly including the ignorance, poverty, disease, and political and religious oppression that have plagued a large proportion of human beings throughout their history.

But the argument cannot be settled at such an abstract level. If we think that there are norms binding on all rational agents—if we think that reasons can be given to show that a particular practice is right or wrong such that those reasons must be accepted by every rational person, regardless of the tradition in which he or she participates—then we should be able to provide an example of such a norm. A good test case might be slavery.

It is easy, of course, to construct an argument against slavery from a modern liberal point of view. But is that argument tied only to modern liberal values? Or does it appeal rather to considerations that any reasonable person should accept?

The primary argument against slavery is, in bare outline, the following. All forms of slavery involve setting apart a class of humans for treatment that is systematically different from that accorded other members of the community. Deprivation of liberty is the feature that these various practices have most in common, although slaves have also been subject to a variety of other unwelcome treatments. Now, the argument is that it is unjust to set some people apart for different treatment unless there is a relevant difference between them that justifies the difference in treatment. But there is no general difference between humans that would justify setting some of them apart as slaves. Therefore slavery is unjust.

Is this argument only a product of modern liberal thought? Or should it be compelling even to those who live in different sorts of societies, with different sorts of traditions? To test this, we might consider a slave society such as Aristotle's. According to one estimate, there were as many slaves in Aristotle's Athens, in proportion to the population, as there were in the slave states of America before the Civil War. Aristotle himself defended slavery. Yet the rational resources available within his tradition seem to have been sufficient for an appreciation of its injustice. Aristotle reports that "some regard the control of a slave by a master as contrary to nature. In their view the distinction of master and slave is due to law or convention; there is no natural difference between them: the relation of master and slave is based on force, and being so based has no warrant in justice."[4]

But, as is well known, Aristotle did not share this enlightened view. A slave owner himself, he held that slavery is justified by the inferior rationality of the slave. Because they are not so rational as other humans, slaves are fitted by nature to be ruled rather than to rule. Aristotle knew that many slaves are inclined to revolt, but he attributed this not to any sense they might have of the injustice of their position but to an excess of "spiritedness." In his sketch of the ideal state, near the end of his *Politics*, he suggests that farm labor should be provided by slaves, "but slaves not drawn from a single stock, or from stocks of a spirited temper. This will at once secure the advantage of a good supply of labour and eliminate any danger of revolutionary designs."[5] But Aristotle was not of a single mind about this, for he also supported provisions for manumission. After recommending that farm labor be performed by slaves, he adds, "It is wise to offer all slaves the eventual reward of emancipation." In his will, Aristotle provided for the emancipation of his own slaves. This is an unexpected concession from someone who held that slaves are fitted for their station by nature itself.

Plainly, Aristotle accepted the principle that differences in treatment are unjustified unless they are correlated with differences between individuals that justify those differences in treatment. In fact, this is just a modern version of an idea that he advances in the *Nicomachean Ethics*, namely, that like cases should be treated alike and different cases differently. That is why he felt it necessary to defend slavery by contending that slaves possess an inferior degree of rationality. But this is a claim that can be shown to be false by evidence that should be counted as evidence as much by him as by us. Therefore, even on Aristotle's own terms, slavery should be recognizable as unjust. In arguing this, we are not simply transporting our standards of rationality back into a culture that was "different," although we might well cite information about the nature of human beings that we have now but that was unavailable to him.

Of course, showing that this argument should be accepted by Aristotle is not the same as showing that it should be accepted by all reasonable people. The possibility still remains that MacIntyre is right and that there are partisans of some traditions for whom this type of argument could have no effect. But I see no good reason to believe this; the argument I have outlined appeals to such a basic principle of reasoning that it should always have some force for reasonable people. At any rate, as we have seen, Aristotle held the sensible view that people in different traditions have enough in common, in virtue of their shared humanity, to make the achievement of common norms a realistic goal. On its face, this seems at least as plausible as the idea that the incompatible standards of different traditions cannot be overcome.

The Psychological Argument

Psychological studies tend to undermine confidence in ethics in a different way, by making us aware of the nonrational ways in which moral beliefs are formed in the individual. The story of how this happens remains remarkably constant, even when we consider radically different psychological theories. Freud was one of the first to set out the central idea. He emphasized that children are utterly dependent on their parents—without the parent's constant attention and help, the child cannot satisfy its most basic needs (it cannot obtain food, for example). Thus, retaining the parent's love becomes the most important thing in the child's life. For their part, parents have definite ideas about how children should behave. They are ready to reward children when they behave in desired ways and to punish them when they behave in unwanted ways. The rewards and punishments may be subtle; they may consist of nothing more than smiles, frowns, and harsh words. But that is enough because, as Freud notes, the parent's disapproval is the thing the child fears most.

This little drama is played out over and over again as the child grows up. As a result, the child learns to behave in "accepted" ways. The child also learns how to talk about her behavior: she learns to call the approved ways "right" and the disapproved ways "wrong." That is the origin of our moral concepts. "Moral" and "immoral" are simply names for the approved and disapproved forms of conduct.

To this is added a distinctively "Freudian" idea. Freud says that there exists within us a psychic mechanism for internalizing the role of the parent. After a while, we no longer need the parent to punish us for acting badly—we come to punish ourselves, through feelings of guilt. This mechanism he calls the "superego." It is, Freud says, the same thing that is commonly called the conscience. But in reality it is nothing more than the internalized voice of the parent.

The story has been repeated often, with minor variations. The behaviorists had no patience with Freudian speculations; nevertheless, their fundamental ideas concerning moral development were quite similar. Where Freud spoke of "the pleasure principle" and of parental approval, the behaviorists spoke of "positive reinforcements." The child is positively reinforced (rewarded) when he behaves in certain ways, and so he tends to repeat that behavior. He is negatively reinforced (punished) for other actions, which he subsequently tends not to repeat. Thus patterns of behavior are established: some types of conduct come to be accepted, others come to be rejected. When the child's vocabulary becomes sufficiently rich, he learns to speak of the former behavior as right and the latter as wrong. Indeed, B. F. Skinner went so far as to suggest that the word "good" could be *defined* as "positively reinforcing."

All this suggests that our values are simply the result of our having been conditioned to behave in certain ways. We may feel that certain actions are good and others are evil, but that is only because we have been trained to have those feelings. If we had been trained differently, we would have different values, and we would feel just as strongly about them. Therefore, to believe that one's values are anything more than the result of this conditioning is simply naïve.

Thus, in many people's minds, psychology swallows up ethics. It does not simply explain ethics; it explains it away. Ethics can no longer exist as a subject having as its aim the discovery of what is right and what is wrong, for this supposes that there is a right and wrong independent of what people already happen to believe. Ethics as a subject matter must disappear, to be replaced, perhaps, by the scientific study of why we have the values we do. We can try to become clearer about what our values are and about the possible alternatives. But we can no longer ask questions about the truth of our convictions.

Yet these psychological facts, like the facts about cultural variations, turn out to be irrelevant to the status of ethics as an autonomous subject. Psychology may tell us that beliefs are acquired in a certain way, but nothing follows from this about the nature or validity of those beliefs. After all, every belief is acquired through the operation of some psychological mechanism or other. A child may learn to respond "George Washington" when asked to name the first American president because she fears the disapproval of the teacher should she say anything else. And, we might add, if she were reinforced differently she might grow up believing that someone else first held that office. Yet it remains a matter of fact that Washington was the first president. The same goes for one's moral beliefs: the manner of their acquisition is logically independent of their status as objectively true or false.

The example of learning history is instructive in another way. In learning history, a student might go through two stages. In the first, he learns by rote. He learns to say things like "George Washington was the first president" even though he has no idea why we think this is true. He has no conception of historical evidence and no understanding of the methods historians use to verify such things. Later, however, he may learn about evidence and historical method. Then he not only believes Washington was the first president; he has good reasons for that belief. Thus he can be confident that this belief is not "merely a matter of opinion."

Something very much like this is true of a child's instruction in how to behave. When a child is very young, she will respond to the parent's instructions even though she has no idea of the reasons behind those instructions. The mother may say, "Don't play in the street," and the child may obey, even though she does not understand why playing in the street is undesirable. She may obey simply because she fears punishment. Later, however, she will become capable of understanding the reasons: she will see that, if she plays in the street, she may be seriously hurt or even killed.

Again, when the child is very young, the mother may say, "Don't kick your brother," and the child may obey because otherwise she will be punished. But later, when she is older, her mother may say something very different. She may say, "When you kick your brother, it *hurts* him," or "How would you like it if someone went around kicking *you*?" In saying these things, and others like them, the mother is bringing the child to understand the most elementary reasons why little brother should not be abused.

At one stage of development, the child learns to behave in certain ways because he will be rewarded if he does and punished if he doesn't. At a later, more mature stage, he learns that there are good reasons for behaving in those ways. At which stage is he learning morality? In one sense, of course, he is learning to behave morally even at the earlier stage: he is learning to do things that it is morally good to do. But in a deeper sense, moral instruction begins only at the later stage. Only at the later stage does the child begin to learn how to reason and act as a moral agent. Rewards and punishments just keep him in line until he is old enough to understand reasons.

Thus the outcome of the psychological account of ethics is reminiscent of the fate of nineteenth-century attempts to reduce mathematics to psychology. In the late 1800s there was considerable interest in explaining mathematics by reference to psychological theories of human thought—but that interest waned when it was realized that little light was being shed on mathematics itself. Regardless of how it might be related to our thought processes, mathematics remained a subject with its own integrity—its own internal rules, procedures, problems, and solutions. The reason ethics resists explanation by sociology or psychology is that, like mathematics, it is also a subject with its own integrity.

The Question of Proof

There is one further skeptical argument that rivals the cultural relativist argument and the psychological argument in influence. To many people, it seems to be a great deficiency of ethics that there is no proof where ethical opinions are concerned. This appears to be a crucial difference between ethics and science. We can prove that the world is round, that there is no largest prime number, and that dinosaurs and human beings did not live at the same time. But can we prove that abortion is right or wrong? The No-Proof Argument, as we might call it, goes like this: "If there were any such thing as objective truth in ethics, we should be able to prove that some moral opinions are true and others are false. But in fact we cannot prove which moral opinions are true and which are false. Therefore, there is no such thing as objective truth in ethics."

The general claim that moral judgments can't be proved sounds right: anyone who has ever argued about a matter like abortion knows how frustrating it can be to try to "prove" that one's point of view is correct. However, if we inspect this claim more closely, it turns out to be dubious.

Suppose we consider a matter that is much simpler than abortion. A student says that a test given by a teacher was unfair. This is clearly a moral judgment—fairness is a basic moral value. Can this judgment be proved? The student might point out that the test was so long that not even the best students could complete it in the time allowed (and the test was to be graded on the assumption that it should be completed). Moreover, the test covered in detail matters that were quite trivial, while ignoring matters the teacher had stressed as important. And the test included questions about some matters that were not covered in either the assigned readings or the class discussions.

Suppose all this is true. And further suppose that the teacher, when asked to explain, has no defense to offer. (In fact, the teacher, who is rather inexperienced, seems muddled about the whole thing and doesn't seem to have had any very clear idea of what he was doing.) Now, hasn't the student proved the test was unfair? What more in the way of proof could we possibly want?

It is easy to think of other examples that make the same point:

Jones is a bad man. Jones is a habitual liar; he manipulates people; he cheats when he thinks he can get away with it; he is cruel to other people; and so on.

Dr. Smith is irresponsible. He bases his diagnoses on superficial considerations; he drinks before performing delicate surgery; he refuses to listen to other doctors' advice; and so on.

A certain used-car salesman is unethical. She conceals defects in her cars; she takes advantage of poor people by pressuring them into paying exorbitant prices for cars she knows to be defective; she runs misleading advertisements in any newspaper that will carry them; and so on.

We can, and often do, back up our ethical judgments with good reasons. Thus it does not seem right to say that they are all unprovable, as though they were nothing more than "mere opinions." If a person has good reasons for her judgments, then she is not merely giving "her opinion." On the contrary, she may be making a judgment with which any reasonable person would have to agree.

The process of giving reasons might be taken a step further. If one of our reasons for saying that Jones is a bad man is that he is a habitual liar, we can go on to explain why lying is bad. Lying is bad because it harms people, because it is a violation of trust, and because the rule requiring truthfulness is necessary for society to exist. (I will not elaborate on these matters here, because they are detailed in chapter 9. The point here is just that such explanations not only are possible in ethics, they are common. There are many examples scattered throughout this book.) So, if we can support our judgments with good reasons, and provide explanations of why these reasons matter, and show that the case on the other side is weak, what more in the way of "proof" could anyone possibly want?

Nevertheless, the impression that moral judgments are "unprovable" is remarkably persistent. What accounts for this persistence? Why is the No-Proof Argument so persuasive? Three reasons might be mentioned.

First, when proof is demanded, people might have in mind an inappropriate standard. They might be thinking, in a vague way, about observations and experiments in science; and when there are no comparable observations and experiments in ethics, they might conclude that there is no proof. But in ethics, rational thinking consists of giving reasons, analyzing arguments, setting out and justifying principles, and the like. The fact that ethical reasoning differs in some ways from reasoning in science does not make it deficient.

Second, when we think of "proving our ethical opinions to be correct," we tend to think automatically of the most difficult moral issues. The question of abortion, for example, is an enormously complicated and difficult matter. No one, to my knowledge, has yet produced a perfectly convincing analysis that would show once and for all where the truth lies. If we think of questions like this, it is easy to believe that "proof" in ethics is impossible. But the same could be said of the sciences. There are complicated matters on which physicists cannot agree, and if we focused our attention entirely on them we might conclude that there is no proof in physics either. But of course there are many simpler matters in physics that can be proved and about which all competent physicists agree. Similarly, in ethics there are many matters far simpler than abortion about which all reasonable people must agree. The examples given above are examples of this type.

Finally, it is easy to conflate two matters that are really very different: (1) proving an opinion to be correct; and (2) persuading someone to accept your proof. It is a common, if frustrating, experience to have an impeccable argument that someone refuses to accept. But that does not mean there is something wrong with the argument or that "proof" is somehow unattainable. It may mean only that someone is being unreasonable. And in ethics we should often expect people not to listen to reason: after all, ethics requires that people do things they don't want to do; so it is only to be expected that sometimes they will try to avoid hearing its demands.

The Difference Science Makes

Somehow it seems *natural,* at the end of the twentieth century, to be skeptical about ethics. It is hard to shake this feeling, regardless of what one makes of arguments such as those we have considered so far. Moral skepticism seems to be our lot. The explanation of why this should be so goes deep into our history and into our understanding of the world and our place in it. The most salient part of this history concerns the rise of modern science. Before modern science, people could reasonably believe that their moral judgments were warranted by the facts of nature. The prevailing view of what the world was like supported such a belief. Today this is no longer true.

Understanding What the World Is Like

The Greeks conceived the world to be an orderly system in which everything has its proper place. A central feature of this conception was the idea that *everything in nature exists for a purpose.* Aristotle incorporated this idea into his system of thought when he said that in order to understand anything, we must ask four questions: What is it? What is it made of? How did it come to exist? And what is it for? (The answers might be: this is a knife, it is made of steel, it was made by a craftsman, and it is used for cutting.) Aristotle assumed that the last question—What is it for?— could sensibly be asked of anything whatever. "Nature," he said, "belongs to the class of causes which act for the sake of something."[6]

It seems obvious that artifacts such as knives have purposes, because we have a purpose in mind when we make them. But what about natural objects that we do not make? Do they have purposes too? Aristotle thought so. One of his examples was that we have teeth so that we can chew. Such biological examples can be quite persuasive; the parts of bodies do seem, intuitively, to have particular purposes—eyes are for seeing, the heart is for pumping blood, and so on. But Aristotle's thesis was not limited to organic beings. He also thought, to take a different sort of example, that rain falls so that plants can grow. As odd as it may seem to a modern reader, Aristotle was perfectly serious about this. He considered other alternatives, such as that the rain falls "of necessity" and that this helps the plants only by "coincidence," and rejected them. He even considered a hypothesis strikingly like Darwinian natural selection: "Wherever then all the parts [of plants and animals] came about just what they would have been if they had come to be for an end, such things survived, being organized spontaneously in a fitting way; whereas those which grew otherwise perished and continue to perish, as Empedocles says his 'man-faced ox-progeny' did."[7] But Aristotle rejects this, too. His considered view was that plants and animals are what they are and that the rain falls as it does "because it is better so."

The world, therefore, is an orderly, rational system, with each thing having its own proper place and serving its own special purpose. There is a neat hierarchy: the rain exists for the sake of the plants, the plants exist for the sake of the animals, and the animals exist—of course—for the sake of people, whose well-being is the point of the whole arrangement:

> [W]e must believe, first that plants exist for the sake of animals, second that all other animals exist for the sake of man, tame animals for the use he can make of them as well as for the food they provide; and as for wild animals, most though not all of these can be used for food or are useful in other ways; clothing and instruments can be made out of them. If then we are right in believing that nature makes nothing without some end in view, nothing to no purpose, it must be that nature has made all things specifically for the sake of man.[8]

It was a stunningly anthropocentric view. Aristotle may be forgiven, however, when we consider that virtually every important thinker in our history has entertained some such thought. Humans are a remarkably vain species.

The Christian thinkers who came later found this view of the world to be perfectly congenial. Only one thing was missing: God was needed to make the picture complete. (Aristotle had denied that God was a necessary part of the picture. For him, the worldview we have outlined was not religious; it was simply a description of how things are.) Thus, the Christian thinkers said that rain falls to help the plants *because that is what the Creator intended* and the animals are for human use *because that is what God made them for.* Values and purposes were, therefore, conceived to be a fundamental part of the nature of things, because the world was believed to have been created according to a divine plan.

The Aristotelian-Christian view of the world had a number of consequences for ethics. On the most general level, it affirmed the supreme value of human life, and it explained why humans are entitled to do whatever they please with the rest of nature. The basic moral arrangement—human beings, whose lives are sacred, dominating a world made for their benefit—was enshrined as the Natural Order of Things.

At a more detailed level, a corollary of this outlook was that the "laws of nature" specify how things ought to be as well as describing how things are. In turn, knowing how things ought to be enables us to evaluate states of affairs as objectively good or bad. Things are as they ought to be when they are serving their natural purposes; when they do not or cannot serve those purposes, things have gone wrong. Thus, teeth that have decayed and cannot be used for chewing are defective; and drought, which deprives plants of the rain they need, is a natural objective evil.

There were also implications for human action. Moral rules could be viewed as one type of law of nature. A leading idea was that some forms of human behavior are "natural," while others are not; and "unnatural" acts are said to be wrong. Beneficence, for example, is natural for us because God has made us social creatures. We want and need the friendship of other people and we have natural affections for them; hence, behaving brutishly toward them is unnatural. Or, to take a different sort of example, the purpose of the sex organs is procreation. Thus the use of them for other purposes is "contrary to nature"—that is why the Christian church has traditionally regarded as impermissible any form of sexual activity that does not result in procreation, such as masturbation, gay sex, or the use of contraceptives.

The Aristotelian worldview began to break up in the sixteenth century when it was discovered that the earth orbits the sun, rather than the other way around. This was an alarming development, because the earth's being at the center of things was an important symbol of mankind's central place in the divine plan. But the heliocentric solar system was by no means the most subversive aspect of the emerging new science. Galileo, Newton, and others developed ways of understanding natural phenomena that made no use of evaluative notions. To their way of thinking, the rain has no purpose. It does not fall in order to help the plants grow. Instead, it falls as a result of physical causes. Is it, then, a mere coincidence that there happen to be plants growing beneath the rain to benefit from it? The Aristotelians and the Christians had found this too far-fetched to believe: how can the wonderful arrangement of nature, with each part supplementing and benefiting the other, be mere coincidence? But the modern thinkers eventually found a way to explain the whole setup: the plants are there because they have evolved, by natural selection, in the rainy climate. Natural selection produces an orderly arrangement that appears to have been designed, but, as Darwin emphasized, that is only an illusion. To explain nature, there is no need to assume teleological principles, neither Aristotle's "final causes" nor the Christians' God. This was by far the most insidious feature of the new science.

This style of explanation—appealing only to physical laws devoid of any evaluative content—was developed in such great and persuasive detail, in connection with so many natural phenomena, that educated people universally gravitated to it. With its superior predictive and explanatory power, this way of thinking transformed people's view of what the world is like. But part of the transformation, inseparable from the rest, was an altered view of the nature of ethics. Right and wrong could no longer be deduced from the nature of things in themselves, for on the new view, the natural world does not, in and of itself, manifest value and purpose. The inhabitants of the world may have needs and desires that generate values special to them, but that is all. The world apart from those inhabitants knows and cares nothing for their values, and it has no values of its own. A hundred and fifty years before Nietzsche declared, "There are no moral facts," David Hume had reached the same conclusion. Hume summed up the moral implications of the new worldview when he wrote: "Take any action allow'd to be vicious: Willful murder, for instance. Examine it in all lights, and see if you can find that matter of fact, or real existence, which you call *vice*. In whichever way you take it, you find only certain passions, motives, volitions and thoughts. There is no other matter of fact in the case."[9] And what of the old idea that "nature has made all things for the sake of man?" In his great essay on suicide, published posthumously in 1783, Hume replied: "The life of a man is of no greater importance to the universe than that of an oyster."[10]

Emotivism and the Eclipse of Ethics

Hume considered belief in an objectively correct ethical system to be part of the old "superstition and false religion." Stripped of false theology, Hume said, we should come to see our morality as nothing more than the expression of our feelings. "When you pronounce any action or character to be vicious," he wrote, "you mean nothing, but that from the constitution of your nature you have a feeling or sentiment of blame from the contemplation of it."[11]

In the twentieth century Hume's thoughts were adapted to support a theory known as *emotivism*. The development of emotivism was one of the great achievements of twentieth-century philosophy. It represented the final, fully worked out form of one of the major options in human thought, ethical subjectivism. Emotivism differed from previous versions of ethical subjectivism in its more sophisticated view of language. A key idea was that not every sentence is meant to be true or false. Utterances such as "Don't do that!" "Hooray for our team!" and "Would that there were more men like Gandhi" are not used to state facts. But that does not mean there is anything defective about them. They serve other purposes.

They give instructions about what to do, and they express (not report) our attitudes and commitments, while encouraging others to adopt similar attitudes and commitments. According to the emotivists, ethical "statements" are like this. They are not used to state facts; they are, really, in the same general family as imperatives and avowals. Even though they may be sincere or insincere, imperatives and avowals are neither true nor false—and similarly, moral judgments are neither true nor false.

To its supporters, emotivism seemed in keeping with a properly scientific outlook. Science describes the facts in an exhaustive way: any state of affairs, any "fact" that is part of the objective world, must be discoverable by scientific methods and describable in the language of science, broadly speaking. The emotivists denied that there are moral facts. One way of putting their argument is this: Facts are the counterparts of true statements; the fact that Buster Keaton made movies is what makes the statement "Buster Keaton made movies" true. We might think there are moral facts because we mistakenly assume that moral "statements" are the kinds of utterances that could be true. Thus, if in saying that Hitler is wicked we are saying something true, there must be a corresponding fact, Hitler's being wicked, that makes it true. However, once we understand that moral "statements" are not really statements at all and, indeed, are not even the sorts of utterances that could be true, the temptation to think there are moral facts disappears. Thus, the belief in moral facts could now be seen not only as the legacy of discarded scientific and religious views but as the symptom of a mistaken assumption about moral language as well.

With the arrival of emotivism as the dominant theory of ethics, many philosophers believed that the final truth about morality had at last been discovered. We can now understand, they said, why ethical disputes go on endlessly, with neither side being able to convert the other. In an ethical dispute, neither side is "correct," because ethical utterances are not the kinds of utterances that are correct or incorrect. Moreover, there are no "proofs" in ethics, because matters of fact and matters of attitude are logically distinct. Two people can agree on all the facts about a situation and yet have utterly different attitudes toward it. Ethical disagreement is like disagreeing about the choice of a restaurant: people might agree on all the facts about restaurants and yet disagree about where to eat, because some prefer Chinese food while others prefer Italian. That's the way ethics is, and that's all there is to it.

During the middle decades of the twentieth century, while emotivism dominated moral philosophy, philosophers rarely wrote about practical issues. Ethics was a nonsubject, beyond the reach of rational methods. For self-respecting philosophers it became a point of pride that, while they might expound upon ethical theory, ethics itself was not to be broached. "A philosopher is not a parish priest or Universal Aunt or Citizens' Advice Bureau,"[12] said P. H. Nowell-Smith in his widely-read book *Ethics*. A moral philosopher might tell you that "Chastity is good" means something like "Hurrah for chastity!" but it was not his business to join in the cheers.

Eventually, however, emotivism fell out of favor, and today it has few adherents. The theory's demise was partly a matter of intellectual fashion. Before his death in 1979, Charles Stevenson, whose book *Ethics and Language* was the definitive statement of emotivism,[13] remarked that while philosophers had abandoned the theory, no one had actually refuted it. But emotivism had failed because it did not do one of the main things that a theory of ethics must do: it did not provide a satisfactory account of the place of reason in ethics. It is a point of logic that moral judgments, if they are to be acceptable, must be founded on good reasons. If I tell you that such-and-such action is wrong, you are entitled to ask why it is wrong; and if I have no adequate reply, you may reject my advice as unfounded. This is what separates moral judgments from mere statements of preference. If I only say "I like so-and-so," I do not need to have a reason; it may just be a brute fact about me that I happen to like it. In making a moral judgment, however, one is at least implicitly claiming that there is some reason for or against what is being recommended or rejected.

The emotivists were able to give only the most anemic account of the relation between moral judgments and the reasons that support them. Moral reasoning, on their view, turned out to be indistinguishable from propaganda—giving reasons is just an effort to persuade someone to do something or to adopt an attitude. If that is all moral reasoning is, then *good* reasons are merely considerations that will have the desired effect. If the thought that Goldberg is Jewish causes someone to distrust him, then "Goldberg is a Jew" becomes a reason in support of the judgment that he is a shady character. Stevenson embraced this consequence of his view without flinching: "Any statement," he said, "about any fact which any speaker considers likely to alter attitudes may be adduced as a reason for or against an ethical judgment."[14]

Something had gone wrong. In the end, not many philosophers could seriously believe that any fact can count as a reason in support of any judgment. For one thing, the fact must be relevant to the judgment, and psychological influence does not necessarily bring relevance with it: Jewishness is irrelevant to shadiness, regardless of the psychological connections in anyone's mind. Moreover, it seems obvious that some facts are reasons in support of some actions, regardless of what anyone thinks. In a moment of rhetorical abandon, Hume had said, "'Tis not contrary to reason to prefer the destruction of the whole world to the scratching of my finger."[15] But surely the fact that doing X will cause the destruction of the world, while doing Y will scratch my finger, must be a reason in favor of doing Y, not X. An adequate theory of morality must explain why this is so. But this is only the tip of an iceberg. Moral judgments can be supported by arguments, and those arguments can be criticized and found adequate or inadequate on any number of grounds. Once this is realized, we have taken a big step away from emotivism and all the other trends of thought I have been describing, toward the recognition of ethics as an autonomous subject.

Ethics and Rationality

Ultimately the case against ethics can be answered only by demonstrating how moral problems are solvable by rational methods. Some of the essays in this book attempt to do that directly, by providing arguments about particular moral issues. But what can be said of a more general nature? How does one go about establishing what is the right thing to do? If there are answers in ethics, how are they to be found? Considered abstractly, these may seem to be impossibly difficult questions. But they are not so hard as one might think.

We have already alluded to the key idea: In any particular case, the right course of action is the one that is backed by the best reasons. Solving moral problems, then, is largely a matter of weighing the reasons, or arguments, that can be given for or against the various alternatives. Consider, for example, euthanasia. Many people feel that mercy killing is wicked, and the American Medical Association condemns it as "contrary to that for which the medical profession stands." Others feel that, in the appropriate circumstances, there is nothing wrong with it. Who is right? We may determine whether euthanasia is right or wrong by formulating and assessing the arguments that can be given for and against it. This is at bottom what is wrong with psychological and cultural relativism: if we can produce good reasons for thinking that this practice (or any other) is wrong and show that the arguments in its support are unsound, then we have proved it wrong, regardless of what belief one has been conditioned to have or what one's cultural code might say. And emotivism runs afoul of the same fact: if a stronger case can be made for euthanasia than against it, then mercy killing is permissible, no matter what one's attitude might be.

But how are arguments to be tested? What distinguishes strong arguments from weak ones? The first and most obvious way that a moral argument can go wrong is by misrepresenting the facts. A rational case for or against a course of conduct must rest on some understanding of the facts of the case—minimally, facts about the nature of the action, the circumstances in which it would be done, and its likely consequences. If the facts are misrepresented, the argument is no good. Even the most skeptical thinkers agree that reason has this role to play in moral judgment.

Unfortunately, however, attaining a clear view of the facts is not always a simple matter. In the first place, we often need to know what the consequences of a course of action will be, and this may be impossible to determine with any precision or certainty. Opponents of euthanasia sometimes claim that if mercy killing were legalized, it would lead to a diminished respect for life throughout society and we would end up caring less about the elderly, the physically handicapped, and the mentally retarded. Defenders of euthanasia, on the other hand, heatedly deny this. What separates the two camps here is a disagreement about "the facts," but we cannot settle the issue in the same easy way we could settle an argument about the melting point of lead. We seem to be stuck with different estimates—all more or less reasonable, with no easy way to decide which to accept—of what would happen if euthanasia were legalized.

Moreover, it is often difficult to determine the facts because the facts are distressingly complex. Take, for example, the question of whether someone who requests euthanasia is "competent"—that is, whether they are rational and in full control of their faculties. I take this to be a question of fact, but it is not a simple matter of fact. In order to decide the matter, we must fit together into a pattern all sorts of other facts about the individual—her state of mind, her attitudes, the quality of her reasoning, the pressures influencing her, and so on. That she is, or is not, competent is a kind of conclusion resting on these other facts; it is a matter of what the simpler facts add up to.

Suppose, though, that we have a clear view of the relevant facts, and so our arguments cannot be faulted on that ground. Is there any other test of rationality the arguments must pass? Hume's official view was that, at this point, reason has done all it can do, and the rest is up to our "sentiments." Reason sets out the facts; then sentiment takes over and the choice is made. This is a tempting idea, but it only illustrates a common trap into which people may fall. Philosophical theses may seduce with their beautiful simplicity. An idea may be accepted because of its appeal at a high level of generality, even though it does not conform to what we know to be the case at a lower level.

In fact, when Hume was considering actual ethical issues and not busy overemphasizing the role of sentiment, he knew very well that appeals to reason are often decisive in other ways. In the essay on suicide, he produced a number of powerful arguments in support of his view that a person has the right to take his own life when he is suffering without hope from a painful illness. Hume specifically opposed the traditional religious view that since life is a gift from God, only God may decide when it shall end. About this he made the simple but devastating observation that we "play God" as much when we save life as when we take it. Each time a doctor treats an illness and thereby prolongs a life, he decrees that this life should not end *now*. Thus if we take seriously that only God may determine the length of a life, we have to renounce not only killing but saving life as well.

Hume's point has force because of the general requirement that our arguments be consistent, and consistency, of course, is the prime requirement of rationality. Hume did not argue that the religious opponent of euthanasia has got his facts wrong—he did not insist that there is no God or that God's will has been misunderstood. If Hume's objection were no more than that, there would be little reason for the religious person to be bothered by it. Hume's objection was much stronger, for he was pointing out that we may appeal to a general principle ("Only God has the right to decide when a life shall end") only if we are willing to accept its consequences. If we accept some of them (the prohibition of suicide and euthanasia) but not others (the abandonment of medicine), then we are inconsistent. This fundamentally important point will be missed if we are bewitched by overly simple doctrines like "Reason establishes the facts; sentiment makes the choice."

There are other ways an ethical view may fail to pass the test of consistency. An ethical view may be based on one's "intuitions"— prereflective hunches about what is right or wrong in particular cases—and, on examination, these may turn out to be incompatible with one another. Consider the difference between killing someone and "merely" allowing someone to die. Many people feel intuitively that there is a big moral difference between these two. The thought of actively killing someone has a kind of visceral repulsiveness about it that is missing from the more passive (but still unpleasant) act of standing by and doing nothing while someone dies. Thus it may be held that although euthanasia is wrong, since it involves direct killing, nevertheless it is sometimes permissible to allow death by refraining from life-prolonging treatment.

To be sure, if we do nothing more than consult our intuitions, there seems to be an important difference here. However, it is easy to describe cases of killing and letting die in which there does *not* seem to be such a difference. Suppose a patient is brought into an emergency room and turned over to a doctor who recognizes him as a man against whom he has a grudge. A quick diagnosis reveals that the patient is about to die but can be saved by a simple procedure—say, an appendectomy. The doctor, seeing his chance, deliberately stalls until it is too late to perform the life-saving procedure, and the patient dies. Now, most of us would think, intuitively, that the doctor is no better than a murderer and that the fact that he did not directly kill the patient, but merely let him die, makes no difference whatever.

In the euthanasia case, the difference between killing and letting die seems important. In the grudge case, the difference seems unimportant. But what is the truth? Is the difference important, or isn't it? Such cases show that unexamined intuitions cannot be trusted. That is not surprising. Our intuitions may be nothing more than the product of prejudice, selfishness, or cultural conditioning; we have no guarantee that they are perceptions of the truth. And when they are not compatible with one another, we can be sure that one or the other of them is mistaken.

Let me mention one other way in which the requirement of consistency can force a change in one's moral views. I have been emphasizing that a moral judgment, if it is to be acceptable, must be backed by reasons. Consistency requires, then, that if there are exactly the same reasons in support of one course of conduct as there are in support of another, those actions are equally right, or equally wrong. We cannot say that X is right but that Y is wrong unless there is a relevant difference between them. This is a familiar principle in many contexts: it cannot be right for a teacher to give students different grades unless there is a relevant difference in the work they have done; it cannot be right to pay workers differently unless there is some relevant difference between the jobs they do; and so on. In general, it is this principle that underlies the social ideal of equality.

But this principle has some surprising consequences. Its implications are much more radical than egalitarians have often realized; for, if applied consistently, it would not only require us to treat our fellow humans better, it would require us to rethink our treatment of nonhuman animals as well. To cite only one instance: We routinely perform experiments on chimpanzees that we would never perform on humans—but what is the difference between the chimps and the humans that justifies this difference in treatment? It might be said that humans are far more intelligent and sensitive than chimpanzees; but this only invites a further query: suppose the humans are mentally retarded and so are *less* intelligent and sensitive than the chimps? Would we be willing to experiment on retarded humans in the same way? And if not, why not? What is the difference between the individuals in question that makes it all right to experiment on one but not the other? At this point, the defender of the status quo may be reduced to asserting that, after all, the humans are *human* and that is what makes the difference. This, however, is uncomfortably like asserting that, after all, women are women, or blacks are black, and that is why they may be treated differently. It is the announcement of a prejudice, and nothing more.

This brings us back to the point at which we started. We have adjusted in many ways to the idea that the earth is not the center of the universe and that we humans are but one race among others that have developed here. But where ethics is concerned, we cling to the idea that humanity is still at the center of the cosmos. The idea that every human life is sacred has been replaced by its secular equivalent, that every human life has special value and dignity just in virtue of being human. As a plea for equality among people, the idea has done noble service; but as a justification for our treatment of the nonhuman world, it won't do.

The Limits of Rationality

This discussion will not have dispelled all the nagging doubts about ethics. Rational methods can be used to construct arguments and to expose factual error and inconsistency in the ways we have described, but is that enough to save ethics from the charge that, at bottom, there is no "truth" in its domain? Couldn't two people who are equally rational—who have all the relevant facts, whose principles are consistent, and so on—still disagree? And if "reason" were inadequate to resolve the disagreement, wouldn't this show that, in the end, ethics really is only a matter of opinion? These questions will not go away.

There is a limit to what rational methods can achieve, which Hume described in the first appendix to his *Inquiry Concerning the Principles of Morals:*

> Ask a man *why he uses exercise;* he will answer, *because he desires to keep his health.* If you then inquire *why he desires health,* he will readily reply, *Because sickness is painful.* If you push your inquiries further and desire a reason *why he hates pain,* it is impossible he can ever give any. This is an ultimate end, and is never referred to any other object.
>
> Perhaps to your second question, *why he desires* health, he may also reply that *it is necessary for the exercise of his calling.* If you ask *why he is anxious on*

that head, he will answer, *because he desires to get money.* If you demand, *Why?*
It is the instrument of pleasure, says he. And beyond this, it is an absurdity to
ask for a reason. It is impossible there can be a progress *in infinitum,* and that
one thing can always be a reason why another is desired. Something must
be desirable on its own account, and because of its immediate accord or
agreement with human sentiment and affection.[16]

The impossibility of an infinite regress of reasons is not peculiar to ethics;
the point applies in all areas. Mathematical reasoning eventually ends
with axioms that are not themselves justified, and reasoning in science
ultimately depends on assumptions that are not proved. It could not be
otherwise. At some point, reasoning must always come to an end, no matter what one is reasoning about.

But there is a difference between ethics and other subjects, and that difference is in the involvement of the emotions. As Hume observed, when
we come to the last reason, we must mention something we care about.
Thus, even though "the right thing to do" always depends on what there
are the best reasons for doing, *what counts as a reason* itself depends on our
emotions. Nothing can count as an ultimate reason for or against a course
of conduct unless we care about that thing in some way. In the absence of
any emotional involvement, there are no reasons for action. On this point
the emotivists were right, whatever defects their overall theory might
have had. And it is the possibility that people might care about different
things, and so accept different ultimate principles between which reason
cannot adjudicate, that continues to undermine confidence in ethics.

I believe this possibility cannot ever be ruled out entirely and that it
will always be the source of a kind of nervousness about ethics. The nervousness cannot be eliminated; we have to live with it. There is, however,
one further point to be considered—a point that goes some way toward
minimizing the worry.[17]

What people care about is itself sensitive to pressure from the deliber-
ative process and can change as a result of thought. This applies as much
to people's "ultimate" cares and desires as to their more passing fancies.
Someone might not care very much about something before he thinks it
through but come to feel differently once he has thought it over. This has
been considered extremely important by some of the major philosophers.
Aristotle, Butler, and others emphasized that responsible moral judgment
must be based on a full understanding of the facts; but, they added, after
the facts are established, a separate cognitive process is required for the
agent to understand fully the import of what he or she knows. It is necessary not merely to know the facts but also to rehearse them carefully in

one's mind, in an impartial, nonevasive way. Only then will one have the kind of knowledge on which moral judgment may be based.

Aristotle even suggested that there are two distinct species of knowledge: first, the sort of knowledge had by one who is able to recite facts, "like the drunkard reciting the verses of Empedocles," but without understanding their meaning; and, second, the sort of knowledge had when one has thought carefully about what one knows. An example might make this clearer. We all know, in an abstract sort of way, that many children in the world are starving; yet for most of us this makes little difference to our conduct. We will spend money on trivial things for ourselves, rather than allowing it to be spent on food for them. How are we to explain this? The Aristotelian explanation is that we "know" the children are starving only in the sense in which the drunkard knows Empedocles' verses—we simply recite the fact.[18] Suppose, though, that we thought carefully about what it must be like to be a starving orphan. Our attitudes, our conduct, and the moral judgments we are willing to make might be substantially altered.

Some years ago, during the Vietnamese War, a wire-service photograph of two Vietnamese orphans appeared in American newspapers. They were sleeping on a Saigon street; the younger boy, who seemed to be about four, was inside a tattered cardboard box, while his slightly older brother was curled up around the box. The explanation beneath the photograph said that while they begged for food during the day, the older boy would drag the box with them, because he didn't want his brother to have to sleep on the sidewalk at night.

After this photograph appeared, a large number of people wrote to relief agencies offering help. What difference did the picture make? It was not a matter of people's being presented with new information—it wasn't as though they did not know that starving orphans have miserable lives. Rather, the picture brought home to them in a vivid way things they already knew. It is easy to think of starving children in an abstract, statistical way; the picture forced people to think of them concretely, and it made a difference to people's attitudes.

In moral discussion we often recognize that thinking through what one knows is a separate matter from merely knowing; and we exploit this in a certain strategy of argument. It is the strategy that begins "Think what it is like. . ."

- Those who favor voluntary euthanasia ask us to consider what it is like, from the point of view of the dying patient, to suffer horribly. If we did, they imply, we would feel more favorably disposed toward mercy killing.

- Albert Camus, in his essay on capital punishment, "Reflections on the Guillotine," argued that people tolerate the death penalty only because they think of it in euphemistic terms ("Pierre paid his debt to society") rather than attending to the sound of the head falling into the basket.[19] If we thought about it nonevasively, he says, we could not avoid detesting it.

- Opponents of abortion show pictures of fetuses to force us to pay attention to what it is that is killed. The assumption is that if we did, we could not approve of killing it.

Often this method of argument is dismissed as nothing more than a demagogic appeal to emotion. Sometimes the charge is true. But this type of argument may also serve as an antidote for the self-deception that Bishop Butler saw as corrupting moral thought. When we do not want to reach a certain conclusion about what is to be done—perhaps we would rather spend money on ourselves than give it for famine relief—we may refuse to face up in a clear-minded way to what we know. Facts that would have the power to move us are put out of mind or are thought of only bloodlessly and abstractly. Rehearsing the facts in a vivid and imaginative way is the needed corrective.

Now let us return to the question of ethical disagreement. When disagreement occurs, two explanations are possible. First, we might disagree because there has been some failure of rationality on the part of one of us. Or, second, the people who disagree might simply be different kinds of people, who care about different things. In principle, either explanation may be correct. But, in practice, when important matters are at issue, we always proceed on the first hypothesis. We present arguments to those who disagree with us on the assumption (in the hope?) that they have missed something: they are ignorant of relevant facts, they have not thought through what they know, they are inconsistent, and so on. We do not, as a practical matter, credit the idea that we are simply and irreconcilably "different."

Is this assumption reasonable? Isn't it possible that sometimes people just care about different things? It is possible; but if such cases do exist, they are notoriously hard to find. The familiar examples of the cultural anthropologists turn out upon analysis to have other explanations. The Eskimos who allow their firstborn daughters to die of exposure and who abandon feeble old people to a similar fate do not have less concern for life than peoples who reject such practices. They live in different circumstances, under threat of starvation in a hostile environment, and the survival of the community requires policies that otherwise they would happily renounce. Or consider the Ik, a tribe of Africans who during the 1970s were observed to be indifferent even to the welfare of their own children. They would not share food with their children and they laughed when others were sick. Surely, one might think, the Ik are radically different from us. But not so: they took on those characteristics only after a prolonged period of near-starvation that virtually destroyed their tribal culture. Of course human behavior will be modified by calamity; but before their calamity, the Ik were much too "normal" to attract attention. To be sure, there may be some disagreements that reflect cultural variables—Herodotus's Greeks and Callatians, for example—but, beyond that, and barring the kind of disaster that reduced the Ik, it is plausible to think that people are enough alike to make ethical agreement possible, if only full rationality were possible.

The fact that rationality has limits does not subvert the objectivity of ethics, but it does suggest the need for a certain modesty in what can be claimed for it. Ethics provides answers about what we ought to do, given that we are the kinds of creatures we are, caring about the things we will care about when we are as reasonable as we can be, living in the sort of circumstances in which we live. This is not as much as we might want, but it is a lot. And it is as much as we can hope for in a subject that must incorporate not only our beliefs but our ideals.

Notes

1. *The History of Herodotus,* trans. George Rawlinson, adapted by John Ladd in *Ethical Relativism* (Belmont, Calif.: Wadsworth, 1973), 12.

2 Alasdair MacIntyre, *Whose Justice? Which Rationality?* (Notre Dame, Ind.: University of Notre Dame Press, 1988), 7.

3. Quoted in Martha Nussbaum, "Recoiling from Reason" (a review of MacIntyre), *New York Review of Books,* 7 December 1989, 41. In this paragraph I am heavily indebted to Nussbaum's excellent discussion.

4. *The Politics of Aristotle,* trans. Ernest Barker (London: Oxford University Press, 1946), 9.

5. *Politics of Aristotle,* 306.

6. Aristotle, *Physics,* in *The Basic Works of Aristotle,* ed. Richard McKeon (New York: Random House, 1941), 249.

7. Aristotle, *Physics,* 249.

8. Aristotle, *Politics,* trans. T. A. Sinclair (Harmondsworth, England: Penguin Books, 1962), 40.

9. David Hume, *A Treatise of Human Nature* (Oxford: Oxford University Press, 1888), 468. Originally published in 1739.

10. David Hume, *Essays Moral, Political, and Literary* (Oxford: Oxford University Press, 1963), 590. Originally published in 1741–42.

11. Hume, *Treatise*, 469.

12. P. H. Nowell-Smith, *Ethics* (Baltimore: Penguin Books, 1954), 12.

13. C. L. Stevenson, *Ethics and Language* (New Haven: Yale University Press, 1944).

14. Stevenson, *Ethics*, 114.

15. Hume, *Treatise*, 416.

16. David Hume, *An Inquiry Concerning the Principles of Morals* (Indianapolis: Bobbs-Merrill, 1957), 111. Originally published in 1752.

17. Among contemporary moral philosophers, W. D. Falk has made this point most forcefully; see, for example, his essay "Action-Guiding Reasons," *Journal of Philosophy* 60 (1963): 702–18.

18. Aristotle, *Nicomachean Ethics* 1147b.

19. Albert Camus, "Reflections on the Guillotine," in *Resistance, Rebellion, and Death* (New York: Knopf, 1961), 175–234.

3

John Dewey and the Truth about Ethics

The deepest philosophical question about ethics is its objectivity. The question appears in various guises: Is morality just a matter of opinion? Do our moral judgments say anything about the world that is true or false independent of our feelings and conventions? Are there any moral facts, in the way that there are facts in physics and chemistry? Or is morality nothing more than a human invention, perhaps merely an expression of the way we feel about things? There was a time, of course, when such questions would not have occurred to people, or if they did occur, when the answers would have seemed easy. Then the world was almost universally regarded as the product of divine creation, and everything in it, including humankind, had its proper place and function. Given such an outlook, there was no problem about ethics: people's duties followed naturally from their assigned place in the scheme of things, from their nature, and from their role as God's children.

But when the world is viewed from a secular perspective, the status of ethics becomes problematic. First, we think that some things *really are* good, and others *really are* bad, in a way that does not depend on how we feel about them. Hitler's concentration camps really were evil, and anyone who thinks otherwise is simply wrong. Therefore we want a theory that will allow for the objectivity of ethics. The most obvious way to construct such a theory is to regard goodness and badness as (nonrelational) properties of actions, or states of affairs, on a par with other straightforward kinds of properties. Thus to say that the concentration camps were evil is to state a fact—the fact that the concentration camps had the property of being evil—in much the same way as it is stating a fact to say that people were killed in them. People were killed in those places, no matter what anyone thinks and no matter how anyone feels about it; and similarly, on this sort of view, those places were evil no matter what anyone

49

thinks and no matter how anyone feels.

The objective-property view accommodates our intuitions about the objectivity of ethics, and it has been defended by such eminent philosophers as G. E. Moore. Nevertheless, there are strong reasons for doubting whether it is correct. One difficulty has to do with the ontology of the theory. It is hard to believe, while maintaining one's sense of reality, that goodness and badness are properties in any simple sense. Hume put his finger on the difficulty when he declared that there is no "matter of fact" concerning vice—if we consider "moral properties" to be qualities that inhere in objects, there is no reason to believe such properties *exist*.

But Hume did not merely assert this; he attempted to prove it by giving arguments. His most influential argument was based on the idea that there is a necessary connection between moral belief and motivation. The test of whether we sincerely believe that we ought to do something, Hume said, is whether in fact we are motivated to do it. (If I say that I believe I ought to do such and such but have not the slightest inclination to do it, my statement is not to be believed.) Thus, having a moral belief is at least in part a matter of being motivated to act, or, as Hume put it, of having a sentiment. On the other hand, a person's capacity to discern truth and falsehood—in Hume's terms, his reason—has no necessary connection with his conduct at all: "Morals excite passions, and produce or prevent actions. Reason of itself is utterly impotent in this particular."[1] If goodness and badness are simply properties of things, the intimate connection between moral judgment and action is lost. How can the fact that an action would have a certain property necessarily provide us with a reason for or against doing it? Why couldn't we be just as indifferent to this "property" as to any other? What do such "facts" have to do with us and our conduct?

Faced with these difficulties, we are pushed toward the opposite view: that our moral judgments merely express our feelings. This view does not require us to believe that actions or states of affairs have any special properties beyond those revealed by a cold scientific analysis of them, so it does not share the ontological problems of the objective-property doctrine. Furthermore, on this view, the connection between moral judgment and action is clear: if, in saying that something is bad, we are expressing our opposition to it, there is no mystery about why such judgments dispose us to act in one way rather than another.

But the subjectivist view is also hard to accept, for now we have given up all pretense of objectivity. It would seem that we could make *any* action or state of affairs (including, for example, concentration camps) good or bad simply by adopting the appropriate attitude toward it. And there are other familiar problems with this view: if, in saying that something is good, I am merely expressing my favorable attitude toward it, am I then infallible in my moral judgments, so long as I express my attitudes honestly? And if someone else says that the same thing is bad, and he is accurately expressing *his* attitudes, are we both right?

So we find ourselves in the dilemma that Dewey describes in his Gifford Lectures, torn between contrary theories, both of which seem somehow necessary, but neither of which seems true. As Dewey puts it, "we oscillate between a theory that, in order to save the objectivity of values, isolates them from experience and nature, and a theory that, in order to save their concrete and human significance, reduces them to mere statements about our own feelings."[2]

How are we to proceed from here? A number of options are available. Noncognitivists such as Stevenson have argued, in subtle and ingenious ways, that the view that moral judgments express attitudes can be freed from the difficulties mentioned above.[3] Another option is to try to work out a form of ethical naturalism that will do justice both to the objectivity of ethics and to its intimate connection with human feelings and conduct, insofar as it is possible to reconcile those two matters. Dewey's theory of ethics is in this latter naturalistic tradition.

Like many students, Dewey tended to accept the views of his teachers, so as a young man he was influenced by the Hegelian idealism then fashionable. Eventually he rejected idealism, but throughout his life he retained the idealist's suspicion of any attempt to understand phenomena apart from their connections and relations with other phenomena. The positivist doctrine that the world consists of "atomic facts," each independent of all the others, was especially abhorrent to him. There is a charming story, told by Ernest Nagel, that points up this aspect of Dewey's thinking:

> I remember one memorable occasion when the late Otto Neurath sought to interest Dewey in the Unity of Science movement, by having him contribute a monograph to the *Encyclopedia of Unified Science* which Neurath was then planning. I accompanied Neurath and Sidney Hook when they called on Dewey at his home; and Neurath was having obvious difficulty in obtaining Dewey's participation in the *Encyclopedia* venture. Dewey had one objection—there may have been others, but this is the only one I recall—to Neurath's invitation. The objection was that since the Logical Positivists subscribed to the belief in atomic facts or atomic propositions, and since Dewey did not think there are such things, he could not readily contribute to the *Encyclopedia*.

Now at this time Neurath spoke only broken English, and his attempts at explaining his version of Logical Positivism were not very successful. Those of us who knew Neurath will remember his elephantine sort of physique. When he realized that his attempts at explanation were getting him nowhere, he got up, raised his right hand as if he were taking an oath in a court of law (thereby almost filling Dewey's living room), and solemnly declared, "I swear we don't believe in atomic propositions." This pronouncement won the day for Neurath. Dewey agreed to write the monograph, and ended by saying, "Well, we ought to celebrate," and brought out the liquor and mixed a drink.[4]

And that is how the *Theory of Valuation* came to be written.

In that book, Dewey emphasizes that we cannot hope to understand the nature of moral judgments apart from the contexts or situations in which they are made. They are made in situations in which "there is something the matter," where there is some conflict or problem to be solved. What typically happens is this. We want or need something that does not exist in the present situation; or we have some purpose or goal that cannot be attained without effort on our part. Therefore, we have to make a decision to act or not to act, and if we choose to act, we have to decide which course of action to adopt from among the available alternatives. Perhaps if we choose one strategy, which satisfies some of our interests, other interests will be frustrated. The question, then, is what to do, and the "valuation" provides the answer by singling out certain actions, but not others, as to-be-done.[5]

Because evaluative judgments have this practical function—they direct conduct—some philosophers have thought that they have a different kind of meaning from ordinary factual judgments. Stevenson, for example, held that insofar as sentences are distinctively ethical, they have *emotive* meaning, which is different from the cognitive meaning of ordinary factual assertions. Ethical sentences express, but do not report, one's attitudes, in much the same way as one expresses, but does not report, an attitude in saying "Alas!" Ethical sentences are also used to influence other people's behavior, much as the cry "Help!" is an attempt to influence other people's behavior. Neither of these sentences describes any state of affairs; they do not, primarily at least, convey information. Their meaning is rather to be understood in terms of the way they express attitudes or influence conduct. And the same goes for ethical sentences.

Dewey argued that this way of thinking involves "a radical fallacy." First, it is a mistake to draw conclusions about the content or meaning of ethical sentences from facts about their use. Dewey agrees that "the *entire* use and function of ethical sentences is directive or 'practical.'" This is what distinguishes them from ordinary factual claims, which only some-times have a directive function. However, he adds, "It is quite another thing to convert the difference in function and use into a differential com-ponent of the structure and contents of ethical sentences."[6] Moreover, Dewey argues that a Stevensonian analysis does not work even for such utterances as "Alas!" and "Help!" for even these utterances have cogni-tive, verifiable contents:

> Take, for example, the case of a person calling "Fire!" or "Help!" There can be no doubt of the intent to influence the conduct of others in order to bring about certain consequences capable of observation and of statement in propositions. The expressions, taken in their observable context, say some-thing of a complex character. When analyzed, what is said is (i) that there exists a situation that will have obnoxious consequences; (ii) that the person uttering the expressions is unable to cope with the situation; and (iii) that an improved situation is anticipated in case the assistance of others is obtained. All three of these matters are capable of being tested by empirical evidence, since they all refer to things that are observable.[7]

> Is there any case in which "alas" has meaning apart from something that is of the nature of a calamity, a loss, a tragic event, or some cause or deed which is mourned? I imagine that when a reader sees the word "emotive," he is likely to think of events like anger, fear, hope, sympathy, and in think-ing of them he thinks necessarily of other things—the things with which they are integrally connected. Only in this way can an event, whether a sigh or a word like "alas," have identifiable and recognizable "meaning."[8]

There is both something right and something wrong in what Dewey says here. He is surely right to insist that, taken in context, utterances such as "Help!" do somehow convey the idea that certain sorts of facts are the case and that if such facts do not obtain, the utterer is seriously mislead-ing her listeners. Dewey goes wrong, however, when he tries to explain this by making it a part of the *content* of such utterances that they *say* such facts are the case. When someone shouts "Help!" she does not literally say that there is an obnoxious situation with which she cannot cope. Dewey does not want us to forget the importance of the total context in analyz-ing acts of communication; but in emphasizing this, he seems to have blurred the valid distinction between the meaning of a bit of language and what we may legitimately infer from the fact that this bit of language has been used.

Nonetheless, Dewey's main contention about ethical language is that ethical sentences may be cognitively meaningful even if their use or func-tion is practical. For unlike such utterances as "Help!" or "Alas!" there is every reason to believe that ethical sentences are true or false. The problem is, if ethical sentences do have a content that is true or false, what is it?

We may approach this question by examining the distinction between what is desired and what is desirable. Dewey gives a naturalistic analysis of this distinction, according to which what is desirable is simply what we would desire as a result of an impartial, intelligent review of the relevant facts. Once again, we must start with the context in which desires arise. We want something, or we need something, in a situation in which that thing does not exist; or there is something in the present situation to which we have an aversion. Thus we are motivated to take some sort of action. We might resolve the situation by simply doing the first plausible thing that occurs to us. But if we pause to deliberate—if we pause to think intelligently about the conditions that gave rise to our desire, about the object of the desire, and about the likely consequences of pursuing it through various means—several things might happen. The original desire might persist. Or it might be strengthened. Or it might be weakened, or even extinguished. New desires and aversions might be formed relative to various alternative actions. The point is that deliberation modifies, changes, and reinforces our desires, and what we desire as a result of this process may be very different from what we desired before. What we desire as a result of this process is, on Dewey's view, what is desirable.

> The contrast referred to [between the desired and the desirable] is simply that between the object of a desire as it first presents itself (because of the existing mechanism of impulses and habits) and the object of desire which emerges as a revision of the first-appearing impulse, after the latter is critically judged in reference to the conditions which will decide the actual result. . . . It points to the difference between the operation and consequences of unexamined impulses and those of desires and interests that are the product of investigation of conditions and consequences.[9]

This is all pretty general, and Dewey is not very good about providing examples. So I will provide one that I think captures the spirit of what Dewey is after. Let us consider the position someone is in when he first confronts the moral arguments for vegetarianism, which are stronger than people usually realize.[10]

Suppose someone enjoys eating meat, and it has never occurred to him to question the morality of this practice. His action follows the pattern of "the existing mechanism of impulses and habits." But then he reads something on the subject of factory farming and is disturbed to learn that raising and slaughtering animals for meat involves making them suffer in various ways that he never considered. Now he finds that two of his desires are in conflict: he wants to continue eating meat, but he doesn't want to participate in a practice that involves such cruelty. A third desire is also involved, namely his desire to remain healthy: he had always believed, in a vague way, that eating meat was necessary for his health. But now suppose he learns that this isn't so, that in fact a vegetarian diet is just as nutritious. So it begins to appear to him that the *only* reason he has for eating meat, and so for supporting the cruelties, is that he likes the way the animals taste. To top it all off, he learns that a diet including meat is wasteful, because we have to feed the animals much more protein in grain form than we get back in the form of meat, so if we did not eat meat, there would be more food to go around for the world's people. As a result of reflecting on all this, he might form a new set of attitudes. His old enjoyment of meat was, as Dewey puts it, one that "reflective judgments condemn."[11]

If I understand Dewey correctly, an enjoyment that "reflective judgments condemn" is one that cannot be sustained in the face of knowledge and reflection. Such enjoyments are unstable in the sense that they can exist only so long as one does not think much about them. The contrast is with likings and enjoyments that are reinforced or even produced by such reflection; these enjoyments "are not repented of; they generate no after-taste of bitterness."[12] If we picture someone whose desires are formed and sustained by their intelligence in this way, we have, I think, not only Dewey's picture of the good person, but also Plato's picture of the "just man": his passions are under the direction of his reason, and the parts of his soul are in harmony.

To return to our question: If ethical sentences have a content that is true or false, what exactly is this content? Dewey's answer, on the reading I am suggesting, can be expressed in this way: "X is desirable" means "X is such that it would be desired by someone who had considered, intelligently and without prejudice, the nature of X and its consequences." And the meaning of "X is good," "X is right," and "X ought to be done" may be explained similarly.

Dewey compares "desirable" with "edible," and the analogy is illuminating.[13] Whether something is edible is a matter of fact; if something is not edible, we cannot simply decide to make it so by adopting a positive attitude toward it. Yet whether something is edible for us depends on the kind of creature we are as much as on the kind of thing it is. If we were different, what is edible for us might be different too. However, we would not say that a certain food was inedible simply because, for special reasons, it could not be eaten by a few people. We have a conception of what is normal for humans, given the kind of creature a human being is, and what is edible for humans is what may be eaten by the representative human being, whether or not it can be eaten by everyone. In the same way, the "someone" in my version of Dewey's definition of "desirable" may be understood as any typical, representative person.

It may be thought that the analogy with "edible" breaks down at a crucial point. "Edible" means, roughly, "*capable* of being eaten," whereas "desirable" (in the sense relevant to ethics) means, again roughly, "*worthy* of being desired." So it may be thought that Dewey's theory trades on a confusion between two senses of "desirable"—"capable of being desired" and "worthy of being desired." The charge is that he thinks he has defined the latter, ethically relevant, sense of "desirable," but really he has only given a definition of the former sense of the term, which is not relevant to ethics. But this charge is not well founded. It is the essence of Dewey's view that to be worthy of being desired *is* to be capable of being desired, under the circumstances of thought and reflection. Perhaps this is not correct, but it certainly is not a *confusion* of the theory: it is the theory itself.

But is the theory correct? From among the many matters relevant to an assessment, we might begin with three central issues. First, it is an important fact about moral judgments that reasons may be given to support them. Does Dewey's sort of naturalistic view provide us with an adequate understanding of the nature of such reasons and their relation to the judgments they support? Second, does this sort of view provide an adequate understanding of the nature of ethical disagreement? And finally, does it commit the naturalistic fallacy?

(1) If I say that you ought to do something—for example, that you ought to stop eating meat—you can ask *why* you should do it, and if there is no reason, you may properly ignore my admonition and conclude that I am wrong. This suggests that there is an important connection between moral judgments and reasons. One test of the adequacy of ethical theories is their ability to explain this connection.

For Stevenson, the connection between reasons and moral judgments is contingent. Since moral judgments are merely devices for influencing attitudes, any fact that will influence someone's attitude may be cited as a reason in support of the judgment. The only test of validity is the reason's effectiveness—good reasons are the ones that work, bad reasons are the ones that don't. This is so implausible that it led many critics to reject Stevenson's view as fundamentally mistaken.[14]

For Dewey, the connection between reasons and moral judgments is a logical one, and not merely the contingent one that Stevenson suggests. This does not mean that the reasons entail moral judgments in the way that the premises of a deductive argument entail its conclusion. Rather, it means that in order for a moral judgment to be true, there must be—logically must be—reasons in its support. "You ought to do X" does not itself state a reason for your doing X, but it implies that there are such reasons, and if there are none, the original proposition is false. Dewey says, "For in my opinion sentences about what *should* be done, chosen, etc., are sentences, propositions, judgments, *in the logical sense* of those words only as matter-of-fact grounds are presented in support of what is advised, urged, recommended to be done—that is, worthy of being done on the basis of the factual evidence available."[15] And not just any facts can be cited in support of "You ought to do X"; they must be facts about the nature and consequences of X which would influence the desires of someone who was being intelligent and reflective about X. Thus I might try to convince you that meat eating is wrong by telling you about the "conditions and consequences" of meat eating, but other means would be irrelevant to the ethical issue.

(2) Another test of the adequacy of ethical theories is their ability to elucidate the nature of ethical disagreement. If you and I disagree about whether meat eating is wrong, exactly what are we disagreeing about? And is there any rational way to resolve our disagreement and determine which of us is right?

On Stevenson's view, our disagreement is not a disagreement about anything at all; rather, it is a disagreement *in* attitude.[16] So our ethical disagreement will be resolved when we come to have the same attitude, no matter how much we continue to disagree over the facts of the matter. There is no difference, then, between showing my view of the morality of meat eating to be correct and persuading you, by any propagandistic or rhetorical means available, to share my attitude.

Dewey's theory permits a much more plausible understanding of ethical disagreement. Rather than assuming that when people disagree, the difference between them is simply in their attitudes, we may begin by asking whether they have exercised their intelligence and reflective abilities in the required way. Dewey emphasizes that when we form our judgments about right and wrong, "If intelligent method is lacking, prejudice, the pressure of immediate circumstance, self-interest and class-interest, traditional customs, institutions of accidental historic origin, are not lacking, and they tend to take the place of intelligence."[17] The point is that in the absence of intelligent thought, there are lots of considerations that might explain why people disagree. Suppose the argument is about meat eating and the vegetarian is convinced that he is right, but he cannot persuade his friend. (Of course, on Dewey's view, no one should ever be *so* convinced he is right that he is unwilling to reconsider his view; but for the moment let us set that aside.) How might the disagreement be explained? There are a number of possibilities. Perhaps his friend is not fully acquainted with the relevant facts—for example, the facts about how animals are treated on factory farms. Or perhaps he has not adequately reflected on such facts as he does know: perhaps he has not considered, in an imaginative way, what it must be like to be treated in the way these animals are treated. Again, perhaps what Dewey calls "prejudice" or "class-interest" is influencing his judgment: it is easy not to take the animals' interests seriously, because we enjoy eating them so much; and besides, "they" are not "us." And, as Dewey notes, the pressure of custom and traditional institutions is always great: eating animals is such a familiar part of our lives that it is hard to take seriously the idea that it may be wrong.

The understanding of ethical disagreement that goes naturally with Dewey's view is this: if we could exercise our intelligence to the fullest, we could agree on evaluations; however, since various forces and interests interfere with our being fully rational, we sometimes disagree, and when we do, the disagreement is explained by the operation of those nonrational forces.

It might be thought that this is much too optimistic, that it seriously underestimates the differences between people. Aren't some people so basically different from others, in their attitudes and outlooks on life, that they would continue to disagree even if they could exercise their rational powers to the fullest? Aren't there differences in attitude between people that are beyond the power of reason to resolve?

It is certainly possible that there should be such differences, and to the extent that there are, what is desirable for one person may not be desirable for all (just as what is edible for one need not be edible for all). A theory such as Dewey's must allow for at least the possibility of a kind of last-ditch relativism. Dewey is right, however, to insist that we should never assume, as an explanation of actual disagreements, that people are simply different. We should always go on the assumption that actual disagreements are due to some failure of rationality and that they are susceptible to rational settlement. We should make this assumption because, even though it is theoretically possible that people are so different that rational methods will not suffice to settle their disagreements, there is reason to think that in fact there are no such basic differences—or, if there are, they are rare and must concern matters of relatively minor importance. The evolutionary history of humankind has produced a species of beings that are so alike in their basic attitudes and needs that the application of intelligence should enable them to reach common decisions. Dewey writes:

Within the content of morals proper there are at least two forces making for stability. One is the psychological uniformity of human nature with respect to basic needs. However much men differ in other respects, they remain alike in requiring food, protection, sex-mates, recognition of some sort, companions, and need for constructive and manipulative activities, and so forth. The uniformity of these needs is at the basis of the exaggerated statements often made about the unchangeability of human nature; it is sufficient to ensure the constant recurrence, under change of form, of certain social patterns. In the second place, there are certain conditions which must be met in order that any form of human association may be maintained, whether it be simple or complex, low or high in the scale of cultures. Some degree of peace, order, and internal harmony must be secured if men are to live together at all. In consequence of these two factors of comparative invariance, the extreme statements sometimes made about the relativity of morals cannot be maintained.[18]

Considering these and other important similarities between them, a common ethic for human beings should not be regarded as an unattainable ideal.

(3) Finally, since Dewey's ethical theory is naturalistic—that is, since it assumes the existence of nothing more than the natural world and defines value in terms of the operation of human interests and intelligence within that world—the question may be raised whether his theory commits "the naturalistic fallacy."[19]

"The naturalistic fallacy" is not a happy name for the subject to which the phrase refers, for it is not concerned solely with naturalism, and it does not refer to a fallacy. The phrase was coined by G. E. Moore, who thought that "good" cannot be defined.[20] Since naturalistic theories, and others as well, try to define "good," Moore thought that all these theories are mistaken. But this does not mean that they all commit a common fallacy (a fallacy is an error in reasoning, such as affirming the consequent or hasty generalization), it only means that they are all mistaken.

The argument that Moore used in attempting to prove that all naturalistic theories (and some others as well) are mistaken is the "open question" argument. It goes like this: First, we note that any definition of "good" can be expressed in this form:

D: "X is good" means "X has the property P."

Then we formulate two questions:

A: X has P, but is it good?
B: X has P, but does it have P?

Now, the open-question argument is simply this:

If D is correct, than A and B have the same meaning.
But A and B do not have the same meaning.

Therefore, D is not correct.

And the reason A and B do not have the same meaning is that A is an open question but B is not.

Can this type of argument be used to show that Dewey's naturalistic conception of value is incorrect? The issue comes down to whether the following is an open question:

X is such that it would be desired by someone who had considered, intelligently and without prejudice, X's nature and consequences; but is X desirable?

I don't think this is an open question—or at the very least, it is not so obviously an open question that Moore's argument is decisive. For if we already know that the intelligent, impartial consideration of every fact about X would lead an unprejudiced, rational person to desire it, is there really room left for doubt as to its desirability? Any reason that could be given to show that X is *not* desirable would, by hypothesis, already have been taken into account and would already have been allowed to have whatever influence it could exert. It may be, of course, that what considerations will have weight for a rational human is relative to human nature; but that is all right, for the logical character of the concept of value may simply reflect this fact.

Notes

1. David Hume, *A Treatise of Human Nature* (Oxford: Oxford University Press, 1888), 457. Originally published in 1739.

2. John Dewey, *The Quest for Certainty* (1929; reprint, New York: Capricorn Books, 1960), 263.

3. Charles L. Stevenson, *Facts and Values* (New Haven: Yale University Press, 1963), chap. 7.

4. Corliss Lamont, ed., *Dialogue on John Dewey* (New York: Horizon Press, 1959), 11–12.

5. Here Dewey is on the side of Plato, Kant, and others who viewed moral notions as essentially conflict-notions—that is, notions we need only because we

sometimes find ourselves in a special sort of quandary about what to do. "When things are going completely smoothly, desires do not arise, and there is no occasion to project ends-in-view, for 'going smoothly' signifies that there is no need for effort and struggle. There is no occasion to investigate what it would be better to have happen in the future, and hence no projection of an end-object." John Dewey, *Theory of Valuation* (Chicago: University of Chicago Press, 1939), 33.

6. John Dewey, "Ethical Subject Matter and Language," *Journal of Philosophy* 42 (1945): 701–12, reprinted in *Pragmatic Philosophy,* ed. A. Rorty (Garden City, N.Y.: Anchor Books, 1966), 285.

7. Dewey, *Theory of Valuation,* 12.

8. Dewey, "Ethical Subject Matter and Language," 292.

9. Dewey, *Theory of Valuation,* 31-32.

10. See chap. 7.

11. Dewey, *Quest for Certainty,* 263.

12. Dewey, *Quest for Certainty,* 267.

13. Dewey, *Quest for Certainty,* 266.

14. See chap. 1.

15. Dewey, "Ethical Subject Matter and Language," 296.

16. Stevenson, *Facts and Values,* chap. 1.

17. Dewey, *Quest for Certainty,* 265.

18. John Dewey, "Anthropology and Ethics," in *The Social Sciences,* ed. W. Ogburn and A. Goldenweiser (Boston: Houghton Mifflin, 1927), 34–35.

19. Kai Nielsen argues in "Dewey's Conception of Philosophy," *Massachusetts Review* 1 (1960), 110–34, that Dewey does commit the naturalistic fallacy.

20. G. E. Moore, *Principia Ethica* (Cambridge: Cambridge University Press, 1903), chap. 1.

4

Active and Passive Euthanasia

The distinction between active and passive euthanasia is thought to be crucial for medical ethics. The idea is that it is permissible, at least in some cases, to withhold treatment and allow a patient to die, but it is never permissible to take direct action to kill a patient. This doctrine seems to be accepted by most doctors, and in 1973 it was endorsed in the first policy statement on euthanasia ever issued by the American Medical Association (AMA). That statement said, in its entirety:

> The intentional termination of the life of one human being by another—mercy killing—is contrary to that for which the medical profession stands and is contrary to the policy of the American Medical Association.
> The cessation of the employment of extraordinary means to prolong the life of the body when there is irrefutable evidence that biological death is imminent is the decision of the patient and/or his immediate family. The advice and judgment of the physician should be freely available to the patient and/or his immediate family.

In subsequent statements the AMA refined its policy, but the central idea—that killing patients is worse than letting them die—has remained. Nonetheless, a strong case can be made against this idea. In what follows we will examine some of the relevant arguments. These arguments suggest that active and passive euthanasia are not as different as people have thought. If one is accepted, the other should be accepted as well.

To begin with a familiar type of case, suppose a patient is dying of incurable cancer of the throat and the pain can no longer be satisfactorily alleviated. He is certain to die within a few days, even if present treatment is continued, but he does not want to go on living for those days since the pain is unbearable. So he asks the doctor for an end to it, and his family supports the request.

The conventional doctrine says that the doctor may agree to withhold treatment and allow the patient to die sooner than he otherwise would. The justification is that the patient is in agony, and since he is going to die soon anyway, it would be wrong to prolong his suffering needlessly. But notice this: if one simply withholds treatment, it may take the patient longer to die, so he may suffer more than he would if more direct action were taken and, say, a lethal injection were given. This fact provides strong reason for thinking that once the decision has been made not to prolong his agony, active euthanasia is preferable to passive euthanasia, rather than the reverse. To say otherwise is to endorse the option that leads to more suffering rather than less and is contrary to the humanitarian impulse that prompts the decision not to prolong his life in the first place.

The process of being "allowed to die" can be relatively slow and painful, whereas being given a lethal injection is relatively quick and painless. Here is a different sort of example. In the United States about one in six hundred babies is born with Down's syndrome. Most of these babies are otherwise healthy—that is, with only the usual pediatric care, they will proceed to a normal infancy. Some, however, have additional defects such as intestinal obstructions so that surgery is needed if they are to live. In such cases, parents and physicians have sometimes decided not to operate and to let the infant die. Writing in the *New York Times* one year before the first AMA statement, Dr. Anthony Shaw described what happens:

> When surgery is denied [the doctor] must try to keep the infant from suffering while natural forces sap the baby's life away. As a surgeon whose natural inclination is to use the scalpel to fight off death, standing by and watching a salvageable baby die is the most emotionally exhausting experience I know. It is easy at a conference, in a theoretical discussion, to decide that such infants should be allowed to die. It is altogether different to stand by in the nursery and watch as dehydration and infection wither a tiny being over hours and days. This is a terrible ordeal for me and the hospital staff—much more so than for the parents who never set foot in the nursery.[1]

It is easy to understand why some people are opposed to all euthanasia and insist that such infants must be allowed to live. It is also understandable that other people might favor destroying these babies quickly and painlessly. But why should anyone want to let "dehydration and infection wither a tiny being over hours and days?" The doctrine that says a baby may be allowed to dehydrate and wither, but may not be given an injection that would end its life without suffering, seems so patently cruel as to require no further refutation. It is a compromise that combines the worst, not the best, features of the two extremes.

A second argument is that the conventional doctrine leads to decisions about life and death being made on irrelevant grounds.

Consider again the Down's-syndrome infants with the obstructed intestines. Sometimes there is no operation and the baby dies. But when there is no such additional defect, the baby lives on. Now, an operation to remove an intestinal obstruction is not prohibitively difficult—it is well within the competence of any good pediatric surgeon. The reason that such operations are not performed in these cases is, clearly, that the child has Down's syndrome and the parents and doctor judge that because of that fact, it is better for the child to die.

But notice that this situation is absurd, no matter what view one takes of the lives and potentials of such babies. If the life of such an infant is worth preserving, what does it matter if the infant needs a simple operation? Or, if one thinks it better that such a baby should not live, what difference does it make that it happens to have an unobstructed intestinal tract? In either case, the matter of life and death is being decided on irrelevant grounds. It is the Down's syndrome, and not the intestines, that is the issue. The matter should be decided, if at all, on that basis and should not be allowed to depend on the essentially irrelevant question of whether the intestinal tract is blocked.

What makes this situation possible is the idea that when there is an intestinal blockage, we can "let the baby die," but when there is no such defect there is nothing that we can do, for we must not "kill" it. The fact that this idea leads to such results as deciding life or death on irrelevant grounds is another good reason it should be rejected.

Why do so many people think there is an important moral difference between active and passive euthanasia? One reason is that they believe the more general proposition that *killing someone is morally worse than letting someone die*. But is it? To investigate this issue, we may consider two cases that are exactly alike except that one involves killing whereas the other involves letting die. Then we can ask whether this difference makes any difference to our moral assessments. It is important that the cases be exactly alike, except for this one thing, since otherwise we cannot be confident that it is this difference and not some other that accounts for any variation in the assessments of the two cases.

In the first case, Smith stands to gain a large inheritance if anything should happen to his six-year-old cousin. One evening while the child is taking his bath, Smith sneaks into the bathroom, drowns the child, and arranges things so that it will look like an accident.

In the second, Jones also stands to gain if anything should happen to his six-year-old cousin. Like Smith, Jones sneaks in, planning to drown the child in his bath. However, as he enters the bathroom Jones sees the child slip, hit his head and fall face down in the water. Jones is delighted; he stands by, ready to push the child's head back under if it is necessary, but it is not necessary. With only a little thrashing about, the child drowns all by himself, "accidentally," as Jones watches and does nothing.

Now Smith killed the child, while Jones merely let the child die. That is the only difference between them. Did either man behave better, from a moral point of view? If the difference between killing and letting die were in itself a morally important matter, we should say that Jones's behavior was less reprehensible than Smith's. But do we really want to say that? Perhaps not. In the first place, both men acted from the same motive, personal gain, and both had exactly the same end in view when they acted. It may be inferred from Smith's conduct that he is a bad man, although that judgment may be withdrawn or modified if certain further facts are learned about him—for example, that he is mentally deranged. But would not the very same thing be inferred about Jones from his conduct? And would not the same further considerations also be relevant to any modification of this judgment? Moreover, suppose Jones pleaded, in his own defense, "After all, I didn't do anything except just stand there and watch the child drown. I didn't kill him; I only let him die." If letting die were in itself less bad than killing, this defense should have at least some weight. But it does not. Such a "defense" can only be regarded as a grotesque perversion of moral reasoning. Morally speaking, it is no defense at all.

It may be pointed out, quite properly, that the cases of euthanasia with which doctors are concerned are not like this at all. They do not involve personal gain or the destruction of normal, healthy children. Doctors are concerned only with cases in which a terminal patient's life has become or will soon become a terrible burden. However, the point is the same even in these cases: the bare difference between killing and letting die does not, in itself, make a moral difference. If a doctor lets a patient die for humane reasons, she is in the same moral position as if she had given the patient a lethal injection for humane reasons. If the decision was wrong—if, for example, the patient's illness was in fact curable—the decision would be equally regrettable no matter which method was used to carry it out. And if the doctor's decision was the right one, the method used would not in itself be important.

The AMA policy statement isolates the crucial issue very well; the crucial issue is "the intentional termination of the life of one human being by another." But after identifying this issue and forbidding "mercy killing," the statement goes on to deny that the cessation of treatment is the intentional termination of a life. This is where the mistake comes in, for what is the cessation of treatment, in these circumstances, if it is not "the intentional termination of the life of one human being by another"? Of course it is exactly that, and if it were not, there would be no point to it.

Many people will find this hard to accept. One reason is that it is easy to conflate the question of whether killing is, in itself, worse than letting die with the very different question of whether most actual cases of killing are more reprehensible than most actual cases of letting die. Most actual cases of killing are clearly terrible (think of all the murders reported in the newspapers), and one hears of such cases every day. On the other hand, one hardly ever hears of a case of letting die except for the actions of doctors motivated by humanitarian reasons. So one learns to think of killing in a much worse light than letting die. But this does not mean that there is something about killing that makes it in itself worse than letting die, for it is not the bare difference between killing and letting die that makes the difference in these cases. Rather, the other factors—the murderer's motive of personal gain, for example, contrasted with the doctor's humanitarian reasons—account for different reactions to the different cases.

All of these arguments suggest that active euthanasia is no worse than passive euthanasia and, therefore, that the conventional doctrine is false. But what arguments can be given on the other side? Perhaps the most common is the following: The morally important difference between active and passive euthanasia is that, in passive euthanasia, the doctor does not *do anything* to bring about the patient's death. The doctor does nothing, and the patient dies of whatever ills already afflict him. In active euthanasia, however, the doctor does something to bring about the patient's death: he kills him. The doctor who gives the cancer patient a lethal injection has himself caused his patient's death; whereas if he merely ceases treatment, the cancer is the cause of the death.

But there is less to this argument than meets the eye. In the first place, it is not exactly correct to say that in passive euthanasia the doctor does nothing, for he does do one thing that is very important: he lets the patient die. "Letting someone die" is certainly different, in some respects, from other types of action—mainly in that it is a kind of action that one may perform by way of not performing certain other actions. One may let a patient die, for example, by not giving medication, just as one may insult someone by not shaking his hand. But for the purpose of moral assessment, it is nonetheless a type of action. The decision to let a patient die is subject to moral appraisal in the same way that a decision to kill would be subject to moral appraisal: it may be assessed as wise or unwise, compassionate or sadistic, right or wrong. If a doctor deliberately let a patient die who was suffering from a routinely curable illness, the doctor would certainly be to blame for what he had done, just as he would be to blame if he had needlessly killed the patient. Charges against him would be appropriate. If so, it would be no defense at all for the doctor to insist that he didn't "do anything." He would have done something very serious indeed, for he let his patient die.

Fixing the cause of death—did the doctor cause the death, or did the cancer cause it?—may be important from a legal point of view, for it may determine whether criminal charges are brought. But can this notion be used to show a moral difference between active and passive euthanasia? The reason it is bad to be the cause of someone's death is that death is a great evil. That is also the reason it is bad to let someone die. However, if it has been decided that euthanasia—even passive euthanasia—is desirable in a given case, it has also been decided that in this instance death is no greater an evil than the patient's continued existence. And if this is true, the usual reason for not wanting to be the cause of someone's death simply does not apply.

Finally, doctors may think that all of this is only of academic interest—the sort of thing that philosophers may worry about but that has no practical bearing on their own work. After all, doctors must be concerned about the legal consequences of what they do, and active euthanasia is forbidden by the law. But even so, doctors should also be concerned with the fact that the law is forcing upon them a moral doctrine that may well be indefensible. Of course, most doctors are not now in the position of being coerced in this matter, for they do not regard themselves as merely going along with what the law requires. Rather, they are endorsing this doctrine as a central point of medical ethics. In the AMA policy statement, active euthanasia is condemned not merely as illegal but as "contrary to that for which the medical profession stands," whereas passive euthanasia is approved. However, the preceding considerations suggest that there is really no moral difference between the two, considered in themselves. (There may sometimes be important moral differences in their *consequences*, but as we have seen, these differences may make active euthanasia, and not passive euthanasia, the preferable option.) So, whereas doctors may have to discriminate between active and passive euthanasia to satisfy the law, they should not do any more than that. They should not give the distinction added weight by writing it into official statements of medical ethics.

Note

1. Anthony Shaw, "Doctor, Do We Have a Choice?" *New York Times Magazine*, 30 January 1972, 54.

5

Killing, Letting Die, and the Value of Life

In 1992 a story appeared in American newspapers about Theresa Ann Campo Pearson, a Florida infant who would be known to the public as "Baby Theresa." Baby Theresa was one of about one thousand anencephalic infants—babies without brains—born each year in the United States. Because anencephaly is a familiar condition, there would have been nothing newsworthy about this particular baby had it not been for an unusual request made by her parents. Knowing that their daughter could not live more than a few days and that even if she could live longer, she could never have a conscious life, Theresa's parents volunteered her organs for transplant. Their thought was that her kidneys, liver, heart, lungs, and eyes should go to other children who could benefit from them. "If my kid can help another baby live, then that is what we want to do," said the father. The physicians agreed, but Florida law would not allow it. So her organs were not taken, and after nine days Theresa died. By then it was too late for the other children. As the doctors had known would happen, her organs had deteriorated too much to be used for transplants.

The newspaper stories about Baby Theresa prompted a great deal of public discussion. Would it have been right to remove the infant's organs, thereby causing her immediate death, to save other children? A number of professional "ethicists"—people employed by universities, hospitals, and law schools whose job it is to think about such matters—were called on by the press to comment. Surprisingly few of them agreed with the parents and the physicians. Instead, they appealed to time-honored philosophical principles to support letting all the children die. "It just seems too horrifying to use people as means to other people's ends," said one such expert. Another explained, "It is unethical to kill in order to save. It's unethical to kill person A to save person B." And a third added: "What the parents are really asking for is: Kill this dying baby so that its organs may be used for someone else. Well, that's really a horrendous proposition."[1]

Why was the parents' request "horrendous"? The principles cited by the ethicists seem insufficient to justify such a conclusion. The idea that "we may not kill in order to save" seems plausible enough when we imagine killing a normal, healthy human being in order to save someone else—after all, we would be depriving the victim of a life that is just as valuable as the life of the person being saved. But if we think of the "life" of someone who can never have a conscious thought or feeling, it is not at all clear why preserving such a life should be so morally important.

The ethicists apparently would disagree. The assumption underlying their comments is that Baby Theresa's life, despite her tragic condition, was of such moral importance that it could not be "sacrificed" even to save the lives of the others. It did not matter that she had no brain and that she was going to die within a few days anyway. It did not matter that she was hardly even a "she" in any significant sense because she did not have, and never could have, a meaningful life as an independent human personality. All that mattered, apparently, was that she was biologically human and that she was alive. Her mere existence as a living member of the species was taken to have such importance that other children should be allowed to die for the sake of it.

What could justify such a remarkable assumption? It could not be based on any concern with the value that her life had *for her*. Her life, such as it was, had no value for her; she would never even know that she existed. Nor could it be based on any concern for the value that her life would have had for others. (Indeed, the only value that her life could have had for others would have been if her organs had been transplanted.) When these options are eliminated, what remains is the idea that human life—all human life, regardless of its condition—is valuable as such, that it is valuable, as one might say, "to the universe."

The belief that human life has a special cosmic importance is in some ways a noble idea. It supports humane moral doctrines that might otherwise seem arbitrary. But it can also be an obstacle to humane thinking—it can lead, paradoxically, to decisions that go against human interests. The refusal to transplant Baby Theresa's organs is one example of this, but there are others as well. Euthanasia is illegal in most of the Western world. (The Netherlands is the one notable exception.) It is forbidden to kill, even at their own request, terminal patients who are dying slow, miserable deaths, and "the sanctity of human life" is cited as a reason that this would be wrong. But who, exactly, benefits from the application of this principle? Certainly not the individuals who are required to suffer, nor their families, nor the medical professionals who care for them. It is another instance of a moral principle working not for, but against, the welfare of human beings.

The irony of this has not been lost on medical practitioners in the United States, many of whom have embraced a set of moral ideas that significantly qualify the thought that it is always wrong to kill. One such idea is that even if it is wrong to kill a patient, it can be permissible to assist that patient in committing suicide. In 1989 a panel of physicians chaired by Dr. Daniel D. Federman of the Harvard Medical School issued a report concluding that physician-assisted suicide is "morally correct" in some circumstances.[2] A good example of what they had in mind was provided two years later, when Dr. Timothy Quill of Rochester, New York, published an article in the *New England Journal of Medicine* describing how he had helped one of his patients end her life.[3] Dr. Quill had advised a woman with leukemia, whom he called "Diane," that she would have a 25 percent chance of prolonging her life if she underwent an arduous program of chemotherapy and bone-marrow transplantation. Diane rejected this possibility, saying that she wanted to live a normal life for as long as possible and then kill herself when her condition became intolerable. She did some research, discovered what drugs she would need, and asked her physician to prescribe them. Dr. Quill prescribed the drugs, eventually Diane used them, and as a result she died. Dr. Quill's thoughtful account of all this elicited considerable sympathy. No action was taken against him.

Physicians also endorse the idea that even if it is wrong to kill, it can be permissible to allow a patient to die by withholding treatment. The American Medical Association confirmed this in policy statements issued in 1973 and 1982, and today the point is conceded by even the most conservative doctors. Initially, the thought was that nontreatment was permissible for terminal patients who were suffering or for patients in irreversible coma; but the idea has been extended to include anencephalic infants as well. When asked about anencephalics, the surgeon general of the United States, who had led a campaign to require aggressive treatment for all handicapped babies, commented that the government "would not attempt to interfere" with physicians whose policy was nontreatment for such infants.[4]

These moral doctrines raise a host of philosophical issues. In what follows I will discuss two of them. First, I will argue that the doctrine of the sanctity of life, if it were interpreted in a reasonable way, would provide no objection either to voluntary euthanasia or to the removal of Baby Theresa's organs. And second, I will argue that the distinction between killing and letting die does not have the moral importance that is commonly attributed to it. If the latter argument is correct, it will follow that, if it is morally permissible in some circumstances to allow patients to die, it may also be morally permissible to actively kill patients in those same circumstances.

The Value of Life

Many people think it is objectionable to compare the values of different lives. The very idea seems an affront to human dignity. If we say "this life is more valuable than that life," the door seems open to ignoring or mistreating those whose lives are deemed less important. Is the life of Bill Clinton "more valuable" than that of a homeless person? Is the life of a physically handicapped individual less important, from a moral point of view, than that of a normal, healthy person? It seems obviously wrong to say such things. Therefore decent people may be tempted to eschew comparisons altogether and fall back on the old cliché that "all human lives are equally valuable."

Yet it is obvious that none of us really believes this. We constantly assess lives as better or worse. A man who is happy, whose days are filled with satisfying activities, and who has a loving family and devoted friends has a better life than someone who has none of these things. We make our own choices based on such assessments—we try to have one sort of life rather than another. Moreover, we would all prefer to live the life of a healthy person than the life of a physically handicapped person—we think such a life is better. In the same vein, we would all wish our children to be intelligent rather than stupid; we would all rather have homes than be homeless; and we would all prefer, in general, that people be happy rather than miserable. So it is obvious that not all human lives are equally worth having. If we say that all human lives are equally valuable, none of this makes any sense.

Nevertheless, the cliché does seem to make an important moral point. But precisely what point is it? The point, I think, is that *regardless of the kind of lives they have, all human beings' interests should be counted as equally important.* Every person, whether she is rich or poor, intelligent or stupid, healthy or ill, has interests that may be helped or harmed by what we do. What we should do, morally speaking, is whatever would give each of these interests equal respect. This explains why it would be wrong to "sacrifice" the lives of some people (the poor or the handicapped, for example) to benefit others. The reason is not that the lives of the less fortunate are as good as other people's lives—often, unfortunately, their lives are not as good. The reason is that, regardless of this, their interests should be given equal respect.

We also need to distinguish the idea that *not all lives are equally good* from the idea that *not all people are equally good*. These are very different notions. The former, as I have said, is obviously true. The latter is more problematic. On the face of it, it does not appear that all people are equally good. Some people are kind and compassionate, while others are cruel and mean spirited. Some work to promote peace and understanding, while others send Jews, Gypsies, and homosexuals to death camps. Despite this, it is a popular idea among some thinkers that all human beings possess an "inner dignity" or "intrinsic worth" that makes them all in some sense moral equals. I will not discuss this difficult issue here, for my subject is the value of lives, not the value of people. Nevertheless, I do want to make this suggestion: regardless of the position one takes on the value of people, the principle that I have already articulated, that each person's interests should be accorded equal respect, should be sufficient to express its reasonable moral implications.

What, exactly, is the value of a life? How should we understand this notion? The question is ambiguous because the word "life" has different meanings, and it is important to keep them separate. On the one hand, "life" can refer to *living things*, to things that are alive. Human beings are living things, but so are fish and snails and even trees and bushes. "Life" in this sense is a term of biology—to be alive is to be a functioning biological organism. When we ask "Is there life on other planets?" we are using the term in this sense. A single blade of grass growing on Mars would justify an affirmative answer.

On the other hand, the word can have a very different meaning, one associated more with biography than biology. The story of a person's life is not just an account of her status as a biological organism. It is the story of her history and character, her aspirations and disappointments, her activities and projects and personal relationships. A person's life, in this sense, includes all that she says and does and thinks. The difference between biological and biographical life is the difference between *being alive* and *having a life*.

Why is this distinction important? It is important because, if the concept of life is ambiguous, then so is the concept of the sanctity of life. The doctrine of the sanctity of life may be interpreted in two ways. First, it may be understood as a moral doctrine that places value on merely being alive. If it is interpreted in this way, then the doctrine protects human life, but it also gives the very same protection to the lives of fish, snails, trees, and bushes—after all, they are living things just as much as we are. The adherents of some Eastern religions take this view. But there is a second way in which the sanctity of life may be interpreted, corresponding to the other sense of "life." It may be understood as a moral doctrine that places value on lives (in the biographical sense) and on the interests that some creatures, including ourselves, have in virtue of the fact that they are the subjects of lives. This will lead to a very different kind of moral position.

Which interpretation is best? We may approach this question by considering the different kinds of value that being alive and having a life have for us. Suppose we try this thought experiment: we are given a choice between (a) dying now, and (b) lapsing into a dreamless coma, from which we will never awaken, and dying after ten years. Which would we choose? Most of us would prefer the first option, both because we would not find the prospect of a vegetable existence very dignified and because we would not want to put our loved ones through the pointless ordeal of caring for our unconscious bodies. But in an obvious sense the choice is indifferent: when we enter the coma, our biographical lives are over. It is *as if* we had died. In the coma, of course, we would still be alive; and if being alive is what matters, then we should prefer that option. The reason we do not prefer that option is that being alive has no value for us if it does not enable us to have some sort of biographical life.

Thus it is biographical life, and not merely being alive biologically, that we care about. In the familiar philosophical terminology, the value of biological life is instrumental, while the value of biographical life is intrinsic. The former is valuable only as a means to the latter. This provides strong evidence that the doctrine of the sanctity of life should be interpreted in the second way. This has clear implications both for voluntary euthanasia and for cases like that of Baby Theresa.

In the Netherlands voluntary euthanasia for terminal patients is permitted provided that seven conditions are satisfied. (1) The patient must be in unbearable pain or in a condition that is otherwise intolerable. (2) There must be no available treatment that could improve the patient's condition. (3) The patient, while competent, must have requested to be killed. (4) The request must be free of doubt, well documented, and repeated. (5) A determination must be made that no one pressured the patient into making the request. (6) The euthanasia must be performed by a physician. (7) Before performing the euthanasia, the physician must consult a second, independent physician. If these conditions are satisfied, the physician's action is not punishable by law.

Is this kind of policy morally acceptable? Of course there are many arguments that might be given on both sides. But let us focus specifically on the question of the sanctity of life. Is there anything in the doctrine of the sanctity of life that would oppose such a policy? A terminal patient is, by definition, approaching the end of his life. If the patient is in "unbearable pain" or some similar condition and nothing can be done to improve things, then all that remains of his life is a period of suffering. Euthanasia would, to be sure, shorten the patient's biographical life. But it would not make that life worse. Indeed, it is the patient's own judgment that it would make the life better. (It is easy to see why one would think this. Suppose you were given the choice of two lives. In one, you live to be eighty-five and die peacefully. In the other, you live to be eighty-five plus two months, but the extra two months are filled with suffering. Which would you think is better?) Thus the doctrine of the sanctity of life—if it were interpreted as placing moral value on biographical lives and on the interests that we have as the subjects of those lives—would offer no objection to euthanasia in this sort of case. Perhaps there are valid reasons for opposing euthanasia, but if this analysis is correct, the sanctity of life is not among them.

The case of Baby Theresa is even simpler. She was, before her death, undoubtedly alive; yet she had no biographical life and could never have one. Moreover, because she did not even have the capacity for consciousness, she had no interests that could have been helped or harmed by anything anyone might have done. It made no difference to her whether she lived for nine days or for two days. Thus neither the doctrine of the sanctity of life nor the principle of equal respect for everyone's interests could pose any objection to transferring her organs to the children who needed them. On the contrary, the principle of respect for everyone's interests would require the transplants, for unlike Baby Theresa the other children did have interests, and those interests were tragically brushed aside.

Killing and Letting Die

These conclusions will strike many people as unacceptable, for they go against very strong moral feelings. The intentional killing of a human being is repugnant to almost all of us; the very idea fills us with horror. It is, no doubt, good that we have such feelings, for they are a bulwark against committing or condoning murder. These feelings also make it difficult to accept euthanasia. At the same time, however, *allowing people to die* does not seem so bad—we do not have the same visceral reaction when we think of a physician standing by and permitting a patient to expire of an incurable disease when further treatment seems pointless.

How are we to explain this combination of feelings? One possibility is that killing is, in fact, much worse than letting die, and our feelings merely reflect this. Killing is wrong, but "merely" letting someone die may be all right. This conclusion is often reached, and as a result this idea has become an established part of medical ethics. Active euthanasia is forbidden, but passive euthanasia is permitted.

We should notice, however, that there is another possible explanation of these feelings, one that leads to a very different moral conclusion. When we think about killing versus letting die, we tend to focus on cases like these:

1. A man murders his wife because he wants to be rid of her.

2. A physician, seeing that further treatment would only prolong the suffering of a hopelessly ill patient, withholds treatment and allows the patient to die.

The first is a case of killing and the second is a case of letting die. What is done in the first case is much worse than what is done in the second case, and so we might naturally conclude that killing is worse than letting die. But suppose instead we were to compare these cases:

1. A man murders his wife because he wants to be rid of her.

2'. An emergency-room physician sees a patient who is suffering from appendicitis. He could operate and save the patient's life, but he recognizes the patient as a woman against whom he holds a grudge. So he delays the operation until the patient's appendix ruptures and then she dies.

Again, the first is a case of killing and the second is a case of letting die. (In [2'], just as in [2], the physician "lets the patient die" by nontreatment. The physician "lets nature take its course" in both instances.) But now things seem very different. What is done in these cases seems equally bad; we have the same reaction of horror in the second case as in the first case. This suggests that our reactions are not based on the relative moral merits of killing and letting die. They are based instead on other features of the cases: for example, on whether the victims have lives that can profitably be continued and on the motives of those who kill or let die. It is not that killing is worse than letting die. It is that killing or letting die is bad when the victim is thereby deprived of biographical life.

This hypothesis can be supported by an independent argument that shows that killing is not, in itself, worse than letting die. This argument begins by appealing to a fundamental idea about the logic of moral judgment, namely that *whether an action, or a type of action, is right or wrong depends on the reasons that can be given for or against it.* If you are told that you should not do something, you may ask why not, and reasons must be provided. If good reasons can be given, then the action would indeed be wrong. The reasons explain why it would be wrong. But, on the other hand, if there are no reasons to be given, the advice is merely arbitrary, and (for moral purposes, at any rate) it may be ignored. This is a familiar point. But it has an important corollary: if there are the same reasons for or against two courses of conduct, then they are equally right or equally wrong.

Let us ask, then, why it is wrong to kill people. Of course, it is not always wrong; there are exceptions. People may disagree about exactly what exceptions should be permitted. Many would say that killing in a just war or in self-defense should be allowed. Others might argue for different exceptions. But that does not matter here. Our question is why killing is *in general* wrong—or, as we might put it, why is ordinary murder wrong?

The answer is undoubtedly connected with the fact that the victim ends up dead. But why is that a bad thing? Of course it is bad for those who love him (they will mourn) and for those who were depending on him for one thing or another (he will be unable to perform as expected). But the evil of death is not to be understood solely in terms of its bad consequences for the survivors. More fundamentally, the victim himself is deprived of something of great value, namely his life. He will never be able to do the things he wanted to do or accomplish what he wanted to accomplish. He will never be able to experience the things he would have liked to experience. This is the fundamental evil that the victim suffers. Notice, however, that the evil done to him is not simply the deprivation of biological life. It is the loss of biographical life that is critical.

Now let us turn to letting die. Why is it wrong to allow someone to die when we could save him? Of course this is not always wrong; there are exceptions. The most obvious exception is the physician who allows a terminal patient to die when further treatment would be pointless. Nevertheless, letting people die when we could save them is in general wrong. Suppose you could save a child drowning in a bathtub simply by reaching down and pulling her out? Obviously, you should. Or think again of the physician in (2'), who lets the patient with appendicitis die. Obviously, he acts wrongly. So we may sensibly ask, why is this wrong?

Once again, the answer is undoubtedly connected with the fact that the person we do not save ends up dead. Of course this will be bad for those who love her (they will mourn) and for those who were depending on her for one thing or another (she will be unable to perform as expected). But the evil of death is not to be understood solely in terms of its bad consequences for the survivors. More fundamentally, the victim herself loses something of great value, namely, her life. She will never be able to do the things she wanted to do or accomplish what she wanted to accomplish. She will never be able to experience the things she would have liked to experience. Once again, this is the fundamental evil that the victim suffers.

But notice that this is the same explanation that we gave of why killing is wrong. Our evaluations of the two kinds of action are exactly parallel. In each case, there are exceptions to be made; in each case, there is the same fundamental harm suffered by the victim; and in each case, there are the same ancillary effects for the survivors. Thus there are precisely the same reasons for objecting to letting die as there are for objecting to killing, so the two kinds of action are equally bad.

Our argument may therefore be summarized as follows:

1. For any two actions (or types of actions), if there are exactly the same reasons for and against one as there are for and against the other, then they are equally good or equally bad. One is neither better nor worse than the other.

2. There are the same reasons for and against killing as there are for and against letting die.

3. Therefore, killing is neither better nor worse than letting die.

This does not mean, of course, that every individual act of killing is morally equivalent to every individual act of letting die. In particular cases there may be reasons why one is worse than the other. When a man murders his wife to be rid of her, he deprives her of biographical life; but when a physician allows a hopelessly ill patient to die because further treatment would be pointless, he does not deprive the patient of further useful biographical life. This explains why the first act is wrong while the second is permissible. What makes one act wrong and the other permissible is not that one is killing and the other is letting die; the moral evaluation depends on other features of the cases.

If this is correct, the implications for euthanasia are obvious. As we have noted, many physicians accept the idea that passive euthanasia—allowing terminal patients to die—is permissible. When this is done, it is because we have reluctantly made the judgment that there is no point in prolonging the patient's life; in these sad circumstances, death is no greater an evil than continued existence. If this is so, however, active euthanasia may also be permissible. We may not say that active euthanasia is wrong merely because it is killing, whereas passive euthanasia is only letting die. In fact, active euthanasia may be preferable to passive euthanasia, because of other features of the case. In many cases, active euthanasia may be kinder because it involves less suffering for the patient.

A similar conclusion follows about Baby Theresa. Despite people's feelings to the contrary, there would have been no moral difference between letting her die and killing her by removing her organs. Thus if it was permissible to allow her to die by not taking steps that would prolong her life, it would also have been permissible to take steps that would have ended her life sooner. Indeed, the other features of the case—the fact that the other babies needed the organs and that the organs would be useless if she were merely allowed to die—made killing the preferable option.

Notes

1. David Briggs, "Baby Theresa Case Raises Ethics Questions," *Champaign-Urbana News-Gazette*, 31 March 1992, A-6.

2. See Sidney H. Wanzer, et al., "The Physician's Responsibility toward the Hopelessly Ill: A Second Look," *New England Journal of Medicine* 320 (1989): 844–49.

3. Timothy E. Quill, "Death and Dignity—A Case of Individualized Decision Making," *New England Journal of Medicine* 324 (1991): 691–94.

4. See Peter Singer and Helga Kuhse, "The Future of Baby Doe," *New York Review of Books*, 1 March 1984.

6

Do Animals Have Rights?

Sometime after World War II, philosophers stopped talking about "natural" rights and started writing books and articles about "human" rights. The change in terminology reflected the political rhetoric of the times, but it was also thought to be a great improvement philosophically—first, because talk about human rights did not bring with it the ontological worries that attended discussions of natural rights; and second, because the new terminology focused more precisely on what everyone wanted to understand: the rights that all human beings have in common. In 1964 Richard Wasserstrom, who began his distinguished career by working in the civil rights movement, was the first philosopher to address the American Philosophical Association about racism. His subject was human rights, and he emphasized that "if any right is a *human* right, . . . it must be possessed by all human beings, as well as only by human beings."[1]

Because human rights are said to be possessed by *all* humans, the doctrine of human rights has been a formidable weapon against slavery, racism, sexism, and the like. The doctrine therefore has a noble history. But, as Wasserstrom notes, human rights are also conceived as being possessed *only* by humans. So when the rights to life and liberty are said to be human rights, the implication is that nonhumans do not have those rights. This aspect of the doctrine may not be so noble. While demanding justice for some creatures, it might permit injustice for a great many more.

How to Decide Whether Animals Have Rights and Which Rights, If Any, They Have

Do animals have rights? It is difficult to know how to go about answering such an abstract question. But the following method seems promising.

81

First we might select a right that we are confident humans have. Then we can ask whether there is a relevant difference between humans and animals that would justify us in denying that right to animals while granting it to humans. If not, then the right is possessed by the animals as well as by the people.

This method has a number of virtues. First, it has a clear rationale in the familiar principle of justice that like cases must be treated alike. Our moral judgments are unacceptably arbitrary if we judge one way in one case and differently in another case, unless there is a relevant difference between the two cases that justifies the difference in assessments. This principle has been used with great effect in arguing against racism. The assumption has been that race is not a morally relevant consideration in determining how people are to be treated. Therefore, racist discrimination is unjustified unless some further differences between blacks and whites can be found that would be relevant to justifying the different modes of treatment. Because there are no such further differences, such discrimination is unjustified.

It seems reasonable to make the similar assumption that a mere difference in species is not enough, in itself, to justify differences in how beings are treated. Thus if we grant a right to humans but deny it to members of other species, we must be able to point to some relevant difference between them other than the mere fact that they are members of different species.

A second advantage of the method is that if we follow it closely, we will avoid the trap of lumping all nonhuman animals together, as though what we say about one species we must say about all. For it may turn out that with respect to some particular right, there is no relevant difference between humans and one species of animal, while there are such differences between humans and some other species.

Finally, we may note one important limitation of this method. Its use does not guarantee that we will identify all the rights that animals have, for it is at least logically possible that they have some rights not possessed by humans. If so, then those rights could not be uncovered by this method.

What sorts of results may be obtained by this method? Here are some examples. Article 5 of the United Nations Universal Declaration of Human Rights says that all people have a right not to be subjected to torture. But is this, in fact, a distinctively human right? If members of other species—say, rabbits or pigs or monkeys—are tortured, they also suffer. Of course, there are many impressive differences between humans and these animals, but are they relevant here? A man can learn mathematics, and a rabbit can't; but what does that have to do with the business of being tortured? A man has an interest in not being tortured because he has the capacity to suffer pain, not because he can do mathematics or anything of that sort. (If we ask, Why is it wrong to torture people? the answer is not, Because they can do mathematics. The answer is, Because it hurts.) But rabbits, pigs, and monkeys also have the capacity to experience pain, so they have the same basic interest in not being tortured. The right not to be tortured, then, is shared by other animals that suffer pain; it is not a distinctively human right at all.

On the other hand, article 18 of the same declaration says that all people have the right to worship as they please. This is a more likely candidate for a right belonging only to humans, because only humans have religious beliefs and a capacity for worship.

The rights not to be tortured and to freedom of worship are relatively clear and unproblematic. But what happens when we consider a more puzzling right, such as the right to property? Once again, we may proceed by asking why it is thought that people have this right—what is the basis of it?—and then asking whether the same case can be made in behalf of animals. Consider, for example, John Locke's classic account of property rights. Locke says that a man has a natural right to his own labor and whatever he produces by it: "The labor of his body and the work of his hands, we may say, are properly his. Whatsoever then he removes out of the state that nature has provided and left it in, he has mixed his labor with, and joined to it something that is his own, and thereby makes it his property." Locke then illustrates his point with this example:

> He that is nourished by the acorns he picked up under an oak, or the apples he gathered from the trees in the wood, has certainly appropriated them to himself. Nobody can deny but the nourishment is his. I ask, then, when did they begin to be his? When he digested or when he ate or when he boiled or when he brought them home? Or when he picked them up? And it is plain, if the first gathering made them not his, nothing else could. That labor put a distinction between them and common; that added something to them more than nature, the common mother of all, had done; and so they became his private right.[2]

If this is right, it follows that animals such as squirrels also have a right to property; for squirrels labor to gather nuts for their own nourishment in exactly the way Locke pictures the man laboring. There is no relevant difference between the man and the squirrel: they both pick up the nuts, take them home, store them away, and eat them. Therefore there is no justification for saying that the man has a right to the nuts he gathers but that the squirrel does not.

The idea of acknowledging a right to property for mere animals may seem a little strange, especially when more basic rights, such as life itself, are still in question. But it is interesting that Locke's famous analysis seems to fit the animals so well. (Indeed, today Locke's discussion of the acorns seems *more* like a description of what squirrels do than of what people do.) And the notion of animals' property rights might actually have some practical significance in environmental ethics, considering the ways in which human use of the environment affects the animals' homes.

The Right to Liberty

The right to liberty has been counted among the most fundamental human rights in all the great liberal manifestos of modern history—the Declaration of Independence of the United States (1776), the French Declaration of the Rights of Man (1789), and the United Nations Universal Declaration of Human Rights (1948), to name but three. Virtually every philosopher who has discussed the subject has followed suit; I have not been able to find any treatment of "human rights" that did not include liberty as a prime example. Considering this, and remembering that some philosophers doubt whether mere animals can have any rights at all, it may not be surprising to find liberty (or freedom, which for present purposes comes to the same thing) being *defined* by some in such a way that only humans could possibly be free. According to J. R. Lucas, for example, "The central sense of Freedom is that in which a rational agent is free when he is able to act as seems best to him without being subject to external constraints on his actions."[3]

If we begin by conceiving freedom in this way, then the question of whether animals have a right to be free will not even arise, since the notion of a "rational agent" who deliberates about which actions are best is so obviously formulated with only humans in mind. But just as obviously, this definition won't do as a general definition of freedom, for that concept applies to animals as well as to people. A lion left alone in his natural habitat is free; a lion in a zoo is not. A chicken in a small wire cage is less free than one allowed to roam about a barnyard. And a bird that is released from a cage and allowed to fly away is "set free" in a perfectly plain sense. So, rewriting the definition to eliminate the prejudice in favor of humans, we get: "The central sense of Freedom is that in which a being is free when he is able to do as he pleases without being subject to external constraints on his actions." This expresses well enough the concept of liberty with which we should be concerned. As before, we may proceed by asking why it is thought that people have this right—what is the basis of it?—and then whether a similar case can be made on behalf of members of other species.

One possibility is to take liberty to be, simply and without need of any further justification, good in itself.[4] If we take this approach, then we might say that humans have a right to liberty simply because they have a right not to be deprived of any intrinsic goods that they are capable of enjoying. (And here the usual qualifications will be added, to the effect that the right will be only as extensive as is compatible with others' having a similar right, that the right may be forfeited or overridden in certain circumstances, and so forth.) But this line of reasoning applies equally well to the members of other species. It is parallel to the right not to be tortured. Any animal that has the capacity for suffering pain has a right not to be tortured, and the reason is connected to the fact that suffering pain is intrinsically bad. Similarly, if we grant humans a right to liberty simply because we regard liberty as something good that they are capable of enjoying, then we must also grant a right to liberty to any other animal that is capable of desiring to act one way rather than another.

Liberty and Harm to Interests

However, not many philosophers would be satisfied with the intrinsic-good approach, because most believe it is possible to provide a rationale for the right to liberty that does not simply stop with calling it good in itself. For example, it may be said that humans have a right to liberty because they have various other interests that will suffer if their freedom is unduly restricted. The right to liberty—the right to be free of external constraints on one's actions—may then be seen as derived from a more basic right not to have one's interests needlessly harmed.

But the interests of many other species are also harmed by a loss of freedom. It is a familiar fact that many wild animals do not fare at all well in captivity. Taken from their natural habitats and put in zoos, they are at first frantic and frustrated because they cannot carry on their normal activities; then they become listless and inactive, shadows of their former selves. Some become vicious and destructive. Often they will not reproduce in captivity, and when they do, their young often will not survive. And finally, members of many species will die sooner in captivity than they would in their natural homes.

Dr. Herbert Ratcliffe, a pathologist, conducted a study of the animals in a Philadelphia zoo. He found that the animals were suffering from sharply increased rates of heart disease, cancer, and ulcers. The metabolism of some white-tailed deer had changed to such an extent that their horns became deformed. The zoo's breeding colony of nutria—small, beaverlike animals—had dwindled because the young animals were born dwarfed, failed to breed, and died early. Dr. Ratcliffe attributes all of this to the effects of the artificial, confined environment of the zoo.[5]

Another example is provided by a widely used psychology textbook, which tells the story of a baboon colony in the London zoo. Investigators

> observed many instances of bloody fighting, brutality, and apparently senseless violence. Some of the females were torn to pieces, and no infant survived to maturity. From these observations, it was concluded that such violence was typical of the "wild" baboons. . . . But later, when baboons were studied under natural conditions in Africa, in the "wild," it was discovered that they lived in well-organized, peaceful groups, in which the only aggressive behavior was directed at predators and intruders.[6]

The effects of confinement on animals have also been studied in the psychology laboratory. For one such series of experiments, reported in 1972, Dr. Harry F. Harlow of the University of Wisconsin built a vertical chamber, "basically a stainless steel trough with sides that slope inward to form a rounded bottom."[7] The device measured about four feet by one foot by a few inches. The idea behind the chamber was explained like this: "Depression in humans has been characterized as embodying a state of 'helplessness and hopelessness, sunken in a well of despair,' and the device was designed on an intuitive basis to reproduce such a well both physically and psychologically for monkey subjects."

Rhesus monkeys were used for the experiments. These animals are often used in psychological studies because they are intelligent, sociable creatures that resemble humans in a great many ways. The experiments were conducted by putting six-week-old monkeys into the "well of despair" for a period of forty-five days. The purpose was to "investigate the chamber's effectiveness in production of psychopathology."

The chamber turned out to be very effective. While confined, the subjects were said to "typically spend most of their time huddled in a corner of the chamber." "Huddling" is defined as a "self-enclosed, fetal-like position incorporating any or all patterns of self-clasp, self-embrace, or lowered head." A nine-month period of observation following the confinement indicated that the effects on the animals were permanent:

> The results indicated that a 45-day period of vertical chamber confinement early in life produced severe and persistent psychopathological behavior of a depressive nature in the experimental subjects. These monkeys failed to

show appreciable changes in home-cage behavioral levels during the 9-month period following removal from the vertical chamber. In comparison to control groups of cage- and peer-reared monkeys, the chambered subjects exhibited abnormally high levels of self-clasp and huddle and abnormally low levels of locomotion and environmental exploration in both the home-cage and playroom situations. Most striking was the virtual absence of social activity among chambered subjects throughout the 8 months of play-room testing.

So there is ample evidence, from many sources, that animals suffer from confinement. Therefore, if the right to liberty is grounded in the fact that the loss of freedom involves harm to one's interests, animals as well as humans qualify for that right. The moral principle might be: Any creature that has interests has at least a prima facie right not to have those interests needlessly harmed. Animals that suffer in captivity have an interest in being free, and so at least a prima facie right to liberty. Lucas, immediately after giving the definition of "freedom" (restricted to "rational agents") quoted above, says that "not to be free is to be frustrated, impotent, futile." He may have been thinking only of humans, but the description applies equally well to animals in zoos, and certainly to the monkeys trapped in the well of despair.

Animals raised for food also suffer in confinement. Before being slaughtered, cows spend their lives crowded into feedlots where they are deprived of any sort of herd life or even adequate exercise. Veal calves are kept in pens so small they cannot even turn around. Peter Singer points out that even the lowly chicken suffers from confinement in the sort of cages used by poultry farmers:

[H]ens are crowded four or five to a cage with a floor area of twenty inches by eighteen inches, or around the size of a single page of the *New York Times*. The cages have wire floors, since this reduces cleaning costs, though wire is unsuitable for the hens' feet; the floors slope, since this makes the eggs roll down for easy collection, although this makes it difficult for the hens to rest comfortably. In these conditions all the birds' natural instincts are thwarted: they cannot stretch their wings fully, walk freely, dust-bathe, scratch the ground, or build a nest. Although they have never known other conditions, observers have noticed that the birds vainly try to perform these actions. Frustrated at their inability to do so, they often develop what farmers call "vices," and peck each other to death. To prevent this, the beaks of young birds are often cut off.[8]

Some of these cruelties have to do with the type of confinement rather than with the bare fact that the birds are confined. So, if the cages had flat, solid floors and perches for the hens, some of the grounds for complaint would be eliminated. But so long as the hens are confined to small cages, their natural desire to scratch the dirt, stretch their wings, build a nest, and so forth, will be frustrated. This is not to say that total freedom is required to satisfy the interests of chickens; no apparent harm would be done to their interests if they were kept captive while being allowed freedom to roam a large area. That is why many vegetarians who refuse to buy eggs produced under the conditions described by Singer nevertheless will buy eggs laid by "free-ranging" hens.

So we need to distinguish two things: first, we need to distinguish the kinds of animals whose interests are harmed by the denial of freedom; and second, we need to distinguish the *degree* of freedom that is required if the animals' interests are not to be harmed. Lions, but not chickens, may need to be set completely free in their natural habitats in order to flourish, whereas the needs of most insects may be so limited that they have no interest in freedom at all.

Rationality

At this point the business about humans' superior rationality might be reintroduced. For even if it is a mistake to define freedom in such a way that only rational agents can be free, it might nevertheless be said that freedom has a special kind of importance for rational agents that it cannot have for nonrational beings. Somehow, it is *the fact that we are rational* that confers on us the right to liberty. In one form or another, this thought is found in the writings of almost all philosophers who discuss the "human right" to liberty. I want to make two preliminary comments about this. The first has only to do with a certain sentiment—so you may want to discount it as an argument—but I will mention it anyway. It is that there is something unbearably sad about a grand animal such as a lion or an elephant being put on exhibit and reduced to nothing more than a spectacle for people's enjoyment. I mention this here because, in the past, humans who lacked "rationality" have suffered the same fate. Henry Salt, the great nineteenth-century champion of animal rights, noted:

> Two or three generations ago, pauper-lunatics used to be caged where passers-by—nurses perhaps with children in their charge—could see them as they passed, and the spectacle was sometimes enjoyed. (I remember hearing from my mother that such was the case at Shrewsbury. The nurse would say, "Where shall we go to-day, children?" and the cry would be, "Oh, to see the madmen, please!")[9]

Most of us recoil at this, and many reasons may be given to show that such practices are barbarous—perhaps because they teach children callous attitudes. But of course making a similar spectacle of animals may also have that effect. However, it is hard to believe that our initial reaction has much to do with such considerations. It has to do rather with the sadness and indignity of the spectacle. The fact that the being on exhibit is not rational hardly matters, in the case of either the lunatic or the lion. The second comment is to express a general doubt about the relevance of rationality to the value of freedom. It may be true, as philosophers have often stressed, that liberty is necessary if we humans are to develop and exercise our powers as rational agents and to have the kinds of lives we want. But it is also true that liberty is necessary for many nonhuman animals if they are to live their own sorts of lives and flourish in ways that are natural to them.

So just what relevance is rationality supposed to have? One popular view, derived from Kant, is that because of their rational powers, humans alone, among all the animals, are moral agents, able to form a conception of right and wrong and guide their actions by it. It is even said that, because of this, there are two kinds of freedom: the natural freedom of any creature to do as it pleases, and the special, *moral* freedom of humans to guide their actions by their sense of right and wrong.[10] The idea is that when we talk of human freedom, it is moral freedom that is especially important and that must be protected. Thus our right to liberty has a foundation and importance that the liberty of mere animals cannot have.

Although the idea of moral freedom is obscure, it is also very powerful, and it is easy to feel the force of it. Here, we need not quarrel with the notion or even analyze it very closely. It is sufficient to note that many nonhuman animals have capacities that might very well be called "moral," so that even if we do hold moral freedom to be an especially important type of liberty, there is still no reason to think it is limited to human beings. For even though animals cannot form an intellectual conception of right and wrong, many of them are nevertheless capable of being motivated to act by desires that, in humans, we would take to be signs of moral goodness. Many nonhuman animals show devotion and love for their offspring and self-sacrificial loyalty to other members of their groups. And if we think it especially important to allow humans the liberty to act on their conceptions of right and wrong, why should it not also be important to allow a nonhuman mother to act from love for her offspring?[11]

The sum of all this is that whatever rationale is provided for granting humans a right to liberty, a relevantly similar one is available in the case of at least some other species. If this is correct, then the right to liberty is not a "human" right at all.

Why Some Philosophers Say Animals Cannot Have Rights

Many philosophers, however, say that animals cannot have rights. In the heyday of "philosophical analysis," when some thinkers believed that philosophical questions could be answered by examining the meanings of words, it was suggested that attributing rights to animals involves a *conceptual* mistake. In his paper "Rights," H. J. McCloskey observed that

> important conclusions follow from the question as to whether animals have rights. If they do, . . . it would seem an illegitimate invasion of animal rights to kill and eat them, if, as seems to be the case, we can sustain ourselves without killing animals. If animals have rights, the case for vegetarianism is prima facie very strong, and is comparable with the case against cannibalism.[12]

But McCloskey thought this unsettling conclusion could be avoided, because it could be shown that nonhuman animals are not even logically possible bearers of rights. He argued that

> A right cannot not be possessed by someone; hence, only beings which can possess things can possess rights. My right to life is mine, I possess it. It is as much mine as any of my possessions—indeed more so—for I possess them by virtue of my rights. . . . All these considerations seem to exclude the lower animals in a decisive way, and the higher animals in a less decisive but still fairly conclusive way as possible bearers of rights. (Consider "possess" in its literal use. Can a horse possess anything, e.g. its stable, its rug, in a literal sense of "possess"?)

But clearly this argument does not prove the point. Why can't animals possess things? When a bird gathers twigs and builds a nest, isn't it his,[13] and not mine or yours or any other bird's? Would we have the right to take the nest from him to satisfy some trivial interest of ours and leave him to build himself another? He made it by his own labor. (Remember Locke's example of the man gathering nuts.) If a larger, stronger bird drives him out and takes over the nest by force, we can recognize an injustice even though neither animal has, or could have, an intellectualized conception of justice. All of this presupposes that the bird possesses the nest as a matter of right, once the nest is built; and although saying this does clash with our usual amoral way of regarding animals, there is nothing *logically* odd about it.

Like McCloskey, D. G. Ritchie believed that if we recognize animal rights, we will have to make drastic changes in our ways of treating them. But he also thought that such changes are not required because animals don't have rights. In his book *Natural Rights*,[14] Ritchie argued that absurd consequences follow from the assumption that they do; for example, if animals have rights, then cats who eat mice violate their rights—but that is silly.

Now, it does sound odd to speak of cats violating mice's rights, but this may be at least partly because we hardly ever think of the matter in this light, and this in turn may be because we don't give much thought to the morality of how animals are treated. Some have thought that there is a deeper, conceptual reason for the oddity but that once this reason is understood, it provides no grounds for doubting that animals have rights. John Plamenatz,[15] for example, suggests that rights be understood as *rights against rational beings*, so that animals have rights against us but not against one another. Thus, even though the cat cannot violate the mouse's rights, we humans can do so.

The Kantian Strategy

Often philosophers have tried to identify some one characteristic that a being must possess in order to have rights. They have sought a simple formula: *Beings have rights if and only if they have X*. More often than not, they have assumed that since only humans have rights, X must be a characteristic that other animals lack.

Kant, for example, held that although we have duties involving nonhuman animals, we can have no duties *to* nonhuman animals—just as we can have duties involving trees but not duties to trees. On Kant's view, we may very well have a duty not to kill an animal. Perhaps it is someone's pet—the person owns the animal and would be unhappy over its death; therefore we should not kill it. The reasons we should not kill it, however, all concern the person's interests and not the animal's. We can never have a duty not to mistreat an animal founded upon the animal's own interests.

If Kant's view is correct, then animals cannot have rights; for if a being has rights, then the duties we have in virtue of those rights are duties to him and not merely duties involving him. The difference between humans and other animals that explains this difference in moral status is that humans are "self-conscious," whereas other animals are not.[16] Thus, on Kant's view, X is self-consciousness: self-conscious beings, and only self-conscious beings, can have rights.

There are three main difficulties with this view.

First, and most obvious, it seems false to say that we can have no duties founded on the interests of animals themselves. If making an animal suffer has adverse effects on human beings, that is certainly a reason it is wrong. But even if there are no adverse effects for humans, wantonly torturing animals is still wrong. Kant maintains, however, that this is not a real possibility: cruelty to animals always involves at least the possibility of harm to persons, because "He who is cruel to animals becomes hard also in his dealings with men."[17] But this seems unlikely. Is there any reason to believe that people in the meat business, or people who experiment on animals, or people who go hunting, are more cruel to their fellow humans than other people? It may be so, but I know of no reason to believe it is so. Those people are, so far as their fellow humans are concerned, moral in the ordinary ways.

Second, the idea that the possession of rights depends on self-consciousness is so obscure as to be deeply problematic. What exactly is "self-consciousness"? In ordinary speech, "self-conscious" means awkward and easily embarrassed, ill at ease—as in, "Johnny went to the party but was too self-conscious to dance." Obviously this is not what Kant has in mind—the Kantian thesis is not that only the ill-at-ease have rights. In what, then, does self-consciousness in the philosopher's sense consist?

One contemporary philosopher who has tried to clarify the notion is Michael Tooley. Like Kant, Tooley believes that self-consciousness is a morally crucial notion; more specifically, he believes that without this characteristic, one cannot have a right to life. In his well-known essay "Abortion and Infanticide," Tooley maintains, "An organism possesses a serious right to life only if it possesses the concept of a self as a continuing subject of experiences and other mental states, and believes that it is itself such a continuing entity."[18] Unlike Kant, Tooley leaves open the possibility that animals might have a right to life by this criterion—but it seems only a bare possibility, unrealized by actual animals.

But in making the Kantian thesis more explicit, Tooley has not made it any more plausible. We may assume that David Hume had a right to life, if anybody has one; yet Hume certainly did not believe that he was a self who was a continuing subject of experiences. In fact, he specifically denied that, and so do many behavioristic psychologists.[19] It might be suggested that Tooley's thesis could be amended so as to avoid this objection by leaving off the last clause. But I do not believe that the difficulty is caused entirely by the reference to belief. It is doubtful that anyone other than philosophers even possesses the concept of such a self— my father, for example, is an intelligent man but not a philosopher, and I doubt that he "possesses the concept of a self as a continuing subject of experiences and other mental states." If he does have this concept, he certainly is not aware of it. Hume argued that this concept is not even intelligible.[20] Others disagree. I do not know who is right, but I would not like the existence of my right to life to depend on the outcome of such a debate.

But the third difficulty for the Kantian view is by far the most interesting one. The Kantian strategy is to identify *one* characteristic that is supposed to be relevant to the possession of *any* right. That is far less plausible than to think that the characteristics one must have in order to have a right vary with the rights themselves. Consider, for example, rights as different as the right to freedom of worship and the right not to be tortured. To have the former right, one must be a creature with a capacity for worship: one must have religious beliefs and the capacity to participate in a form of life in which worship could have some place. For this reason, it seems senseless to think that rabbits could have such a right. At the same time, rabbits might very well have a right not to be tortured, for the capacity to worship has little or nothing to do with that right.

Perhaps, by some convoluted reasoning, it might be shown that only self-conscious beings can have a right to worship. But does having a right not to be tortured depend on being self-conscious? One way to get a grip on this is to ask whether a person's self-consciousness figures into the reasons we object to torture. Do we object to a person's being tortured because he is a self-conscious being? Or, to use Tooley's explication of the idea, because he possesses a concept of the self as a continuing subject of experiences? I do not believe that this is the reason torture is wrong; the explanation is much simpler. Torture is wrong because it hurts. It is the capacity for suffering, and not the possession of sophisticated concepts, that underlies the wrongness of torture. This is true for both people and rabbits; in both cases, torture is wrong because of the suffering that is caused. The characteristic of humans that qualifies them as bearers of a right not to be tortured is, therefore, a characteristic also possessed by rabbits, and by many other animals as well. And it is a *different* capacity from the capacity necessary to have a right to worship.

This argument contains an important gap. We might concede that we have the same reason for objecting to torturing animals that we have for objecting to torturing humans but still maintain that torturing humans violates their rights, whereas torturing animals does not. For it may be wrong to treat an animal in a certain way without any question of *rights* being involved. To address this issue, we need to ask what the difference is between merely having a duty not to treat someone in a certain way and violating their rights by treating them in that way. Three differences come immediately to mind.

(1) When it is a matter of an individual's rights not to be treated in a certain way, treating that person in that way is objectionable *for that person's own sake,* and not merely for the sake of someone or something else. Thus if a pet-owner's animal is harmed and the only objection we have is that the owner's interests are violated, we are not considering the animal to have any rights of its own in the matter.

(2) When rights are involved, the rights bearer may protest, in a special way, if he or she is not treated properly. Suppose you think you ought to give money for famine relief, but you consider this to be simply an act of generosity on your part. You ought to do it because you ought to be generous to those in need. However, you do not consider the starving to have a *right* to your money; you do not owe it to them in any sense. Then, you will not think them entitled to complain if you choose not to give; it will not be proper for them to insist that you contribute or to feel resentment if you do not. Whether you do your moral duty is in this case strictly up to you, and you owe them no explanation if you choose not to do so. On the other hand, if they have a *right* to your money, it is permissible for them to complain, to insist, and to feel resentment if you do not give them what they have coming.

(3) When rights are involved, the position of third parties is different. If you are violating someone's rights, it is permissible for a third party to intervene and compel you to stop. But if you are not violating anyone's rights, then even though you are not behaving as you should, no third party is entitled to force you to do otherwise. Since giving for famine relief is widely considered not to involve the rights of the starving but only to involve "charity" toward them, it is not considered permissible for anyone to compel you to contribute. But if you had contracted to provide food, so that they now had a claim of right on your aid, compulsion would be thought proper if you reneged.[21]

When judged by these measures, it appears that animals do have a right not to be tortured and not merely that we are wrong to torture them. (1) Torturing animals is objectionable for reasons having to do with the animals' own interests. (2) Someone speaking for the animals could legitimately complain in their behalf and insist that you not torture them. For this complaint to be heard, the animals would need surrogates only in the same way that mentally deficient humans and infants require surrogates to assert their rights. (3) Finally, the position of third parties is the same as where rights are involved: it is permissible for third parties to compel you not to do it. The weight of this evidence, then, is that the animals have a right not to be tortured—it is not simply that we are being nice in not harming them.

The Kantian strategy is common among contemporary philosophers who theorize that eligibility for rights depends on possession of certain characteristics without considering that the relevant characteristics might change as different rights are in question. In *Anarchy, State, and Utopia,* Robert Nozick holds that a being has rights only if it is a rational, free moral agent with "the ability to regulate and guide its life in accordance with some overall conception that it chooses to accept."[22] McCloskey's idea is that the capacity for moral self-direction qualifies one for basic moral rights. Other examples could easily be cited. These thinkers are all up to the old Kantian trick: the attempt to divide rights bearers from non–rights bearers on the basis of their possession, or lack, of some one (set of) very general characteristic(s). The primary objection must be to the form, not the content, of these proposals. Why should we believe that the *same* characteristics that make one eligible for one right also make one eligible for the others? Surely the sensible approach is to take up the rights, and the characteristics that qualify us for them, one at a time.

Reciprocity

There is, however, a somewhat deeper reason for doubting that animals can have rights. It is plausible to think that moral requirements can exist only where certain conditions of reciprocity are satisfied. The basic idea here is that a person is obligated to respect the interests of others and acknowledge that they have claims against her only if the others are willing to respect her interests and acknowledge her claims. This may be thought of as a matter of fairness: if we are to accept inconvenient restrictions on our conduct in the interests of benefiting (or at least not harming) others, then it is only fair that the others should accept similar restrictions on their conduct for the sake of our interests.

The requirement of reciprocity is central to contract theories of ethics. Hobbes, for example, conceived of moral rules as rules that rational, self-interested people will agree to obey on condition that others will obey them as well.[23] Each person can be motivated to accept such an arrangement by considering the benefits she will gain if others abide by the rules; and her own compliance with the rules is the fair price she pays to secure the compliance of others. That is the point of the "contract." It is a natural part of such theories that nonhuman animals are not covered by the same moral rules that govern the treatment of humans, for the animals cannot participate in the mutual agreement on which the whole setup depends.

This implication is made explicit in John Rawls's *A Theory of Justice.*[24] Rawls identifies the principles of justice as those that would be accepted by rational, self-interested people in what he calls "the original position"; that is, a position of ignorance with respect to particular facts about oneself and one's own position in society. The question then arises as to what sorts of beings are owed the guarantees of justice. Rawls's answer is:

> We use the characterization of the persons in the original position to single out the kinds of beings to whom the principles chosen apply. After all, the parties are thought of as adopting these criteria to regulate their common institutions and their conduct toward one another; and the description of their nature enters into the reasoning by which these principles are selected. Thus equal justice is owed to those who have the capacity to take part in and to act in accordance with the public understanding of the initial situation.

This, he says, explains why nonhuman animals do not have the "equal basic rights" possessed by humans; "they have some protection certainly but their status is not that of human beings." And of course this result is not surprising, for if rights are determined by agreements of mutual interest and animals are not able to participate in the agreements, then how can *their* interests give rise to rights?

The requirement of reciprocity may seem plausible, and I think that it does contain the germ of a plausible idea—I will say more about this in a moment—but nevertheless there are good reasons to reject it. We need to distinguish the conditions necessary for *having* a moral obligation from the conditions necessary for being the *beneficiary* of a moral obligation.

Normal adult humans have the moral obligation not to torture one another. What characteristics make it possible for people to have this obligation? For one thing, they must be able to understand what torture is, and they must be capable of recognizing that it is wrong. When someone (a severely retarded person, perhaps) lacks such capacities, we do not think he has such obligations, and we do not hold him responsible for what he does. On the other hand, it is a different question what characteristics qualify someone to be the beneficiary of this obligation. It is wrong to torture people—they are the beneficiaries of our obligation not to torture—not because of their capacity for understanding what torture is, or for recognizing that it is morally wrong, but simply because of their capacity for experiencing pain. Thus a person may lack the characteristics necessary for having a certain obligation and yet may still possess the characteristics necessary to qualify him as the beneficiary of that obligation. A severely retarded person may not be able to understand what torture is, or see it as wrong, and yet still be able to suffer pain. So we have an obligation not to torture him, even though he cannot have a similar obligation not to torture us.

The requirement of reciprocity says that a person is morally required to accept restrictions on his conduct in the interests of not harming others only if the others reciprocate. The example of the retarded person shows this to be false. He is not capable of restricting his conduct in this way; nevertheless, we have an obligation to restrict ours. We are in the same position with respect to nonhuman animals; like the retarded person, they lack characteristics necessary for having obligations; but they may still be the beneficiaries of our obligations. The fact that they cannot reciprocate, then, does not affect our basic obligations to them.

I said that the requirement of reciprocity, although unacceptable, does contain the germ of a plausible idea. What I have in mind is the idea that if a person is capable of acting considerately of our interests and *refuses* to do so, then we are released from any similar obligations we might have had to him. This may very well be right. But whether or not this point is accepted makes no difference to our duties to nonhuman animals, since they lack the capacity to "refuse" to recognize obligations to us, just as they are not able to accept such obligations.

Notes

1. Richard Wasserstrom, "Rights, Human Rights, and Racial Discrimination," *Journal of Philosophy* 61 (1964): 631.

2. John Locke, *The Second Treatise of Government* (1690), chap. 5, para. 27.

3. J. R. Lucas, *The Principles of Politics* (Oxford: Oxford University Press, 1966), 144.

4. For an account of this type, see Gregory Vlastos, "Justice and Equality," in *Social Justice,* ed. Richard B. Brandt (Englewood Cliffs, N.J.: Prentice-Hall, 1962), 51.

5. "The Shame of the Naked Cage," *Life,* 8 November 1968, 77. For a more recent discussion, see Stephen St. C. Bostock, *Zoos and Animal Rights* (London: Routledge & Kegan Paul, 1993).

6. Floyd L. Ruch and Philip G. Zimbado, *Psychology and Life,* 8th ed. (Glenview, Ill.: Scott, Foresman & Co., 1967), 539.

7. Stephen J. Suomi and Harry F. Harlow, "Depressive Behavior in Young Monkeys Subjected to Vertical Chamber Confinement," *Journal of Comparative and Physiological Psychology* 80 (1972): 11–18. The quotations that follow are from p. 11, 12, 13, and 14.

8. Peter Singer, "All Animals Are Equal," *Philosophic Exchange* 1, no. 5 (Summer 1974): 108.

9. Henry Salt, *The Creed of Kinship* (New York: Dutton, 1935), 60–61.

10. See Edith Watson-Schipper, "Two Concepts of Human Freedom," *Southern Journal of Philosophy* 11 (1973): 309–15.

11. For an extended discussion of the moral capacities of nonhumans, see James Rachels, *Created from Animals: The Moral Implications of Darwinism* (Oxford: Oxford University Press, 1990), chap. 4.

12. H. J. McCloskey, "Rights," *Philosophical Quarterly* 15 (1965): 122. The next quotation is from p. 126.

13. I say "his" rather than "its" deliberately, although either choice may be thought prejudicial: "Words and names are not without their effect upon conduct; and to apply to intelligent beings such terms as *brute, beast, live-stock, dumb*, etc., or the neuter pronouns *it* and *which*, as if they had no sex, is a practical incitement to ill-usage, and certainly a proof of misunderstanding. For example, the *Morning Post* (September 26th, 1933) thus described a case of cruelty to a cow: 'He (the culprit) struck the cow with a milking-stool. It fell to the ground and died.' It! One's thoughts turn to the milking-stool, but the allusion was to the cow!" Salt, *Creed of Kinship*, 62.

14. D. G. Ritchie, *Natural Rights* (London: Allen & Unwin, 1894), 109.

15. John Plamenatz, *Consent, Freedom, and Political Obligation*, 2d ed. (Oxford: Oxford University Press, 1968), 83.

16. Immanuel Kant, *Lectures on Ethics* (New York: Harper & Row, 1963), 239.

17. Kant, *Lectures on Ethics*, 240.

18. Michael Tooley, "Abortion and Infanticide," *Philosophy and Public Affairs* 2 (1972): 64.

19. Leonard S. Carrier makes this point about Tooley's thesis in "Abortion and the Right to Life," *Social Theory and Practice* 3 (1975): 292–93.

20. David Hume, *A Treatise of Human Nature* (Oxford: Oxford University Press, 1888), 1.4. 6. Originally published in 1739.

21. Philosophers suspicious of the concept of rights have wondered exactly what it means and how it might be rendered in terms of the less puzzling notion of permissibility. The preceding observations suggest this analysis. X has a right to be treated in a certain way by Y if and only if: first, it is not permissible for Y not to treat X in that way, for reasons having to do with X's own interests; second, it is permissible for X to insist that Y treat him in that way, and to complain or feel resentment if Y does not; and third, it is permissible for a third party to compel Y to treat X in that way if Y will not do so voluntarily. The *understanding* of rights that goes with this analysis is that rights are correlates of duties the performance of which we are not willing to leave to individual discretion.

22. Robert Nozick, *Anarchy, State, and Utopia* (New York: Basic Books, 1974), 49.

23. Thomas Hobbes, *Leviathan* (1651), chaps. 13–16.

24. John Rawls, *A Theory of Justice* (Cambridge: Harvard University Press, 1971). The quotations that follow are from p. 505.

7

The Moral Argument for Vegetarianism

The idea that it is morally wrong to eat meat may seem faintly ridiculous. After all, eating meat is a normal, well-established part of our lives; people have always eaten meat; and many find it difficult even to conceive of what an alternative diet would be like. So it is not easy to take seriously the possibility that it might be wrong. Moreover, vegetarianism is commonly associated with Eastern religions whose tenets we do not accept and with extravagant, unfounded claims about health. A quick perusal of vegetarian literature might confirm the impression that it is all a crackpot business; tracts have titles like "Victory through Vegetables" and promise that if we will only keep to a meatless diet, we will have perfect health and be filled with wisdom. Of course we can ignore this kind of nonsense. However, there are other arguments for vegetarianism that must be taken seriously. The most powerful argument appeals to the principle that it is wrong to cause unnecessary suffering.

The wrongness of cruelty to animals is often explained in terms of its effects on human beings. The idea seems to be that although the animals themselves are not morally important, cruelty has bad consequences for humans, and so it is wrong for that reason. In legal writing, cruelty to animals has been included among the "victimless crimes," and the problem of justifying legal prohibitions has been viewed as comparable to justifying the prohibition of other behavior, such as prostitution or the distribution of pornography, where no one is hurt. In 1963 the distinguished legal scholar Louis Schwartz wrote that, in prohibiting the torturing of animals, "It is not the mistreated dog who is the ultimate object of concern. . . . Our concern is for the feelings of other human beings, a large proportion of whom, although accustomed to the slaughter of animals for food, readily identify themselves with a tortured dog or horse and respond with great sensitivity to its sufferings."[1]

Philosophers have also adopted this attitude. Kant, for example, held that we have no direct duties to nonhuman animals. "The Categorical Imperative," the ultimate principle of morality, applies only to our dealings with people: "The practical imperative, therefore, is the following: Act so that you treat humanity, whether in your own person or in that of another, always as an end and never as a means only."[2] And of other animals, Kant says: "But so far as animals are concerned, we have no direct duties. Animals are not self-conscious, and are there merely as means to an end. That end is man."[3] He adds that we should not be cruel to animals only because "he who is cruel to animals becomes hard also in his dealings with men."[4]

Surely, this is unacceptable. Cruelty to animals ought to be opposed, not only because of the ancillary effects on humans, but also because of the direct effects on the animals themselves. Animals that are tortured suffer, just as tortured humans suffer, and that is the primary reason it is wrong. We object to torturing humans on a number of grounds, but the main one is that the victims suffer so. Insofar as nonhuman animals also suffer, we have the same reason to oppose torturing them, and it is indefensible to take the one suffering but not the other as grounds for objection.

Although cruelty to animals is wrong, it does not follow that we are never justified in inflicting pain on an animal. Sometimes we are justified in doing this, just as we are sometimes justified in inflicting pain on humans. It does follow, however, that there must be a good reason for causing the suffering, and if the suffering is great, the justifying reason must be correspondingly powerful. As an example, consider the treatment of the civet cat, a highly intelligent and sociable animal. Civet cats are trapped and placed in small cages inside darkened sheds, where fires keep the temperature up to 110 degrees Fahrenheit.[5] They are confined in this way until they die. What justifies this extraordinary mistreatment? These animals have the misfortune to produce a substance that is useful in the manufacture of perfume. Musk, which is scraped from their genitals once a day for as long as they can survive, makes the scent of perfume last a bit longer after each application. (The heat increases their "production" of musk.) Here Kant's rule—"Animals are merely means to an end; that end is man"—is applied with a vengeance. To promote one of the most trivial interests we have, animals are tormented for their whole lives.

It is usually easy to persuade people that this use of animals is not justified and that we have a moral duty not to support such cruelties by consuming their products. The argument is simple: Causing suffering is not justified unless there is a good reason; the production of perfume made with musk causes suffering; our enjoyment of this product is not a good enough reason to justify causing that suffering; therefore, the use of animals in this way is wrong. Once people learn the facts about musk production, they come to regard using such products as morally objectionable. They are surprised to discover, however, that an exactly analogous argument can be given in connection with the use of animals as food. Animals that are raised and slaughtered for food also suffer, and our enjoyment of the way they taste is not a sufficient justification for mistreating them.

Most people radically underestimate the amount of suffering that is caused to animals who are raised and slaughtered for food.[6] They believe, in a vague way, that slaughterhouses are cruel and perhaps that methods of slaughter ought to be made more humane. But after all, the visit to the slaughterhouse is a relatively brief episode in the animal's life; and beyond that, people imagine that the animals are treated well enough. Nothing could be further from the truth. Today the production of meat is big business, and the helpless animals are treated more as machines in a factory than as living creatures.

Veal calves, for example, spend their lives in pens too small to allow them to turn around or even to lie down comfortably—exercise toughens the muscles, which reduces the quality of the meat; and besides, allowing the animals adequate living space would be prohibitively expensive. In these pens the calves cannot perform such basic actions as grooming themselves, which they naturally desire to do, because there is not room for them to twist their heads around. It is clear that the calves miss their mothers, and like human infants they want something to suck; they can be seen trying vainly to suck the sides of their stalls. In order to keep their meat pale and tasty, they are fed a liquid diet deficient in iron and roughage. Naturally, they develop cravings for these things, because they need them. The calf's craving for iron is so strong that if it is allowed to turn around, it will lick at its own urine, although calves normally find this repugnant. The tiny stall, which prevents the animal from turning, solves this problem. The craving for roughage is especially strong since without it the animal cannot form a cud to chew. It cannot be given any straw for bedding, since the animal would be driven to eat it and that would spoil the meat. For these animals the slaughterhouse is not an unpleasant end to an otherwise contented life. As terrifying as the process of slaughter is, for them it may actually be a merciful release.

Similar stories can be told about the treatment of other animals on which we dine. In order to produce animals by the millions, it is necessary to keep them crowded together in small spaces. Chickens are commonly kept four or five to a space smaller than a newspaper page. Unable to walk around or even stretch their wings—much less build a nest—the birds become vicious and attack one another. The problem is exacerbated because the birds are so crowded that because they are unable to move, their feet sometimes grow around the wire floors of the cages, anchoring them to the spot. An anchored bird cannot escape attack no matter how desperate it becomes. Mutilation of the animals is an efficient solution. To minimize the damage they can do to one another, poultry farmers cut off their beaks. The mutilation is painful but probably not as painful as other sorts of mutilations that are routinely practiced. Cows are castrated, not to prevent the unnatural "vices" to which overcrowded chickens are prone, but because castrated cows put on more weight and there is less danger of meat being tainted by male hormones.

> In Britain an anesthetic must be used, unless the animal is very young, but in America anesthetics are not in general use. The procedure is to pin the animal down, take a knife and slit the scrotum, exposing the testicles. You then grab each testicle in turn and pull on it, breaking the cord that attaches it; on older animals it may be necessary to cut the cord.[7]

It must be emphasized that such treatment is not out of the ordinary. It is typical of the way that animals raised for food are treated, now that meat production is big business. As Peter Singer puts it, these are the sorts of things that happened to your dinner when it was still an animal.

What accounts for such cruelties? As for the meat producers, there is no reason to think they are unusually cruel people. They simply accept the common attitude expressed by Kant: "Animals are merely means to an end; that end is man." The cruel practices are adopted not because they are cruel but because they are efficient, given that one's only concern is to produce meat (and eggs) for humans as cheaply as possible. But clearly this use of animals is immoral if anything is. Since we can nourish ourselves very well without eating them, our only reason for doing all this to the animals is our enjoyment of the way they taste. And this will not even come close to justifying the cruelty.

Does this mean that we should stop eating meat? It is tempting to say: "What is objectionable is not *eating* the animals, but only making them suffer. Perhaps we ought to protest the way they are treated and even work for better treatment of them. But it doesn't follow that we must stop eating them." This sounds plausible until we realize that it would be impossible to treat the animals decently and still produce meat in sufficient quantities to make it a normal part of our diets. Cruel methods are used in the meat-production industry because such methods are economical; they enable the producers to market a product that people can afford.

Humanely produced chicken, beef, and pork would be so expensive that only the very rich could afford them. (Some of the cruelties might be eliminated without too much expense—the cows could be given an anesthetic before castration, for example, even though this alone would mean a slight increase in the cost of beef. But others, such as overcrowding, could not be eliminated without really prohibitive cost.) So to work for better treatment for the animals would be to work for a situation in which most of us would have to adopt a vegetarian diet.

Still, there remains the interesting theoretical question: If meat could be produced humanely, without mistreating the animals before killing them painlessly, would there be anything wrong with it? The question has only theoretical interest, because the actual choice we face in the supermarket is whether to buy the remains of animals that were not treated humanely. Still, the question has some interest, and we may take a quick look at it.

First, it is a vexing issue whether animals have a "right to life" that is violated when we kill them for trivial purposes; but we should not simply assume until it is proved otherwise that they don't have such a right. We assume that humans have a right to life—it would be wrong to murder a normal, healthy human even if it were done painlessly—and it is hard to think of any plausible rationale for granting this right to humans that does not also apply to other animals. Other animals live in communities, as do humans; they communicate with one another and have ongoing social relationships; killing them disrupts lives that are perhaps not as complex emotionally and intellectually as our own but that are nevertheless quite complicated. They suffer and are capable of happiness as well as fear and distress, as we are. So what could be the rational basis for saying that we have a right to life but that they don't? Or even more pointedly, what could be the rational basis for saying that a severely retarded human, who is inferior in every important respect to an intelligent animal, has a right to life but that the animal doesn't? Philosophers often treat such questions as "puzzles," assuming that there must be answers even if we are not clever enough to find them. But perhaps there are no acceptable answers to this question. If it seems, intuitively, that there must be some difference between us and the other animals that confers on us, but not on them, a right to life, perhaps this intuition is mistaken. At the very least, the difficulty of answering such questions should make us hesitant about asserting that it is all right to kill animals so long as we don't make them suffer, unless we are also willing to take seriously the possibility that it is all right to kill people so long as we don't make them suffer.

But let me make a more definite suggestion about this. If we want to know whether animals have a right to life, we should start by asking why

humans have such a right. What is it about humans that gives them a right
to life? If humans have a right to life, but plants, say, do not, then there
must be some difference between them that explains why one has a right
the other lacks. There must be characteristics possessed by humans but not
by plants that qualify the humans for this right. Therefore, one way to
approach our question is by trying to identify those characteristics. Then
we can ask whether any nonhuman animals have those characteristics.

With respect to the characteristics that qualify one for a right to life, my
suggestion is that an individual has a right to life if that individual has a
life. Like many philosophical ideas, this one is more complicated than it
first appears.

Having a life is different from merely being alive. The latter is a biological notion—to be alive is just to be a functioning biological organism.
It is the opposite of being dead. But "a life," in the sense that concerns us
here, is a notion of biography rather than of biology. "The life of Babe
Ruth" will be concerned not with the biological facts of Ruth's existence—
he had a heart and liver and blood and kidneys—but with facts about his
history, beliefs, actions, and relationships:

> He was born George Herman Ruth in Baltimore in 1895, the troubled child
> of a poor family. He was sent to live at St. Mary's School when he was eight;
> he learned baseball there and started pitching for the Red Sox at nineteen.
> Babe was an outstanding pitcher for six seasons before switching to the
> Yankee outfield and going on to become the most idolized slugger in the
> history of the game. He hit 60 home runs in a single season and 714 overall.
> He was the beer-guzzling friend of Lou Gehrig and was married to Claire.
> He died of cancer at age fifty-three.

These are some of the facts of his life. They are not biological facts.

Death is an evil when it puts an end not simply to being alive but to a
life. Some humans, tragically, do not have lives and never will. An infant
with Tay-Sachs disease will never develop beyond about six months of
age, there may be some regression at that point, and it will die. Suppose
such an infant contracts pneumonia; the decision might be made not to
treat the pneumonia and to allow the baby to die. The decision seems justified because in the absence of any possibility of a life in the biographical
sense, life in the biological sense has little value. The same sort of consideration explains why it seems so pointless to maintain persons in irreversible coma. The families of such patients are quick to realize that merely being alive is unimportant. The mother of a man who died after six
years in a coma told a newspaper reporter, "My son died at age 34 after
having lived for 28 years."[8] It was a melodramatic remark, and on the sur-

face a paradoxical one—how can one die at 34 and have lived only 28 years?—yet what she meant is clear enough. The man's life was over when he entered the coma, even though he was alive for 6 years longer. The temporal boundaries of one's being alive need not be the same as the temporal boundaries of one's life.

Therefore, it is unwise to insist that any animal, human or nonhuman, has a right to life simply because it is a living being. The doctrine of the sanctity of life, interpreted as applying merely to biological life, has little to recommend it. My suggestion about the right to life is that an individual has a right to life if that individual has a life in the biographical sense. By this criterion, at least some nonhuman animals would have such a right. Monkeys, to take the most obvious example, have lives that are quite complex. They are remarkably intelligent, they have families and live together in social groups, and they apparently have forward-looking and backward-looking attitudes. Their lives do not appear to be as emotionally or intellectually complex as the lives of humans; but the more we learn about them, the more impressed we are with the similarities between them and us.

Of course we do not know a great deal about the lives of the members of most other species. To make intelligent judgments about them, we need the sort of information that could be gained by observing animals in their natural homes rather than in the laboratory—although laboratory-acquired information can be helpful. When baboons, dogs, and wolves have been studied in the wild, it has been found that the lives of individual animals, carried out within pack societies, are surprisingly diverse. But we are only beginning to appreciate the richness of the animal kingdom.

In our present state of semi-ignorance about other species, the situation seems to be this. When we consider the mammals with which we are most familiar, it is reasonable to believe that they do have lives in the biographical sense. They have emotions and cares and social systems and the rest, although perhaps not in just the way that humans do. Then the further down the old phylogenetic scale we go, the less confidence we have that there is anything resembling a life. When we come to bugs, or shrimp, the animals pretty clearly lack the mental capacities necessary for a life, although they certainly are alive. Most of us already have an intuitive sense of the importance of these gradations—we think that killing a human is worse than killing a monkey, but we also think that killing a monkey is a more morally serious matter than swatting a fly. And when we come to plants, which are alive but to which the notion of a biographical life is not applicable at all, our moral qualms about killing vanish altogether. If my suggestion about the right to life is correct, these feelings have a rational basis: insofar as we have reason to view other creatures as having lives, as we do, we have reason to view them as having a right to life, if we do.

Finally, it is important to see the slaughter of animals for food as part of a larger pattern that characterizes our whole relationship with the non-human world. Animals are taken from their natural homes to be made objects of our entertainment in zoos, circuses, and rodeos. They are used in laboratories, not only for experiments that are themselves morally questionable, but also in testing everything from shampoo to chemical weapons. They are killed so that their heads can be used as wall decorations or their skins as ornamental clothing or rugs. Indeed, simply killing them for the fun of it is thought to be sport. This pattern of cruel exploitation flows naturally from the Kantian attitude that animals are nothing more than things to be used for our purposes. It is this whole attitude that must be opposed, and not merely its manifestation in our willingness to hurt the animals we eat. Once one rejects this attitude and no longer regards the animals as disposable at one's whim, one ceases to think it all right to kill them, even painlessly, just for a snack.

But for those of us who do not live on old-fashioned family farms, the question of whether it would be permissible to eat humanely treated, painlessly slaughtered animals is merely theoretical. The meat available to us at the supermarket was not produced by humane methods. To provide this meat, animals were abused in ways similar to the ones we have described; and millions of other animals are being treated in these ways now, with their flesh to appear soon in the markets. The practical issue is, should we support such practices by purchasing and consuming their products?

It is discouraging to realize that no animals will actually be helped simply by one person ceasing to eat meat. One consumer's behavior, by itself, cannot have a noticeable impact on an industry as vast as the meat business. However, it is important to see one's behavior in a larger context. There are already millions of vegetarians, and because they don't eat meat, there *is* less cruelty than there otherwise would be. The question is whether one ought to side with that group or with the people whose practices cause the suffering. Compare the position of someone thinking about whether to buy slaves in 1820. He might reason as follows: "The whole practice of slavery is immoral, but I cannot help any of the poor slaves by keeping clear of it. If I don't buy these slaves, someone else will. One person's decision can't by itself have any impact on such a vast business. So I may as well own slaves like everyone else." The first thing we notice is that this fellow was too pessimistic about the possibilities of a successful movement; but beyond that, there is something else wrong with his reasoning. If one really thinks that a social practice is immoral, that is sufficient grounds for refusing to participate in it. In 1848 Henry David Thoreau remarked that even if someone did not want to devote himself to the abolition movement and actively oppose slavery, "it is his duty, at least, to wash his hands of it, and, if he gives it no thought longer, not to give it practically his support."[9] In the case of slavery, this seems clear. If it seems less clear in the case of the cruel exploitation of nonhuman animals, perhaps it is because the Kantian attitude has so tenacious a hold on us.

Notes

1. Louis B. Schwartz, "Morals Offenses and the Model Penal Code," in *Philosophy of Law*, ed. Joel Feinberg and Hyman Gross (Encino, Calif.: Dickenson, 1975), 156. First published in *Columbia Law Review* 63 (1963): 669–84.

2. Immanuel Kant, *Foundations of the Metaphysics of Morals*, trans. Lewis White Beck (Indianapolis: Bobbs-Merrill, 1959), 47.

3. Immanuel Kant, *Lectures on Ethics*, trans. Louis Infield (New York: Harper, 1963), 239.

4. Kant, *Lectures on Ethics*, 240.

5. Muriel the Lady Dowding, "Furs and Cosmetics: Too High a Price?" in *Animals, Men, and Morals*, ed. Stanley Godlovitch, Roslind Godlovitch, and John Harris (New York: Taplinger, 1972), 36.

6. The best account is chap. 3 of Peter Singer's *Animal Liberation* (New York: New York Review Books, 1975). I have drawn on Singer's work for the factual material in the following two paragraphs.

7. Singer, *Animal Liberation*, 152.

8. *Miami Herald*, 26 August 1972, sec. A, p. 3.

9. Henry David Thoreau, *Walden and Civil Disobedience*, ed. Owen Thomas (New York: W. W. Norton & Co., 1966), 229–30. First published in 1848.

8

God and Moral Autonomy

_Kneeling down or grovelling on the ground, even to express your rev-
erence for heavenly things, is contrary to human dignity._

—Kant

God, if he exists, is worthy of worship. Any being who is not worthy
of worship cannot be God, just as any being who is not omnipotent
or perfectly good cannot be God.[1] This is reflected in the attitudes of religious believers who recognize that whatever else God may be, he is a
being before whom we should bow down. Moreover, he is unique in this;
to worship anyone or anything else is blasphemy. But can such a being
exist? In what follows I will present an argument against the existence of
God that is based on the conception of God as a fitting object of worship.
The argument is that God cannot exist, because there could not be a being
toward whom we should adopt such an attitude.

Worship

The concept of worship has received surprisingly little attention from
philosophers of religion. When it has been treated, the usual approach is
by way of referring to God's awesomeness or mysteriousness: to worship
is to "bow down in silent awe" when confronted with a being that is "ter-
rifyingly mysterious."[2] But neither of these notions is of much help in
understanding worship. Awe is certainly not the same thing as worship;
one can be awed by a performance of _King Lear_, or by witnessing an
eclipse of the sun or an earthquake, or by meeting one's favorite film star,
without worshiping any of these things. And a great many things are both
terrifying and mysterious that we have not the slightest inclination to

109

worship—the Black Death probably fits that description for many people. So we need an account of worship that does not rely on such notions as awesomeness and mysteriousness.

Consider McBlank, who worked against America's entry into the Second World War, refused induction into the army, and went to jail. He was active in the "ban the bomb" movements of the 1950s; he made speeches, wrote pamphlets, led demonstrations, and went back to jail. He opposed the war in Vietnam; and in old age he angrily denounced the short-lived Gulf War. In all of this McBlank acted out of principle. He thinks that all war is evil and that no war is ever justified.

We might note three features of McBlank's pacifist commitment. (1) He recognizes that certain facts are the case. History is full of wars; war causes the massive destruction of life and property; in war people suffer on a scale hardly matched in any other way; the large nations now have weapons that, if used, could virtually wipe out the human race; and so on. These are just facts that any normally informed person will admit without argument. (2) But of course they are not *merely* facts that people recognize to be the case in some indifferent manner. They are facts that have special importance to human beings. They form an ominous and threatening backdrop to people's lives—even though for most people they are a backdrop only. But not so for McBlank. He sees the accumulation of these facts as having radical implications for his conduct; he behaves in a very different way from the way he would behave were it not for these facts. His whole style of life is different; his conduct is altered, not just in its details, but in its pattern. (3) Not only is his overt behavior affected; so are his ways of thinking about the world and his place in it. His self-image is different. He sees himself as a member of a race with an insane history of self-destruction, and his self-image becomes that of an active opponent of the forces that lead to this self-destruction. He is an opponent of militarism just as he is a father or a musician. When the existentialists said that we "create ourselves" by our choices, they may have had something like this in mind.

The worshiper has a set of beliefs about God that function in the same way as McBlank's beliefs about war. First, the worshiper believes that certain sorts of things are the case: for example, that the world was created by an all-powerful, all-wise being who knows our every thought and action; that this being cares for us and regards us as his children; that we are made by him in order to return his love and live in accordance with his laws; and that if we do not live in a way pleasing to him, we may be punished. (I use these beliefs as my example. But I do not mean that these particular beliefs are accepted, in just this form, by all religious people.

They are, however, the sorts of beliefs that are required for the business of worshiping God to make sense.)

Second, like the facts about warfare, these are not facts that one notes with an air of indifference. They have important implications for one's conduct. An effort must be made to discover God's will both for people generally and for oneself in particular; and to this end, the believer consults the church authorities and the theologians, reads the scripture, and prays. The degree to which this will alter his behavior will depend, of course, on exactly what he decides God would have him do and on the extent to which his behavior would have followed the prescribed pattern in any case.

Finally, the believer's recognition of these facts will influence his self-image and his way of thinking about the world and his place in it. The world will be regarded as having been made for the fulfillment of divine purposes; the hardships that befall men will be regarded either as "tests" in some sense or as punishments for sin; and most important, the believer will think of himself as a child of God and of his conduct as reflecting either honor or dishonor upon his Heavenly Father.

Wittgenstein's View

What will be most controversial in what I have said so far (to some philosophers, though perhaps not to most religious believers) is the treatment of claims such as "God regards us as his children" as in some sense factual. Wittgenstein is reported to have thought this a misunderstanding of religious belief, and others have followed him in this.[3] Religious utterances, it is said, do not report putative facts. Instead, we should understand such utterances as revealing the speaker's *form of life*. To have a form of life is to accept a language game; the religious believer accepts a language game in which there is talk of God, Creation, Heaven and Hell, a Last Judgment, and so forth, which the skeptic does not accept. Such language games can be understood only in their own terms; we must not try to assimilate them to other sorts of games. To see how this particular game works, we need only to examine the way the language of religion is used by actual believers; in its proper habitat the language game will be "in order" as it stands. We find that the religious believer uses such utterances for a number of purposes—for example, to express reasons for action, to show the significance that she attaches to various things, to express her attitudes, and so on—but not to state facts in the ordinary sense. So when the believer makes a typically religious assertion and the nonbeliever denies the same, *they are not contradicting one another;* rather, the nonbeliever is simply refusing to play the believer's (very serious) game. Wittgenstein (as recorded by his pupils) said:

> Suppose that someone believed in the Last Judgement, and I don't, does this mean that I believe the opposite to him, just that there won't be such a thing? I would say: 'not at all, or not always.'
> Suppose I say that the body will rot, and another says 'No. Particles will rejoin in a thousand years, and there will be a Resurrection of you.'
> If some said: 'Wittgenstein, do you believe in this?' I'd say: 'No.' 'Do you contradict the man?' I'd say: 'No.'[4]

Wittgenstein goes on to say that the difference between the believer and the skeptic is not that one holds something to be true that the other thinks false but that the believer takes certain things as "guidance for life" that the skeptic does not—for example, that there will be a Last Judgment. He illustrates this by reference to a person who "thinks of retribution" when he plans his conduct or assesses his condition:

> Suppose you had two people, and one of them, when he had to decide which course to take, thought of retribution, and the other did not. One person might, for instance, be inclined to take everything that happened to him as a reward or punishment, and another person doesn't think of this at all.
> If he is ill, he may think: 'What have I done to deserve this?' This is one way of thinking of retribution. Another way is, he thinks in a general way whenever he is ashamed of himself: 'This will be punished.'
> Take two people, one of whom talks of his behavior and of what happens to him in terms of retribution, the other does not. These people think entirely differently. Yet, so far, you can't say they believe different things.
> Suppose someone is ill and he says: 'This is punishment,' and I say: 'If I'm ill, I don't think of punishment at all.' If you say: 'Do you believe the opposite?'—you can call it believing the opposite, but it is entirely different from what we would normally call believing the opposite.
> I think differently, in a different way. I say different things to myself. I have different pictures.[5]

But it is not at all clear that this account is true to the intentions of those who engage in religious discourse. If a believer (at least, the great majority of those whom I have known or read about) says that there will be a Last Judgment and a skeptic says that there will not, the believer certainly will think that he has been contradicted. Of course, the skeptic might not think of denying such a thing except for the fact that the believer asserts it; and in this trivial sense, the skeptic might "think differently"— but that is beside the point. Moreover, former believers who become skeptics frequently do so because they come to believe that religious assertions are *false;* then they consider themselves to be denying exactly what they previously asserted.

Moreover, a belief does not lose its ordinary factual import simply because it occupies a central place in one's way of life. McBlank takes the facts about war as guidance for life in a perfectly straightforward sense; but they remain facts. I take it that just as the man in Wittgenstein's example thinks of retribution often, McBlank thinks of war often. So, we do not need to give religious utterances any peculiar interpretation in order to explain their importance for one's way of life.

Finally, we do not need a view of religious belief that is deep and difficult. If the impact of religious belief on conduct and thinking can be explained by appeal to nothing more mysterious than putative facts and their impact on conduct and thinking, then the need for a more obscure theory is obviated. And if people believe that, as a matter of fact, their actions are subject to review by a just God who will mete out rewards and punishments on a day of final reckoning, that will explain very nicely why they think of retribution when they reflect on their conduct.

The Point of the Ritual

Worship is something that is done; but it is not clear just what is done when one worships. Other actions, such as throwing a ball or insulting one's neighbor, seem transparent enough; but not so with worship. When we celebrate Mass in the Roman Catholic Church, for example, what are we doing (apart from eating a wafer and drinking wine)? Or when we sing hymns in a Protestant church, what are we doing (other than merely singing songs)? What is it that makes these acts of *worship?* One obvious point is that these actions, and others like them, are ritualistic in character; so before we can make any progress in understanding worship, perhaps it will help to ask about the nature of ritual.

First we need to distinguish the ceremonial form of a ritual from what is supposed to be accomplished by it. Consider, for example, the ritual of investiture for an English prince. The prince kneels; the queen (or king) places a crown on his head; and he takes an oath: "I do become your liege man of life and limb and of earthly worship, and faith and trust I will bear unto thee to live and die against all manner of folks." By this ceremony the prince is elevated to his new station, and by this oath he acknowledges the commitments that, as prince, he will owe the queen. In one sense, the ceremonial form of the ritual is unimportant; it is possible that some other procedure might have been laid down, without the point of the ritual being affected in any way. Rather than placing a crown on his head, the queen might break an egg into his palm (that could symbolize all sorts of things). Once this was established as the procedure, it would do as well as the other. It would still be the ritual of investiture, so long as it was understood that by the ceremony a prince is created. The performance of a ritual, then, is in certain respects like the use of language. In speaking, sounds are uttered, and, thanks to the conventions of the language, something is said, or affirmed, or done; and in a ritual performance, a ceremony is enacted, and, thanks to the conventions associated with the ceremony, something is done, or affirmed, or celebrated.

How are we to explain the point of the ritual of investiture? We might explain that certain parts of the ritual symbolize specific things; for example, that the prince's kneeling before the queen symbolizes his subordination to her (it is not merely to make it easier for her to place the crown on his head). But it is essential that in explaining the point of the ritual as a whole, we include that a prince is being created, that he is henceforth to have certain rights in virtue of having been made a prince, and that he is to have certain duties that he is now acknowledging, among which are complete loyalty and faithfulness to the queen, and so on. If the listener already knows about the complex relations between queens, princes, and subjects, then all we need to say is that a prince is being installed in office; but if he is unfamiliar with this social system, we must tell him a great deal if he is to understand what is going on.

So, once we understand the social system in which there are queens, princes, and subjects, and therefore understand the role assigned to each within that system, we can sum up what is happening in the ritual of investiture in this way: someone is being made a prince, and he is accepting that role with all that it involves. Similar explanations could be given for other rituals, such as the marriage ceremony: two people are being made husband and wife, and they are accepting those roles with all that they involve.

The question to be asked about the ritual of worship is what analogous explanation can be given of it. The ceremonial form of the ritual may vary according to the customs of the religious community; it may involve singing, drinking wine, counting beads, sitting with a solemn expression on one's face, dancing, making a sacrifice, or what have you. But what is the point of it?

As we have already observed, the worshiper thinks of himself as inhabiting a world created by an infinitely wise, infinitely powerful, perfectly good God; and it is a world in which he, along with other people, occupies a special place in virtue of God's intentions. This gives him a certain role to play: the role of a "child of God." In worshiping God, one is acknowledging and accepting this role, and that is the point of the ritual of worship. Just as the ritual of investiture derives its significance from its place within the social system of queens, princes, and subjects, the ritual of worship gets its significance from an assumed system of relationships between God and human beings. In the ceremony of investiture, the prince assumes a role with respect to the queen and the citizenry. In marriage, two people assume roles with respect to one another. And in worship, a person accepts and affirms his role with respect to God.

Worship presumes the superior status of the one worshiped. This is reflected in the logical point that there can be no such things as mutual or reciprocal worship, unless one or the other of the parties is mistaken as to his own status. We can very well comprehend people loving one another or respecting one another, but not (unless they are misguided) worshiping one another. This is because the worshiper necessarily assumes his own inferiority; and since inferiority is an asymmetrical relation, so is worship. (The nature of the "superiority" and "inferiority" involved here is of course problematic; but in the account I am presenting, it may be understood on the model of superior and inferior positions within a social system.) This is also why humility is necessary on the part of the worshiper. The role to which he commits himself is that of the humble servant, "not worthy to touch the hem of his garment." Compared to God's gloriousness, "all our righteousnesses are as filthy rags."[6] So in committing oneself to this role, one is acknowledging God's greatness and one's own relative worthlessness. This humble attitude is not a mere embellishment of the ritual: on the contrary, worship, unlike love or respect, requires humility. Pride is a sin, and pride before God is incompatible with worshiping him.

The function of worship as "glorifying" or "praising" God, which is often taken to be primary, may be regarded as derivative from the more fundamental nature of worship as commitment to the role of God's child. "Praising" God is giving him the honor and respect due to one in his position of eminence, just as one shows respect and honor in giving fealty to a king.

In short, the worshiper is in this position: He believes that there is a being, God, who is the perfectly good, perfectly powerful, perfectly wise Creator of the universe; and he views himself as the child of God, made for God's purposes and responsible to God for his conduct. And the ritual of worship, which may have any number of ceremonial forms according to the customs of the religious community, has as its point the acceptance of, and commitment to, this role as God's child, with all that this involves. If this account is accepted, then there is no mystery as to the relation between the act of worship and the worshiper's other activity. Worship will be regarded not as an isolated act taking place on Sunday morning, with no necessary connection to one's behavior the rest of the week, but as a ritualistic expression of, and commitment to, a role that dominates one's whole way of life.[7]

Acting Consistently with One's Role as God's Child

An important feature of roles is that they can be violated: we can act and think consistently with a role, or we can act and think inconsistently with it. The prince can, for example, act inconsistently with his role as prince by giving greater importance to his own interests and welfare than to the queen's; in this case, he is no longer her liege man. And a father who does not attend to the welfare of his children is not acting consistently with his role as a father, and so on. What would count as violating the role to which one is pledged in virtue of worshiping God?

In Genesis two familiar stories, both concerning Abraham, are relevant. The first is the story of the near sacrifice of Isaac. We are told that Abraham was "tempted" by God, who commanded him to offer Isaac as a human sacrifice. Abraham obeyed—he prepared an altar, bound Isaac to it, and was about to kill him until God intervened at the last moment, saying, "Lay not thine hand upon the lad, neither do thou any thing unto him: for now I know that thou fearest God, seeing thou hast not withheld thy son, thine only son from me" (Gen. 22:12). So Abraham passed the test. But how could he have failed? What was his temptation? Obviously, his temptation was to disobey God; God had ordered him to do something contrary both to his wishes and to his sense of what would otherwise have been right. He could have defied God, but he did not—he subordinated himself, his own desires and judgments, to God's command, even when the temptation to do otherwise was strongest.

It is interesting that Abraham's record in this respect was not perfect. We also have the story of him bargaining with God over the conditions for saving Sodom and Gomorrah from destruction. God had said that he would destroy those cities because they were so wicked; but Abraham gets God to agree that if fifty righteous men can be found there, the cities will be spared. Then he persuades God to lower the number to forty-five, then forty, then thirty, then twenty, and finally ten. Here we have a different Abraham, not servile and obedient, but willing to challenge God and bargain with him. However, even as he bargains with God, Abraham realizes that there is something radically inappropriate about it: he says,

"Behold now, I have taken upon me to speak unto the Lord, which am but dust and ashes. . . . Oh let not the Lord be angry" (Gen. 18:27, 30).

The fact is that Abraham could not, consistent with his role as God's subject, set his own judgment and will against God's. The author of Genesis was certainly right about this. We cannot recognize any being *as* God and at the same time set ourselves against him. The point is not merely that it would be imprudent to defy God, since we certainly can't get away with it. Rather, there is a stronger, logical point involved—namely, that if we recognize any being as God, then we are committed, in virtue of that recognition, to obeying him.

To see why this is so, we must first notice that "God" is not a proper name like "Richard Nixon" but a title like "president of the United States" or "king."[8] Thus, "Jehovah is God" is a nontautological statement in which the title "God" is assigned to Jehovah, a particular being, just as "Richard Nixon is president of the United States" assigns the title "president of the United States" to a particular man. This permits us to understand how statements like "God is perfectly wise" can be logical truths, which is problematic if "God" is regarded as a proper name. Although it is not a logical truth that any particular being is perfectly wise, it nevertheless is a logical truth that if any being is God (that is, if any being properly holds that title), then that being is perfectly wise. This is exactly analogous to saying that although it is not a logical truth that Richard Nixon has the authority to veto congressional legislation, nevertheless it is a logical truth that if Richard Nixon is president of the United States, then he has that authority.

To bear the title "God," then, a being must have certain qualifications: he must be all-powerful and perfectly good in addition to being perfectly wise. And in the same vein, to apply the title "God" to a being is to recognize him as one to be obeyed. The same is true, to a lesser extent, of "king"; to recognize anyone as king is to acknowledge that he occupies a place of authority and has a claim on one's allegiance as his subject. And to recognize any being as God is to acknowledge that he has unlimited authority and an unlimited claim on one's allegiance. Thus, we might regard Abraham's reluctance to defy Jehovah as grounded not only in his fear of Jehovah's wrath but as a logical consequence of his acceptance of Jehovah as God. Albert Camus was right to think that "from the moment that man submits God to moral judgment, he kills Him his own heart."[9] What a man can "kill" by defying or even questioning God is not the being that (supposedly) *is* God but his own conception of that being as God. That God is not to be judged, challenged, defied, or disobeyed is at bottom a truth of logic. To do any of these things is incompatible with taking him as one to be worshiped.

As a sidelight, this suggestion might also provide some help with the old problem of how we could, even in principle, verify God's existence. Skeptics have argued that even though we might be able to confirm the existence of an all-powerful cosmic superbeing, we still wouldn't know what it means to verify that this being is *divine*. And this, it is said, casts doubt on whether the notion of divinity and related notions such as "sacred," "holy," and "God" are intelligible.[10] Perhaps this is because in designating a being as God, we are not only describing him as having certain properties (such as omnipotence), but we are also ascribing to him a certain place in our devotions and taking him as one to be obeyed, worshiped, and praised. If this is part of the logic of "God," we shouldn't be surprised if God's existence, insofar as that includes the existence of divinity, is not empirically confirmable. But once the reason for this is understood, it no longer seems such a serious matter.

The Moral Autonomy Argument

So the idea that any being could be worthy of worship is much more problematic than we might have at first imagined. In saying that a being is worthy of worship, we would be recognizing him as having an unqualified claim on our obedience. The question, then, is whether there could be such an unqualified claim. It should be noted that the description of a being as all-powerful, all-wise, and so on would not automatically settle the issue; for even while admitting the existence of such an awesome being, we might still question whether we should recognize him as having an unlimited claim on our obedience.

There is a long tradition in moral philosophy, from Plato to Kant, according to which such a recognition could never be made by a moral agent. According to this tradition, to be a moral agent is to be autonomous, or self-directed. Unlike the precepts of law or social custom, moral precepts are imposed by the agent upon himself, and the penalty for their violation is, in Kant's words, "self-contempt and inner abhorrence."[11] The virtuous person is therefore identified with the person of integrity, the person who acts according to precepts that she can, on reflection, conscientiously approve in her own heart.

On this view, to deliver oneself over to a moral authority for directions about what to do is simply incompatible with being a moral agent. To say "I will follow so-and-so's directions no matter what they are and no matter what my own conscience would otherwise direct me to do" is to opt out of moral thinking altogether; it is to abandon one's role as a moral agent. And it does not matter whether "so-and-so" is the law, the customs of one's society, or Jehovah. This does not, of course, preclude one from seeking advice on moral matters and even on occasion following that advice blindly, trusting in the good judgment of the adviser. But this is justified by the details of the particular case—for example, that you cannot form any reasonable judgment of your own because of ignorance or inexperience or lack of time. What is precluded is that a person should, while in possession of his wits, adopt this style of decision making (or perhaps we should say this style of abdicating decision making) as a general strategy of living, or abandon his own best judgment when he can form a judgment of which he is reasonably confident.

We have, then, a conflict between the role of worshiper, which by its very nature commits one to total subservience to God, and the role of moral agent, which necessarily involves autonomous decision making. The role of worshiper takes precedence over every other role the worshiper has; when there is any conflict, the worshiper's commitment to God has priority over everything. But the first commitment of a moral agent is to do what in his own heart he thinks is right. Thus the following argument might be constructed:

1. If any being is God, he must be a fitting object of worship.

2. No being could possibly be a fitting object of worship, since worship requires the abandonment of one's role as an autonomous moral agent.

3. Therefore, there cannot be any being who is God.

Objections and Replies

The concept of moral agency underlying this argument is controversial, and although I think it is sound, I cannot give it here the detailed treatment that it requires. Instead, I will conclude by considering some of the most obvious objections to the argument.

(1) What if God lets us go our own way and issues no commands other than that we should live according to our own consciences? In that case there would be no incompatibility between our commitment to God and our commitments as moral agents, since God would leave us free to direct our own lives. The fact that this supposition is contrary to major religious traditions (such as the Christian tradition) doesn't matter, since these traditions could be mistaken. The answer is that this is a mere contingency,

and that even if God did not require obedience to detailed commands, the worshiper would still be committed to the abandonment of his role as a moral agent if God required it.

(2) God is perfectly good; it follows that he would never require us to do anything except what is right. Therefore, in obeying God, we would only be doing what we should do in any case. So there is no incompatibility between obeying him and carrying out our moral responsibilities. Our responsibility as moral agents is to do right, and God's commands are right, so that's that. This objection rests on a misunderstanding of the idea that (necessarily) God is perfectly good. This can be intelligibly asserted only because of the principle that *no being who is not perfectly good may bear the title "God."* The catch is that we cannot determine whether some being is God without first checking on whether he is perfectly good;[12] and we cannot decide whether he is perfectly good without knowing (among other things) whether his commands to us are right. Thus our own judgment that some actions are right and others wrong is logically prior to our recognition of any being as God. The upshot is that we cannot justify the suspension of our own judgment on the grounds that we are deferring to God's command; for if, by our own best judgment, the command is wrong, this gives us good reason to withhold the title "God" from the commander.

(3) People are sinful; their very consciences are corrupt and unreliable guides. What is taken for conscientiousness is nothing more than self-aggrandizement and arrogance. Therefore, we cannot trust our own judgment; we must trust God and do what he wills. Only then can we be assured of doing what is right.

This is a view that has always had its advocates among theologians. But this Augustinian view suffers from a fundamental inconsistency. It is said that we cannot know for ourselves what is right and what is wrong, because our judgment is corrupt. But how do we know that our judgment is corrupt? Presumably, in order to know that, we would have to know (a) that some actions are morally required of us, and (b) that our own judgment does not reveal that these actions are required. However, (a) is just the sort of thing that we cannot know, according to this view. Now, it may be suggested that while we cannot know (a) by our own judgment, we can know it as a result of God's revelation. But even setting aside the practical difficulties of distinguishing genuine from bogus revelation (a generous concession), there is still this problem: if we learn that God (some being we take to be God) requires us to do a certain action and we conclude on this account that the action is morally right, then we have still made at least one moral judgment of our own, namely, that whatever this being requires is morally right. Therefore, it is impossible to maintain the view that we have moral knowledge and that all of it comes from God's revelation.

(4) Some philosophers have held that the voice of individual conscience is the voice of God speaking to the individual, whether the individual realizes it or not and whether he is a believer or not. This would resolve the conflict, because in following one's conscience, one would at the same time be discharging one's obligation as a worshiper to obey God. However, this maneuver is unsatisfying because if it were taken seriously, it would lead to the conclusion that in speaking to us through our "consciences," God is merely tricking us, for he is giving us the illusion of self-governance while all the time he is manipulating our thoughts from without. Moreover, in acting from conscience, we are acting under the view that our actions are right and not merely that they are decreed by a higher power. Socrates' argument in the *Euthyphro* can be adapted to this point. If in speaking to us through the voice of conscience, God is informing us of what is right, then there is no reason to think that we could not discover this for ourselves—the notion of "God informing us" is eliminable. On the other hand, if God is only giving us arbitrary commands, which cannot be thought of as right independent of his promulgating them, then the whole idea of conscience, as it is normally understood, is a sham.

(5) Finally, it might be objected that the question of whether any being is worthy of worship is different from the question of whether we *should* worship him. In general, that X is worthy of our doing Y with respect to X does not entail that we should do Y with respect to X. Mrs. Brown, being a fine woman, may be worthy of a marriage proposal, but we ought not to propose to her, since she is already married. Or, Seaman Jones may be worthy of a medal for heroism, but still there could be reasons why we should not award it. Similarly, it may be that there is a being who is worthy of worship and yet we should not worship him since it would interfere with our lives as moral agents. Thus God, who is worthy of worship, may exist; and we should love, respect, and honor him, but not worship him in the full sense of the word. If this is correct, then the Moral Autonomy Argument is fallacious.

But this objection will not work because of a disanalogy between the cases of proposing marriage and awarding the medal, on the one hand, and the case of worship on the other. It may be that Mrs. Brown is worthy of a proposal, yet there are circumstances in which it would be wrong to propose to her. However, these circumstances are contrasted with others in which it would be perfectly all right. The same goes for Seaman Jones's medal: there are some circumstances in which awarding it would be proper. But in the case of worship—if the foregoing arguments have been sound—there are no circumstances under which anyone should worship God. And if one should never worship, then the concept of a fitting object of worship is empty.

The Moral Autonomy Argument will probably not persuade anyone to abandon belief in God—arguments rarely do—and there are certainly many more points that need to be worked out before it can be known whether this argument is even viable. Perhaps it isn't. Yet it does raise an issue that is clear enough. Theologians are already accustomed to speaking of theistic belief and commitment as taking the believer "beyond morality." The question is whether this should not be regarded as a severe embarrassment.

Notes

1. Charles Hartshorne and Nelson Pike have suggested that St. Anselm's famous definition of God, "that than which none greater can be conceived," should be understood as meaning "that than which none more worthy of worship can be conceived." Charles Hartshorne, *Anselm's Discovery* (LaSalle, Ill.: Open Court, 1966), 25–26; and Nelson Pike, *God and Timelessness* (London: Routledge & Kegan Paul, 1970), 149–60.

2. These phrases are from John Hick, *Philosophy of Religion* (Englewood Cliffs, N.J.: Prentice-Hall, 1963), 13–14.

3. Ludwig Wittgenstein, *Lectures and Conversations on Aesthetics, Psychology, and Religious Belief,* ed. Cyril Barrett, from notes taken by Yorick Smythies, Rush Rhees, and James Taylor (Berkeley: University of California Press, 1967). See also, for example, Rush Rhees, *Without Answers* (London: Routledge & Kegan Paul, 1969), chap. 13.

4. Wittgenstein, *Lectures,* 53.

5. Wittgenstein, *Lectures,* 54–55.

6. Isa. 64:6 AV. All biblical citations are to the Authorized (King James) Version.

7. This account of worship, specified here in terms of what it means to worship God, may easily be adapted to the worship of other beings, such as Satan. The only changes required are (a) that we substitute for beliefs about God analogous beliefs about Satan, and (b) that we understand the ritual of worship as committing the Satan-worshiper to a role as Satan's servant in the same way that worshiping God commits theists to the role of his servant.

8. Cf. Nelson Pike, "Omnipotence and God's Ability to Sin," *American Philosophical Quarterly* 6 (1969): 208–9; and C. B. Martin, *Religious Belief* (Ithaca, N.Y.: Cornell University Press, 1964), chap. 4.

9. Albert Camus, *The Rebel,* trans. Anthony Bower (New York: Vintage, 1956), 62.

10. See Kai Nielsen, "Eschatological Verification," *Canadian Journal of Theology* 9 (1963).

11. Immanuel Kant, *Foundations of the Metaphysics of Morals*, trans. Lewis White Beck (Indianapolis: Bobbs-Merrill, 1959), 44.

12. In one sense, of course, we could never know for sure that such a being is perfectly good, since that would require an examination of all his actions and commands, which is impossible. However, if we observed many good things about him and no evil ones, we would be justified in accepting the hypothesis that he is perfectly good. The hypothesis would be confirmed or disconfirmed by future observations in the usual way.

9

Lying and the Ethics of Absolute Rules

A re moral rules inviolable? Most philosophers would reject the notion out of hand, for, it would be said, every rule has its exceptions. Generally speaking, one ought not to lie, but circumstances might arise in which lying is justified. Generally speaking, one ought not to kill another human being, but circumstances might arise in which even killing is justified; and so on. The worse the action, the rarer the circumstances in which it would be justified. Some actions might be so bad that in fact no such desperate circumstances ever arise; however, even in these extreme cases, such circumstances could be imagined and written into a fanciful story.

The circumstances in which generally bad actions are nevertheless justified, it is said, are those in which the consequences of not doing the action are worse than the evil involved in the action itself, or, alternatively, in which the consequences are so good as to outweigh the evil of the action. Then we are justified in doing the bad act—in violating the moral rule prohibiting actions of that sort—by the expectation of redeeming consequences. But Professor Anscombe will have no part of such thinking. She protests that philosophers who defend this sort of view—"every single English academic moral philosopher since Sidgwick," she says—are assuming a great deal more than they ought:

> It is noticeable that none of these philosophers displays any consciousness that there is such an ethic, which he is contradicting: it is pretty well taken for obvious among them that a prohibition such as that on murder does not operate in the face of some consequences. But of course the strictness of the prohibition has as its point *that you are not to be tempted by fear or hope of consequences.*[1]

She approves of such prohibitions: there are "certain things" that should be prohibited "simply in virtue of their description as such-and-such identifiable kinds of action, regardless of any further consequences." We may call this kind of view *moral absolutism*.[2]

Moral absolutists might disagree about which types of action should be prohibited altogether. Anscombe, in the passage just quoted, mentions murder as an example. However, someone might agree that *some* kinds of actions should be absolutely prohibited but disagree that murder is one of them. He might say that the evil must be greater than that of simple murder and offer as an alternative example genocide. Others might think that the standard of evil could be set much lower and that the absolute prohibitions could be extended to such lesser sins as lying, breaking one's promises, and so forth. Thus absolutists may disagree among themselves as to which prohibitions are inviolable, and the plausibility of the view may depend on which version we are considering.

The most extreme form of moral absolutism is the view that *every* sort of bad action—that is, every sort of action that is prima facie objectionable just in virtue of the kind of action it is—should be utterly prohibited. On this view, *no* general prohibition could ever be set aside by considerations of consequences. If an act, considered merely as the kind of action it is, is a bad sort of thing to do, then it should never be done, and that's that. A good person, recognizing that the action would be an act of a bad type, will deliberate no further; he or she will not "be tempted by fear or hope of consequences."

It is not clear whether Anscombe would endorse this strong version of moral absolutism. There is, however, at least one philosopher who does, namely, P. T. Geach. Geach argues that the principle "We must not do evil that good may come" is applicable to all actions that are, considered in themselves, evil.[3] Lying, for example, is usually considered bad, but not so bad that on occasion it is not justified. But in saying this, we are admitting that lying is a bad sort of action; so, for Geach, lying is out: It is not even to be considered, no matter how extreme the circumstances and no matter what the results of lying would be in the particular case at hand. The moral decision of what to do will be settled when the action has been seen to fall under the prohibition against lying—"That would be lying, so I can't do it"—and no further deliberation is necessary or even proper.

The Standard Way of Understanding the Debate

There is a conventional way of understanding absolutism that goes like this. Absolutists believe that certain sorts of actions are *intrinsically wrong*—wrong simply because of the kinds of actions they are. Such actions might sometimes have good consequences, but that does not matter. The intrinsic character of the act makes it impermissible.

An example might help to define the issue more sharply. Suppose you have a friend who, after years of saving and planning, has recently bought a house. He proudly shows it to you and asks what you think. Your opinion means a lot to him. You think the house is awful. What do you do? Lie and make your friend happy, or tell the truth and make him unhappy? Of course there may be a third option: you might find some way to finesse the situation. Geach suggests that this is always possible. He tells the story of how St. Athanasius once encountered persecutors who, not recognizing him, demanded to know "Where is the traitor Athanasius?" "Not far away," the saint replied, and went on his way unmolested. Geach, who thinks that lying is always wrong, nevertheless applauds this deception—"Such," he says, "is the snakish cunning of the Saints, commended in the Gospel"[4]—and cites it as an example of how clever people can find a way out of difficult situations without having to lie.

But suppose there is no way to finesse the situation with your friend—he's looking you in the eye and he will take any hesitation to mean you don't like his house. The Geachean absolutist would say that you mustn't lie. Others might say that the right thing to do is to lie, on the grounds that your friend would be pleased and no harm would be done. (This is an example of what many people regard as an innocent lie, or a "little white lie.") If we make a list of the reasons for and against telling this particular lie, it might look like this:

A. Reasons for the action
    1. *Reasons having to do with the intrinsic character of the act:* in this case there are none.
    2. *Reasons having to do with the consequences of the act:* it would make your friend happy.
B. Reasons against the action
    1. *Reasons having to do with the intrinsic character of the act:* it would be lying.
    2. *Reasons having to do with the consequences of the act:* in this case there are none.

We can distinguish at least five possible views.

(1) It might be held that, in assessing an action, only its consequences are of any importance; the intrinsic character of the action itself counts for nothing at all. Therefore, every reason for or against an action will be classified under A2 or B2. This view has the consequence, which many

philosophers have found objectionable, that if there is a situation in which the effects of lying are exactly the same as the effects of truthfulness, then there is nothing to choose between the two options—one is as good as the other.

(2) A less extreme consequentialist view would be that the intrinsic character of the act has some importance but not enough to overcome any contrary considerations as to consequences. Reasons of type A2 will always outweigh reasons of type B1, and reasons of type B2 will always outweigh reasons of type A1. If there are reasons of types A2 and B2 in a single case, then the decision of what to do will depend on which are stronger. Only if these considerations are of equal weight should we bring reasons of types A1 or B1 into our deliberations. On this view, in the case where the effects of lying are just the same as the effects of telling the truth, we can conclude that we should tell the truth.

(3) On the other side, it could be said that only the intrinsic character of the action has any importance and that consequences never matter at all; that is, that the only reasons for or against any action are those found under A1 or B1. On this view, if an action considered in itself is not bad but a consequence of the action would be the destruction of the world, there would nonetheless be no reason to avoid doing it.

(4) A second anticonsequentialist position would be the view that the consequences of an act have some importance, but not enough to justify doing the act when there are reasons against it having to do with its intrinsic character. That is, reasons of type B1 always override reasons of type A2; and similarly, reasons of type A1 always override reasons of type B2.

(5) Finally, there is what we might call the "compromise" view, the view that both the intrinsic character of the action and its consequences are important in determining whether it ought to be done and that the decision of which overrides which is a matter for judicious assessment in each case. On this view, no general formula such as those proposed in views 1 through 4 is possible; each case must be judged on its own merits.

Views 1 and 2 are versions of consequentialism that have been defended by utilitarians. View 3 is an utterly insane view that no one has ever defended, so far as I know; I mention it only because it occupies a position in logical space. View 4 seems to be Geach's view, and also Kant's view; and view 5 is the view of Sir David Ross. As crude as this classification may be, it shows the usual distinction between utilitarians and deontologists to be even cruder: to lump Kant and Ross together as "deontologists" is to conceal a crucial difference between them: that Ross was willing to allow an importance to consequences that Kant was not.

Why Is Lying Wrong?

There is something deeply unsatisfactory about the preceding discussion. The conventional way of understanding the debate between absolutists and their critics assumes that we can make a firm distinction between the intrinsic character of an action and the action's consequences. It also assumes that we can make sense of the notion that an act is wrong because of its intrinsic character—that lying is wrong simply because it is lying. But both these assumptions are questionable.

To say that lying is wrong "simply because it is lying" leaves the wrongness utterly mysterious. It is not difficult to see why some things—pain, for example—are thought to be intrinsically bad. The badness of pain is transparent. But lying is not like that. In order to understand why lying is wrong, we need to be told more than that it is intrinsically so.

Why, then, is lying wrong? Part of the answer is that lying to people harms them. If I lie to you and you believe what I say, you end up with a false belief. Then, if you act on that belief, things can go wrong for you in a variety of ways. Suppose I tell you the concert starts at nine o'clock, when I know it starts at seven. Believing me, you arrive at nine, only to find that you have missed it. Or you desperately need a job, and I tell you the interviews are at nine . . .

But there is also a more general reason why the rule against lying must be part of any rational scheme of action guidance. It would not be possible for people to live together in societies if they could not communicate with one another, and communication would not be possible without the presumption that people will speak the truth. Suppose I ask you what time it is; if I could not assume that you will tell the truth, there would be no point in asking and no reason to pay any attention to your answer. Without the assumption of truthfulness, communication could not take place. So lying violates a condition that is necessary for social living.

These points go a long way toward explaining why lying is wrong, but they do not tell the whole story. There is a special offensiveness to lying that so far is unexplained. To be lied to by someone who is looking you straight in the eye is offensive in a very personal way; if the lie does harm your interests, it is not like being harmed by the impersonal actions of someone you have never met. Conversely, to be caught in a lie is acutely embarrassing above and beyond the embarrassment that goes with other sorts of exposures; it has a humiliating quality that is terrible to experience. What accounts for this?

I suggest that the special offensiveness of being lied to is connected with the fact that the liar takes advantage of the victim's trust. Trusting another person involves leaving oneself vulnerable. When I trust you to tell me the truth, I put my beliefs in your hands. I will believe whatever you say, and if you lie, I will end up with false beliefs. When I trust you to keep your promise, I go ahead with my plans, depending on you to perform as expected. If you break the promise, you let me down. The metaphor of being "let down" is apt: it is as though I had built on a foundation I thought was solid but that now crumbles beneath me. When I trust you not to cheat me, I allow you into a position in which you can do me harm, and then I refrain from guarding against that harm.

In all these cases, I leave some part of my welfare in your hands; I leave myself at your mercy. Thus the harm that you may do me by violating my trust is different in an important way from a gratuitous assault by a stranger whom I have never trusted, for it is harm that was made possible *by* the trust. You were able to cause me to have false beliefs, or let me down, or cheat me, precisely because I trusted you, because I left myself open. This explains why a violation of trust is experienced as so personally offensive. It explains why one might say, in a particularly bitter way, "You took advantage of me"; or, accusingly, "And I trusted you." This is a matter about which not only the one who trusts, but also the one who is trusted, may be sensitive.

To these arguments, Alan Donagan adds another. In his book *The Theory of Morality,* Donagan appeals to the Kantian principle of respect for persons to explain why lying is wrong. Kantian respect for persons involves, first and foremost, not manipulating them. But giving people false information is a way of manipulating them, of causing them to choose as we wish rather than as they would wish if they knew the truth. For example, a doctor who thinks his patient should have an operation but who fears the patient will not choose the operation if he knows how dangerous it is may mislead the patient concerning the dangers. The fact that the patient is manipulated explains why the paternalistic lying is offensive—what right does the doctor have to decide whether the patient will have the operation? Thus Donagan says that "the duty of veracity appears . . . to rest simply on the fact that the respect due to another as a rational creature forbids misinforming him, not only for evil ends, but even for good ones. In duping another by lying to him, you deprive him of the opportunity of exercising his judgment on the best evidence available to him."[5]

It is clear, then, that we can say a lot about why lying is wrong without resorting to the mysterious and unhelpful idea that it is "intrinsically bad." But there is a reason the notion of intrinsic badness is so natural a part of absolutist ethics: if we base our understanding of the wrongness of lying on the preceding sorts of considerations, we have no grounds for laying down an absolute prohibition. There is nothing in the idea that lying harms people, or that lying violates a condition necessary for social living, or that lying violates trust, that compels the conclusion that lying is *always* wrong. Donagan defends a moderate form of absolutism—he holds that we should never lie when we are freely communicating with fully responsible rational creatures—but his explanation of why lying is wrong, although it avoids obscurantism, fails to support even the qualified absolutist conclusion. The idea that lying is intrinsically wrong, however, seems to be just the sort of conception that absolutism needs. Because it is cognitively impenetrable, it is impossible to tell what it supports and what it does not.

Geach's Argument

One obvious way to defend absolutism is to view the moral rules as divine commandments, and Geach does just this. He rejects the widely held view that belief in God has no logical consequences for morality. Belief in God, he says, makes this difference: the believer must be an absolutist. To prove this, Geach offers an argument with premises taken from natural theology. He does not argue whether these premises are true (though he clearly believes them to be true); the point is only that if one accepts these premises, one must adopt an absolutist ethic. The argument goes as follows:[6]

Unlike other creatures he has made, God has created people to be voluntary agents. Given this, it is reasonable to think that God will "direct men to his own ends" by "command and counsel" as well as by foisting his will on them "willy-nilly." Now, all rational people know that some sorts of actions, such as lying, are generally undesirable. Following the principles of natural theology, such knowledge is to be regarded as knowledge of divine prohibitions. The question is then whether these prohibitions are to be taken as absolute, holding without exception, or only as guidelines to be applied at our discretion. If the latter, then it is puzzling that God has left us incompetent to judge when we should follow the rules and when we should not. Geach asks rhetorically, "But what man is competent judge in his own cause, to make exception in a particular case? Even apart from bias, our knowledge of the present relevant circumstances is grossly fallible; still more, our foresight of the future." This incompetence would not matter so much if God were to provide individ-

ual guidance for each of us in each case—a kind of continual personal revelation—but obviously this does not happen. But if we do not know when
a rule applies and when it does not, then we might as well not have the
rule. Therefore, if God's commands are not absolute, then he has in fact
left us without any directions whatever:

> So unless the rational knowledge that these practices are *generally undesir-
> able* is itself a promulgation of the Divine law *absolutely forbidding* such prac-
> tices, God has left most men without any promulgation of commands to
> them on these matters at all, which, on the theological premises I am assum-
> ing, is absurd.

The situation, then, is this: although everyone can know that some practices are generally undesirable, only the believer can know that these
practices are absolutely forbidden. In this way knowledge of God makes
a difference to one's moral code. The unbeliever has no reason to be an
absolutist, but the believer does.

The first thing to notice about this argument is that it does have the
exceedingly strong conclusion that I have already described: If it is valid,
it shows that every practice that is correctly thought to be generally undesirable is in fact absolutely forbidden; thus there are no practices that are
merely "generally undesirable."

But the second thing to notice is that the theological content is in fact
unnecessary to the argument. It does no work in generating the conclusion.
These are the argument's steps, with the theological references retained:

1. We possess knowledge that certain sorts of actions are generally
   undesirable. According to natural theology, this knowledge is
   understood as a promulgation of divine commands.

2. Either God forbids us to do these actions in all cases, or he permits
   exceptions in some special cases.

3. Since the actions in question are known to be generally undesirable,
   we would be justified in doing them in special cases only if we knew
   that a greater good would be accomplished.

4. However, owing to our incorrigible ignorance and prejudice, we
   cannot judge in particular cases whether a greater good would be
   accomplished. Moreover, this deficiency is not made good by divine
   revelation.

5. Therefore, we are never justified in doing these acts. God's commands are absolute prohibitions.

Now the argument may be secularized as follows, deleting the theological trappings, without the loss of anything important:

6. We possess knowledge that certain sorts of actions are generally undesirable.

7. Generally undesirable actions should either be avoided in all cases or done in some special cases only as circumstances require.

8. Since the actions in question are known to be generally undesirable, we would be justified in doing them in special cases only if we knew that a greater good would be accomplished.

9. However, owing to our incorrigible ignorance and prejudice, we cannot judge in particular cases whether a greater good would be accomplished.

10. Therefore, we are never justified in doing these acts.[7]

If this is correct, then Geach's argument does not provide the believer with reasons unavailable to the nonbeliever for accepting an absolutist code. If the argument in (1) through (5) is conclusive for the believer, the argument in (6) through (10) should be equally conclusive for the nonbeliever. There is then no difference in their respective situations; if one should be an absolutist on these grounds, so should the other. And in assessing the argument, there is no need to consider the merits (or demerits) of the theological trappings, since they are logically idle.

The crucial move in this argument is the appeal to people's incompetence in judging when to make exceptions to moral rules. This is not an unfamiliar move in the dispute between absolutists and consequentialists. The absolutist argues that in making actual choices, we do not know for certain exactly what our circumstances are or what the effects of our action will be; we are condemned to act in situations that at best we understand only partially. Kant, for example, in arguing that one ought never to lie, emphasizes that even the well-intentioned liar cannot be certain of the consequences he seeks. His famous case has a man being asked directions by a scoundrel intent on murder:

> After you have honestly answered the murderer's question as to whether his intended victim is at home, it may be that he has slipped out so that he does not come in the way of the murderer, and thus that the murder may not be committed. But if you had lied and said he was not at home when he had really gone out without your knowing it, and if the murderer had then met him as he went away and murdered him, you might justly be accused

as the cause of his death. For if you had told the truth as far as you knew it, perhaps the murderer might have been apprehended by the neighbors while he searched the house and thus the deed must have been prevented. . . .

To be truthful (honest) in all deliberations, therefore, is a sacred and absolutely commanding decree of reason, limited by no expediency.[8]

Add to this fallibility the fact that people are inescapably prejudiced in their own interests, and the situation is made even worse. The upshot is that consequentialism (and a fortiori the compromise view) is unworkable because we cannot accurately gauge in advance the actual results of any act. The alternative, it is said, is an arrangement in which we do not even try to judge individual cases, but only "do our duty" according to a set of predetermined rules.

Reasons and Principles

The Geach-Kant argument should be rejected, but not too hastily, for even though it is ultimately unsatisfactory, it contains the germ of an important truth. In order to uncover this truth, it will be helpful to examine the relation between acting from a consideration of reasons and acting on principles.

It is a widely held view, propounded by Kant and championed in our own time by Richard Hare, that every rational decision about what to do must be based on principles. In *The Language of Morals* Hare argues that giving reasons for a decision is the same thing as appealing to principles.[9] Hare points out that reasons are, by their nature, universal; if some consideration is a reason in one case, it follows that it must also be a reason in relevantly similar cases. It would be inconsistent for someone to say in one circumstance "I won't do that because it would be lying" and in the next to put no special weight on the fact that a contemplated action would be lying. Therefore, the argument goes, to accept "It would be lying" as a reason for not doing an action on a particular occasion is to commit oneself to the principle "Do not lie" as valid for all such occasions.

But this does not seem right. It is one thing to accept a reason and quite another to accept a principle. To accept "It would be lying" as a reason against doing a certain action does not rule out the possibility that one might do the action anyway, since there might be weightier reasons in its favor. But if we accept the principle "Do not lie" as applicable in this situation, then we are bound not to do the action. This is because reasons are things that are to be *taken into account*, given weight in one's deliberations, and so on, whereas principles are things that are to be *acted on*. When we make an exception to a principle, we say that the principle *does not apply* in that case—it is set aside, abandoned, not acted on, perhaps for the sake of a supposedly greater good. But the abandonment of the principle does not necessarily mean that the agent has not given the corresponding reason due consideration; she may have set aside the principle that would forbid the action, but without ignoring any of the reasons against it.

Hare denies that principles are abandoned in these cases. Rather, he says, they are *modified.*

> Suppose then that we find ourselves in circumstances that fall under the principle, but that have certain other peculiar features, not met before, that make us ask 'Is the principle really intended to cover cases like this, or is it incompletely specified—is there here a case belonging to a class which should be treated as exceptional?' . . . If we decide that this should be an exception, we thereby modify the principle by laying down an exception to it.[10]

Thus, if I subscribe to the principle "Do not lie" and I encounter circumstances X in which lying seems the thing to do, then I must conclude that I had not formulated the principle correctly. The improved formulation would be "Do not lie except in circumstances X."

There are serious difficulties with this. If we meet circumstances Y, in which lying also seems the thing to do, the principle would become "Do not lie except in circumstances X and Y." Then if we meet circumstances Z in which lying again seems the thing to do, the principle becomes "Do not lie except in circumstances X, Y, and Z"—and so on, and so on. The original principle, which seemed to give clear-cut instructions for what to do, now begins to look suspiciously like "Do not lie except when it's all right to lie." It may well be asked whether having such an open-ended principle is any different from having no principle at all. Since we can never be sure that the amendments are all in, we must make a fresh choice in each case about whether the principle applies as it stands or whether yet another qualification is to be attached. We are not following a principle. Instead, we are judging each case on its own merits and then modifying the "principle" to bring it into line.

In *Freedom and Reason* Hare makes a somewhat different suggestion.[11] There he says that, in making a rational choice, the only principle to which one is committing oneself is the principle that *in all cases precisely like the one at hand, the same sort of action is to be done.* Thus the foregoing difficulty is circumvented; there is no question of whether the principle applies in other cases unless they are exactly like the original case, and then, of course, it does apply. But it could be argued that "principles" this specific really don't deserve the name. If someone proposed to give us his principles about lying and proceeded to give us a catalogue of very definite sorts of situations in which he would lie and equally definite sorts of situations in which he would be truthful, we would probably conclude that he does not know what the word means. On this understanding of "principles," we are not in the business of applying fixed standards to new cases as we meet them; rather, we are making new decisions for each case. Therefore, when we invoke principles to justify such decisions, it is mere rationalization; for we are first deciding on the merits of each case what is to be done, and then we are formulating the principle ad hoc. This is certainly not what is ordinarily meant by "acting on principle."

In light of these rather obvious difficulties, why should anyone want to insist that every rational decision is made on the basis of a principle? The only motive, so far as I can see, is to preserve the universal applicability of reasons. But surely we can do that simply by insisting that whatever considerations are given weight in one case must also be given weight in other cases. We need not bring in (and inevitably distort) the concept of a principle at all.

The difference between considering reasons and having principles is at bottom a difference between sharply contrasting styles of decision making. The "man of principle" is the man who insists that some things are to be done (or not done), come what may. Geach, not Hare, is right about this. Where his principles are concerned, this man tends to be stern and inflexible, as Geach says he should be, for to say "It's a matter of principle" is a prelude to closing off debate and to closing one's mind to contrary considerations. We sometimes admire such people if they stick to their principles even when it means personal sacrifice on their part; but, contrary to Geach, we feel differently when such inflexibility leads to an unfeeling disregard for other people, as when the man of principle will not lie on a trivial matter even to avert a disaster. And sometimes such people are admired because they are deeply "committed" on moral issues; the man of principle is equated with the man of integrity. But integrity does not necessarily involve the acceptance of inviolable rules; it only means being true to one's own sense of right.

The alternative style of decision making—acting from a consideration of reasons as opposed to acting on fixed principles—is represented by the person who makes her decisions by considering the reasons in each case, by weighing one consideration against another, and then deciding what seems best in the particular case at hand. Such a person must be consistent, of course—she must not give considerations weight in one case that she will not give them in other cases; and she must avoid prejudice and self-deception as best she can. She may have principles, to be sure, but she will be ready to set her principles aside if the situation demands it.

Now we may return to Geach's argument. On his view, this sort of deliberation is impossible, because no one has the resources to judge the merits of individual cases. Therefore, the wise man, recognizing his own limitations, will be a man of principle. I said that this argument, though unsatisfactory in the end, contains the germ of an important truth. It is unsatisfactory because it is false that we can never know what the relevant consequences of our actions will be. But the germ of truth is that there *is* a connection between the need for principles and uncertainty as to the effects of one's action. In making decisions, we need principles most in just those cases in which the likely effects of our action are least clear. If I must reply to a question put to me in circumstances in which I cannot judge what will come of my answer, I may have to say to myself, "Well, honesty is the best policy," and tell the truth, because that principle is the only guide I have. Even if I am no absolutist, I have no alternative but to act on principle in cases where I am in the dark as to the likely outcome of my action. And, as a practical matter, we don't have the time or opportunity to investigate the likely outcome of every action we perform; so we need habits of action—"principles"—to guide our everyday conduct. These are the cases of relative ignorance in which the need for principles is most clearly felt. But in cases in which I know very well what the effects of my action will be, things are different. Then I do not have to rely on my principles for guidance.

Conflict Cases

The most obvious objection to moral absolutism has to do with the possibility of conflict cases. If it is absolutely wrong to do A in any circumstances and also wrong to do B in any circumstances, then what of the case in which someone is faced with the choice between A and B, when she must do something and when there are no other alternatives open?

In keeping with his general theological approach, Geach tries to close off this possibility by appealing to God's power to prevent such cases from arising:

> "But suppose circumstances are such that observance of one Divine law, say the law against lying, involves breach of some other absolute Divine prohibition?"—If God is rational, he does not command the impossible; if God governs all events by his providence, he can see to it that circumstances in which a man is inculpably faced by a choice between forbidden acts do not occur. Of course such circumstances (with the clause "and there is no way out" written into their description) are consistently describable; but God's

providence could ensure that they do not in fact arise. Contrary to what
unbelievers often say, belief in the existence of God does make a difference
to what one expects to happen.[12]

What is needed, then, is not a fictitious example but a real-life case.
During World War II, Dutch fishermen smuggled Jewish refugees to
England in their fishing boats, and the following sort of situation sometimes arose. A Dutch boat, with refugees in the hold, would be stopped by
a Nazi patrol boat. The Nazi captain would call out and ask the Dutch
captain where he was bound, who was on board, and so forth. The fishermen would lie and be allowed to pass. (Only in the movies do the Nazis
have the resources to board and search every suspicious boat.) Now, it is
clear that the fishermen had only two alternatives: to lie or to allow themselves and their passengers to be taken; and the latter would mean certain
death for at least some of them. No third alternative was available; they
could not, for example, remain silent or outrun the Nazis. This seems just
the sort of case that Geachean absolutism could not handle, and it is a real
case, God's power notwithstanding. However, we must not be too quick
here. There are at least two rejoinders that might be attempted.

First, it might be said that the fishermen's choice was not between lying
and murdering, both of which are prohibited, but only between lying and
not lying, only one of which is prohibited. For it would not be the fishermen who murdered the refugees, but the Nazis—and the fishermen are
not responsible for what the Nazis do. But on the other hand the fishermen would be responsible for having lied. So there is no conflict; the fishermen should tell the truth.

The question here is whether there is a morally relevant difference
between murder and failing to save a life. Murdering and refraining from
saving life are certainly different sorts of actions; in fact, it might be said
that whereas murdering someone is an action, refraining from saving a
life is not an action at all but only an omission of action. But surely no
moral conclusion can be drawn from this difference; for if any action is
morally required in any situation, then at least some omission is morally
blameworthy, namely, the omission of that required action. So we cannot
say that only actions, as opposed to omissions, are blameworthy.

Again, it might be said that murder is much worse than omitting to
save a life. This may be so; if Smith murders Brown while Jones watches
and does nothing to stop him, it is Smith who will be taken to trial and
punished, not Jones; and surely this is as it should be, for it is Smith, not
Jones, who did the evil deed. But even if this is true, it does not matter
here. Even if murder is worse than omitting lifesaving, it does not follow

that omitting lifesaving is not bad and that we do not have a duty to save life whenever we can. And while we may not think as badly of Jones as we do of Smith, we may still think quite badly of Jones.

Another retort would be that we cannot assert a general duty to save life in the same way that we can assert a general duty not to murder, because it would result in the requirement of supererogatory actions. For example, if I hear of a terrible natural disaster—say, an earthquake or flood—in some distant place, I might be able to save a life by going there and working with the relief forces. But this does not mean that I have a duty to do that; such action would be above and beyond the call of mere duty. I should be praised if I do it; but I cannot reasonably be condemned for not doing it. However, as an argument to show that we never have an obligation to save life, this clearly will not do. While I may not be blameworthy for failing to perform actions requiring exceptional effort and sacrifice, it does not follow that I will not be blameworthy for failing to save a life when doing so would not require exceptional effort. A man who watches a child drown in a bathtub and does nothing is, if not the moral equivalent of a murderer, at least very close.

Thus there appears to be no difference between the duty to save life and the duty not to murder that would aid the absolutist in explaining away the conflict case. So this rejoinder may be judged a failure.

The second absolutist rejoinder would go like this. If the fishermen lie, they will be doing a bad sort of action (lying) in order to achieve an admittedly good result (lives will be saved). If they tell the truth, they will be doing a good sort of action (telling the truth), but unfortunately there will be bad consequences (people will be killed). Now, on absolutist grounds there is no conflict here, because it is not necessary for the fishermen to do one bad action in order to avoid doing another bad action. To be sure, there would be bad consequences of the good action, but that is beside the point, for the absolutist admits that sometimes there will be bad consequences of good actions. His view is simply that in these cases the good actions should be done anyway. The point is that insofar as the *actions* are concerned, the choice is simply between a good action and a bad action, between a permitted action and a forbidden action. So even though this might be a conflict case for the compromiser, it would not be a conflict case for the absolutist. Therefore, even if the absolutist is charged with moral obtuseness, he cannot be charged with logical failings.

The question here is whether the distinction between actions and consequences can bear the weight required of it. Just why is "lying" the name of an action while "saving a life" is not? Certainly, if we describe the action as lying, then *under that description* it is a consequence of the action, rather than a part of the action itself, that a life is saved. But we could always describe the act from the beginning as an act of saving life. Then we could say that the fishermen's choice is between truth telling and life-saving, both of which are actions and both of which cannot be done; then this case *would* be a conflict case of the sort that Geach says cannot arise. To avoid this and say that this is not a genuine conflict case, the absolutist must maintain that "saving a life," contrary to appearances, cannot be the name of an action.

Earlier, we noted that the standard way of understanding the debate about absolutism assumes that we can make a firm distinction between the intrinsic character of an action and the action's consequences. Now we need to see why this is a questionable assumption. The problem is that an act can be given many different descriptions, none of which captures its "essence" any more than the others. For example, a single action might be described in these ways:

Jones moved his finger
Jones pulled the trigger
Jones fired the gun
Jones shot Smith
Jones killed Smith
Jones started a riot

and so on. This list illustrates what Joel Feinberg calls the "accordion effect": the description of an action can be expanded or contracted so that what was a consequence of the action under the old description becomes a part of the action itself under the new description, or vice versa.[13] Thus, Smith's being shot is a consequence of what Jones did under the second description listed, but not under the fourth. Clearly, the absolutist cannot accept such a view of act descriptions, because it would vitiate the whole point of "not doing evil that good may come"—the good to come could simply be written into the description of the action, making it a good action rather than an evil one, and thus reversing the original judgment.[14]

The absolutist needs a way to freeze the accordion, so that we can firmly distinguish between actions and consequences. A natural way to do this is by appealing to Arthur Danto's conception of a "basic action."[15] An action A is a *basic action* of an agent X if and only if A is an action performed by X and there is no action B such that X does B and B causes A. In other words, basic actions are those that are not done by way of doing something else; they are done "directly." Jones's shooting Smith is not a basic action because there is another action, pulling the trigger, such that

Jones does the latter action and that "causes" the former. Similarly, in the case of the fishermen confronting the Nazis, saving life is not a basic action because there is another action, lying, such that the lie causes the life to be saved. Utilizing this concept, we can interpret Geachean absolutism as the doctrine that if the performance of a basic action is, considered in itself, a bad thing to do, then that action must not be done no matter what other nonbasic actions may be done by way of it. This interpretation would at least have the advantage of extricating the absolutist from the pinch of Feinberg's accordion.

Unfortunately, this move creates other, equally serious difficulties for the absolutist. The only really clear examples of basic actions are simple bodily movements—blinking one's eyes, moving one's arms, kicking one's legs, and things like that. Obviously none of these are intrinsically good or evil sorts of things to do, and it would be absurd to make them the objects of absolute prohibitions. On the other hand, the actions that the absolutists are most eager to prohibit are not basic actions, such as "procuring the judicial execution of the innocent," the favorite example of both Geach and Anscombe. So, on this interpretation, absolutism would be an absurd view that would attract no serious proponents.

There are, of course, other arbitrary points at which we might try to freeze the accordion, but none of them is sufficient to make absolutism reasonable. It might be suggested that the act-consequence distinction be drawn in terms of the agent's *expectations:* the description of the act proper will include the upshots that she expects to bring about, while the consequences will consist in the unexpected upshots. Not only is this completely counterintuitive (this is not so important in itself, for now the distinction is a purely technical one that is purported to be important for moral philosophy even if it is not reflected by our ordinary understanding of actions and consequences); it gives no assistance to the absolutist. For since the fishermen do expect their lying to save life—that is why they do it—their lying should, on this reading of the distinction, be described as an act of saving life.

Again, it might be suggested that the distinction be marked in terms of the agent's *aims, wants,* or *intentions.* The action is to be described by reference to what the agent aims, wants, or intends to accomplish, while other results, even though they are expected, are to be put down as consequences. This is somewhat more plausible than the previous suggestion, but it is clearly of no more help to the absolutist. For on this way of drawing the distinction, the fishermen's lying should also be described as an act of saving life, since that is what they aim at, want, and intend.[16]

The upshot of all this is that we have found no way for the absolutist to accommodate the conflict cases. And, in the absence of a way to treat these cases, absolutism stands convicted of logical as well as moral shortcomings. The conflict cases inevitably push us away from moral absolutism toward an approach that attends to the details of each particular case. Making a moral decision becomes a matter of weighing the relevant considerations, balancing the pros and cons, and, in the words of Bishop Butler, seeing what course of action "sits most easy on the mind." Moral judgments will have to be made one at a time as the cases arise, for one of the results of abandoning absolutism is that we are deprived of any easy mechanical way of making decisions. But if this is consonant with the moral good sense of most thoughtful people, including "every single English academic moral philosopher since Sidgwick," it may be a virtue, not a vice, of rejecting absolutism.

Notes

1. G. E. M. Anscombe, "Modern Moral Philosophy," *Philosophy* 33 (1958): 10. Emphasis Anscombe's.

2. The phrase *moral absolutism* is sometimes used to name the idea that moral judgments are objectively true or false independent of human feelings and conventions. This is different from the idea that moral rules have no exceptions.

3. P. T. Geach, *God and the Soul* (London: Routledge & Kegan Paul, 1969), 120.

4. P. T. Geach, *The Virtues* (Cambridge: Cambridge University Press, 1977), 115.

5. Alan Donagan, *The Theory of Morality* (Chicago: University of Chicago Press, 1977), 89.

6. Geach, *God and the Soul*, 124.

7. This form of the argument is unnecessarily cumbersome; I put it this way only to retain the parallel with Geach's version. A simpler formulation would be: If an action is a generally bad sort of thing to do, then we would be justified in doing it only if we know that a greater good would be accomplished. But, owing to ignorance and prejudice, we can never know that a greater good will be accomplished; therefore, if an action is a generally bad sort of thing to do, we are never justified in doing it.

8. Immanuel Kant, "On a Supposed Right to Lie from Altruistic Motives," trans. Lewis White Beck, in *Kant's Critique of Practical Reason and Other Writings in Moral Philosophy* (Chicago: University of Chicago Press, 1949), 348. Compare Kant's remarks in *The Metaphysical Principles of Morals*, pt. 2 of *The Metaphysics of Morals*, trans. James Ellington (Indianapolis: Bobbs-Merrill, 1964), 92–93. Sartre presents a case very much like the one described by Kant in his short story "The Wall," trans. Lloyd Alexander, in Jean-Paul Sartre, *Intimacy and Other Stories* (New York: New Directions, 1948).

9. R. M. Hare, *The Language of Morals*, (Oxford: Oxford University Press, 1952),

I.4.2. For a similar identification of reasons and principles, see William K. Frankena, *Ethics* (Englewood Cliffs, N.J.: Prentice-Hall, 1963), 22–23.

10. Hare, *Language of Morals*, I.4.3.

11. R. M. Hare, *Freedom and Reason* (Oxford: Oxford University Press, 1963), II.7.6.

12. Geach, *God and the Soul*, 128. If Geach's previous argument were accepted along with this, it would follow that the occurrence of such circumstances would be sufficient grounds for concluding that God does not exist.

13. Joel Feinberg, "Action and Responsibility," in *Philosophy in America*, ed. Max Black (London: Allen & Unwin, 1965), 134–60.

14. Cf. Andrew Oldenquist, "Rules and Consequences," *Mind* 75 (1966): 180–92. As Oldenquist points out, if this line of criticism is correct, then no ethical theory that depends on the act-consequence distinction is sound. In *Anarchy, State, and Utopia* (New York: Basic Books, 1974) Robert Nozick refers to the strategy of redefining actions to include their consequences as "gimmicky," but a number of subsequent thinkers have argued, like Oldenquist, that any classification of moral theories that relies on the act-consequence distinction cannot be sustained. See Robert Dreier, "Structures of Normative Theories," *Monist* 76 (1993): 22–40.

15. Arthur Danto, "What We Can Do," *Journal of Philosophy* 60 (1963), 435–45; and Arthur Danto, "Basic Actions," *American Philosophical Quarterly* 2 (1965): 141–48.

16. For a more detailed treatment of various ways of marking the act-consequence distinction that also supports the conclusion that none of the available ways is sufficient for absolutist purposes, see Jonathan Bennett, "'Whatever the Consequences,'" *Analysis* 26 (1966): 83–102; and, more recently, Jonathan Bennett, *The Act Itself* (Oxford: Oxford University Press, 1995).

10

Why Privacy Is Important

Privacy is one of those familiar values that seem unproblematic until we start thinking about them, and then puzzles appear at every turn. The first puzzle is why, exactly, privacy is important. According to Justice Brandeis, it is "the right most valued by civilized men."[1] But why should we care so much about it? At first it may appear that no unitary explanation is possible, because people have so many interests that may be harmed by invasions of their privacy:

(1) Privacy is sometimes necessary to protect people's interests in competitive situations. For example, it obviously would be a disadvantage to Bobby Fischer if he could not analyze the adjourned position in a chess game in private, without his opponent learning his results.

(2) In other cases someone may want to keep some aspect of his life or behavior private simply because it would be embarrassing for other people to know about it. There is a splendid example of this in John Barth's novel *End of the Road*. The narrator of the story, Jake Horner, is with Joe Morgan's wife, Rennie, and they are approaching the Morgan house where Joe is at home alone:

> "Want to eavesdrop?" I whispered impulsively to Rennie. "Come on, it's great! See the animals in their natural habitat."
>
> Rennie looked shocked. "What for?"
>
> "You mean you never spy on people when they're alone? It's wonderful! Come on, be a sneak! It's the most unfair thing you can do to a person."
>
> "You disgust me, Jake!" Rennie hissed. "He's just reading. You don't know Joe at all, do you?"
>
> "What does that mean?"
>
> "*Real* people aren't any different when they're alone. No masks. What you see of them is authentic."
>
> . . .Quite reluctantly, she came over to the window and peeped in beside me.

It is indeed the grossest of injustices to observe a person who believes himself to be alone. Joe Morgan, back from his Boy Scout meeting, had evidently intended to do some reading, for there were books lying open on the writing table and on the floor beside the bookcase. But Joe wasn't reading. He was standing in the exact center of the bare room, fully dressed, smartly executing military commands. About *face!* Right *dress!* *'Ten-shun!* Parade *rest!* He saluted briskly, his cheeks blown out and his tongue extended, and then proceeded to cavort about the room—spinning, pirouetting, bowing, leaping, kicking. I watched entranced by his performance, for I cannot say that in my strangest moments (and a bachelor has strange ones) I have surpassed him. Rennie trembled from head to foot.[2]

The scene continues even more embarrassingly.

(3) There are several reasons medical records should be kept private, having to do with the consequences to individuals of facts about them becoming public knowledge. The president of the American Medical Association warned, "The average patient doesn't realize the importance of the confidentiality of medical records. Passing out information on venereal disease can wreck a marriage. Revealing a pattern of alcoholism or drug abuse can result in a man's losing his job or make it impossible for him to obtain insurance protection."[3]

(4) When people apply for credit (or for large amounts of insurance or for jobs of certain types), they are often investigated, and the result is a fat file of information about them. There is something to be said in favor of such investigations, for business people surely do have the right to know whether credit applicants are financially reliable. The trouble is that all sorts of other information can find its way into such files—information about the applicant's sex life, his political views, and so on. Clearly, it is unfair for one's application for credit to be influenced by such irrelevant matters.

These examples illustrate the variety of interests that may be protected by guaranteeing people's privacy, and it would be easy to give further examples of the same general sort. However, I do not think that examining such cases will provide a complete understanding of the importance of privacy, for two reasons.

First, these cases all involve relatively unusual sorts of situations, in which someone has something to hide or in which information about a person might provide someone with a reason for mistreating him in some way. Thus, reflection on these cases gives us little help in understanding the value that privacy has in *normal* or *ordinary* situations. By this I mean situations in which there is nothing embarrassing or shameful or unpopular in what we are doing and nothing ominous or threatening connected with its possible disclosure. For example, even married couples whose sex lives are normal (whatever that is), and so who have nothing to be ashamed of, by even the most conventional standards, and certainly nothing to be blackmailed about, do not want their bedrooms bugged. We need an account of the value that privacy has for us not only in the few special cases but in the many common and unremarkable cases as well.

Second, even those invasions of privacy that do result in embarrassment or in some specific harm are objectionable on other grounds. A woman may rightly be upset if her credit rating is adversely affected by a report about her sexual behavior, because the use of such information is unfair; however, she may also object to the report simply because she feels—as most of us would—that her sex life is *nobody else's business*. This is an extremely important point. We have a sense of privacy that is violated in such affairs, and this sense of privacy cannot adequately be explained merely in terms of our fear of being embarrassed or disadvantaged in one of the obvious ways. An adequate account of privacy should help us to understand what makes something "someone's business" and why intrusions into things that are "none of your business" are, as such, offensive.

These considerations suggest that there is something important about privacy that we will miss if we confine our attention to examples such as (1)–(4). In what follows I will try to bring out what this something is.

Social Relationships and Appropriate Behavior

I will give an account of the value of privacy based on the idea that there is a close connection between our ability to control who has access to us and to information about us and our ability to create and maintain different sorts of social relationships with different people. According to this account, privacy is necessary if we are to maintain the variety of social relationships with other people that we want to have, and that is why it is important to us. By a "social relationship" I do not mean anything unusual or technical; I mean the sort of thing that we usually have in mind when we say of two people that they are friends or that they are husband and wife or that one is the other's employer.

We may begin by noticing that there are fairly definite *patterns of behavior* associated with these relationships. Our relationships with other people determine, in large part, how we act toward them and how they behave toward us. Moreover, there are different patterns of behavior associated with different sorts of relationships. Thus a man may be playful and affectionate with his children (although sometimes firm), businesslike with his employees, and respectful and polite with his mother-in-law. And to his close friends he may show a side of his personality that others never see—perhaps he is secretly a poet, and rather shy about it, and shows his verse only to his closest friends.

It is sometimes suggested that there is something deceitful or hypocritical about such variations in behavior. It is suggested that underneath all the role-playing there is the "real" person and that the various "masks" that we wear are some sort of phony disguise that we use to conceal our "true" selves. I take it that this is what is behind Rennie's remark, in the passage from Barth: "*Real* people aren't any different when they're alone. No masks. What you see of them is authentic." According to this way of looking at things, the fact that we observe different standards of conduct with different people is merely a sign of dishonesty. Thus the coldhearted businessman who reads poetry to his friends is "really" a gentle, poetic soul whose businesslike demeanor in front of his employees is only a false front; and the man who curses and swears when talking to his friends, but who would never use such language around his mother-in-law, is just putting on an act for her.

This is wrong. Of course the man who does not swear in front of his mother-in-law may be just putting on an act so that, for example, she will not disinherit him, when otherwise he would curse freely in front of her without caring what she thinks. But it may be that his conception of how he ought to behave with his mother-in-law is simply different from his conception of how he may behave with his friends. (Or it may not be appropriate for him to swear around *her* because "she is not that sort of person.") Similarly, the businessman may be putting up a false front for his employees, perhaps because he dislikes his work and has to make a continual, disagreeable effort to maintain the role. But on the other hand he may be, quite comfortably and naturally, a businessman with a certain conception of how it is appropriate for a businessman to behave; and this conception is compatible with his also being a husband, a father, and a friend, with different conceptions of how it is appropriate to behave with his wife, his children, and his friends. There need be nothing dishonest or hypocritical in any of this, and neither side of his personality need be the "real" him, any more than any of the others.

It is not merely accidental that we vary our behavior with different people according to the different social relationships that we have with them. Rather, the different patterns of behavior are (partly) what define the different relationships; they are an important part of what makes the different relationships what they are. The relation of friendship, for example, involves bonds of affection and special obligations, such as the duty of loyalty, that friends owe to one another; but it is also an important part of what it means to have a friend that I welcome her company, confide in her, tell her things about myself, and show her sides of my personality that I would not tell or show to just anyone.[4] Suppose I believe someone is my close friend, and then I discover that she is worried about her job and is afraid of being fired. But while she has discussed this situation with several other people, she has not mentioned it at all to me. And then I learn that she writes poetry and that this is an important part of her life; but while she has shown her poems to other people, she has not shown them to me. Moreover, I learn that she behaves with her other friends in a much more informal way than she behaves with me, that she makes a point of seeing them socially much more than she sees me, and so on. In the absence of some special explanation of her behavior, I would have to conclude that we are not as close as I had thought.

The same general point can be made about other sorts of human relationships: employer to employee, minister to congregant, doctor to patient, husband to wife, parent to child, and so on. In each case, the sort of relationship that people have to one another involves a conception of how it is appropriate for them to behave with each other and, what is more, a conception of the kind and degree of knowledge concerning one another that it is appropriate for them to have. Of course such relationships are not structured in exactly the same way for everyone. Some parents are casual and easygoing with their children, while others are more formal and reserved. Some doctors want to be friends with at least some of their patients; others are businesslike with all. Moreover, the requirements of social roles may vary from community to community—the role of wife may not require exactly the same sort of behavior in rural Alabama that it does in New York or New Guinea. And the requirements of social roles may change; the women's movement, for example, has made a tremendous impact on our understanding of the husband-wife relationship. The examples that I have been giving are drawn, loosely speaking, from contemporary American society, but this is mainly a matter of convenience. The important point is that however one conceives one's relations with other people, there is inseparable from that conception an idea of how it is appropriate to behave with and around them and what information about oneself it is appropriate for them to have.

Privacy and Personal Relationships

All of this has to do with the way that a crucial part of our lives—our relations with other people—is organized, and as such. its importance to us can hardly be exaggerated. Therefore, we have good reason to object to anything that interferes with these relationships and makes it difficult or impossible for us to maintain them in the way that we want. That is why the loss of privacy is so disturbing. Our ability to control who has access to us and to information about us allows us to maintain the variety of relationships with other people that we want to have.

Consider what happens when close friends are joined by a casual acquaintance. The character of the group changes; one of the changes is that conversation about intimate matters is now out of order. Suppose these friends could never be alone; suppose there were always third parties (let us say casual acquaintances or strangers) intruding. Then they could do either of two things. They could carry on as close friends do, sharing confidences, freely expressing their feelings about things, and so on. But this would mean violating their sense of how it is appropriate to behave around casual acquaintances or strangers. Or they could avoid doing or saying anything that they think inappropriate to do or say around the third party. But this would mean that they could no longer behave with one another in the way that friends do and, further, that, eventually, they would no longer *be* close friends.

Again, consider the differences between the way that a husband and wife behave when they are alone and the way they behave in the company of third parties. Alone, they may be affectionate, sexually intimate, have their fights and quarrels, and so on; but with others, a more "public" face is in order. If they could never be alone together, they would either have to abandon the relationship that they would otherwise have as husband and wife or else behave in front of others in ways they now deem inappropriate.[5]

These considerations suggest that we need to separate our associations, at least to some extent, if we are to maintain a system of different relationships with different people. Separation allows us to behave with certain people in the way that is appropriate to the sort of relationship we have with them, without at the same time violating our sense of how it is appropriate to behave with, and in the presence of, others with whom we have different kinds of relationships. Thus if we are to be able to control the relationships that we have with other people, we must have control over who has access to us.

We now have an explanation of the value of privacy in ordinary situations in which we have nothing to hide. The explanation is that even in the most common and unremarkable circumstances, we regulate our behavior according to the kinds of relationships we have with the people around us. If we cannot control who has access to us, sometimes including and sometimes excluding various people, then we cannot control the patterns of behavior we need to adopt (this is one reason that privacy is an aspect of liberty) or the kinds of relations with other people that we will have.

What about our feeling that certain facts about us are "nobody else's business"? Here, too, it is useful to consider the nature of our relationships. If someone is our doctor, then it literally is her business to keep track of our health; if someone is our employer, then it literally is his business to know what salary we are paid; our financial dealings literally are the business of the people who extend us credit; and so on. In general, a fact about ourselves is someone's business if there is a specific relationship between us that entitles him to know. We are often free to choose whether or not to enter into such relationships, and those who want to maintain as much privacy as possible will enter them only reluctantly. What we cannot do is accept such a social role with respect to another person and then expect to retain the same degree of privacy relative to him or her that we had before. Thus, if we are asked how much money we have in the bank, we cannot say "It's none of your business" to our banker, prospective creditors, or our spouses. But, at the risk of being boorish, we could say that to others with whom we have no such relationship.

Thomson's View

In an important essay,[6] Judith Jarvis Thomson suggests that the key to understanding the right to privacy is to realize that there is nothing special about it. She suggests, "as a simplifying hypothesis, that the right to privacy is itself a cluster of rights, and that it is not a distinct cluster of rights but itself intersects with the cluster of rights which the right over the person consists of, and also with the cluster of rights which owning property consists of." This is an appealing idea because these other rights seem less puzzling than the right to privacy. Therefore, if the simplifying hypothesis is correct, the right to privacy may be much easier to understand.

Thomson explains that "the right over the person" consists of such "un-grand" rights as the right not to have various parts of one's body looked at, the right not to have one's elbow painted green, and so on. She understands these rights as analogous to property rights. The idea is that our bodies are *ours* and so we have the same rights with respect to them that we have with respect to our other possessions.

Is this plausible? Is a woman's right to prevent a Peeping Tom from looking at her breasts no different from her right to control who drives her car or who uses her fountain pen? These seem importantly different because the kind of interest we have in controlling who looks at what parts of our bodies is different from the interest we have in our cars or pens. For most of us, physical intimacy is a part of special sorts of personal relationships. Exposing one's knee or one's face to someone does not count for us as physical intimacy, but exposing a breast, and allowing it to be seen and touched, does. Of course the details are to some extent a matter of social convention; it is easy to understand that for a Victorian woman an exposed knee could be a sign of intimacy. She would be right to be distressed at learning that she had left a knee uncovered and that someone was staring at it. By dissociating the body from ideas of physical intimacy and the complex of personal relationships of which such intimacies are a part, we can make this "right over the body" seem to be an ungrand kind of property right; but that dissociation separates this right from the matters that make privacy important.

Thomson suggests the following case as a possible source of trouble for the simplifying hypothesis:

> Some acquaintances of yours indulge in some very personal gossip about you. Let us imagine that all of the information they share was arrived at without violation of any right of yours, and that none of the participants violates a confidence in telling what he tells. Do they violate a right of yours in sharing the information? If they do, there is trouble for the simplifying hypothesis, for it seems to me there is no right not identical with, or included in, the right to privacy cluster which they could be thought to violate.[7]

But, she adds, this case does not really cause trouble, because the gossips "don't violate any right of yours. It seems to me we simply do not have rights against others that they shall not gossip about us."

This is, as Thomson says, a debatable case, but if our account of why privacy is important is correct, we have at least some reason to think that your right to privacy can be violated in such a case. Let us fill in some details. Suppose you are recently divorced, and the reason your marriage failed is that you became impotent shortly after the wedding. You have shared your troubles with your closest friend, but this is not the sort of thing you want everyone to know. Not only would it be humiliating for everyone to know, it is none of their business. It is the sort of intimate fact about you that is not appropriate for strangers or casual acquaintances to know. But now the gossips have obtained the information. Perhaps one of them innocently overheard your conversation with a friend; it was not his fault, so he did not violate your privacy in the hearing, but then you did not know he was within earshot. And now the gossips are spreading it around to everyone who knows you and to some who do not. Are they violating your right to privacy? Surely they are. If so, it is not surprising, for the interest involved in this case is just the sort of interest that the right to privacy typically protects. Since the right that is violated in this case is not also a property right or a right over the person, the simplifying hypothesis fails. But this should not be surprising, either, for if the right to privacy has a different point than these other rights, we should not expect it always to overlap with them. And even if it did always overlap, we could still regard the right to privacy as a distinctive sort of right in virtue of the special kind of interest it protects.

Notes

1. *Olmstead v United States*, 277 US 438, 478 (1928).
2. John Barth, *End of the Road* (New York: Avon, 1960), 57–58.
3. Dr. Malcolm Todd, quoted in the *Miami Herald*, 26 October 1973, sec. A, p. 18.
4. This is similar to Charles Fried's view of the relation between friendship and privacy in his illuminating book *An Anatomy of Values* (Cambridge: Harvard University Press, 1970).
5. This is from a television program guide in the *Miami Herald*, 21 October 1973, p. 17:

> "I think it was one of the most awkward scenes I've ever done," said actress Brenda Benet after doing a romantic scene with her husband, Bill Bixby, in his new NBC-TV series, "The Magician."
> "It was even hard to kiss him," she continued. "It's the same old mouth, but it was terrible. I was so abnormally shy; I guess because I don't think it's anybody's business. The scene would have been easier had I done it with a total stranger because that would be real acting. With Bill, it was like being on exhibition."

On the view presented here, it is not "abnormal shyness" or shyness of any type that is behind such feelings. Rather, it is a sense of what is appropriate with and around people with whom one has various sorts of personal relationships. Kissing *another actor* in front of the camera crew, the director, and so on, is one thing; but kissing *one's husband* in front of all these people is quite another thing. What made Ms. Benet's position confusing was that her husband was another actor, and the behavior that was permitted by one relationship was discouraged by the other.

6. Judith Jarvis Thomson, "The Right to Privacy," *Philosophy and Public Affairs* 4 (1975): 295–314.
7. Thomson, "Right to Privacy," 311–12.

11

Reflections on the Idea of Equality

In philosophy, labels often say as much about one's temperament as about the doctrines to which one subscribes. Some philosophers who call themselves egalitarians accept all sorts of social inequalities as necessary for the general welfare and for the protection of individual rights. Yet they call themselves egalitarians because they dislike having to concede the inequalities—they would rather see the inequalities eliminated, if only that were possible. Meanwhile, other philosophers scoff at the very idea of "equality." They would never dream of calling themselves egalitarians, because they see egalitarianism as a false ideal, incompatible with social welfare and individual rights. Yet the pattern of equalities and inequalities they envision as characterizing the good society may be indistinguishable from the one endorsed by the so-called egalitarians.

Kai Nielsen's Egalitarianism

Kai Nielsen is an egalitarian, but not a wishy-washy one. As the title of his book *Equality and Liberty: A Defense of Radical Egalitarianism* suggests, Nielsen defends about as extreme a version of egalitarian social philosophy as one will find in the contemporary literature. Although much of his book is devoted to the kind of abstract argument that is the bread and butter of philosophy, the moral seriousness that Nielsen brings to this work is evident from the first page. His philosophical theory, he says, gives expression to

> the sense of unfairness which goes with the acceptance, where something non-catastrophic could be done about it, of the existence of very different life prospects of equally talented, equally energetic children from very

155

different social backgrounds: say the children of a successful businessman and a dishwasher. Their whole life prospects are very unequal indeed and, given the manifest quality of that difference, that this should be so seems to me very unfair. It conflicts sharply with my sense of justice.[1]

"My egalitarian ideal," he adds, "is a generalization of that."

The unfairness of some children being condemned to inferior life prospects is, for Nielsen, one of the incontrovertible "bedrock" judgments that moral philosophy may take as its starting point. It may be difficult to provide arguments that this is unfair—"If someone sees no unfairness here," he says, "nothing that, other things being equal, should be corrected in the direction of equality, then I do not know where to turn"[2]—but that is only because the unfairness is of such a fundamental kind. At any rate, it is a judgment that any morally decent person should accept.

In a just society, there would be no such disparities in life prospects; all children would have an equal chance of prospering. What would such a society be like? As Nielsen sees it, in a perfectly just society people would be equals not only in legal protection and political power but in economic status as well. There would be no social classes and no one would be significantly richer or poorer than anyone else. Life's goods would be available to all on an equal basis. Nielsen devotes considerable space to countering the arguments of philosophers, such as Robert Nozick,[3] who say that respecting people's liberty necessarily leads to unequal distributions because liberty empowers people to make decisions that affect their holdings for good or ill. Against such partisans of inequality, Nielsen defends a robust conception of the egalitarian society.

Present-day societies, of course, are nothing like the egalitarian community that Nielsen envisions. Therefore, in the present scheme of things, equality of the more radical sort must be conceived of as a *goal* toward which we should strive. Only after substantial progress has been made can it be reconceived as a *right* that all people will have—complete equality will become a right only in "situations of plenty where this is possible."[4] (Thus Nielsen sidesteps the problems that arise when we try to apply moral principles in the context of social structures with which they are not congenial and frees himself to focus on the principles that would fit more comfortably in a different and, in his view, a better society.) "What starts as a goal . . . turns into a right when that goal can realistically be achieved."[5] But that day is still in the future. In the meantime, it is morally mandatory that we take all appropriate steps toward transforming basic social institutions so that the goal can be realized. This means, on Nielsen's view, moving toward socialism: the ideal of equality "requires socialist institutions for anything even approximating its implementation."[6]

But we want something more specific. In a properly egalitarian society, precisely what principles would govern relations between people? And perhaps more important, what principles would determine the structure of basic social institutions? The principles espoused by liberal egalitarians such as John Rawls do not, in Nielsen's view, go far enough. His own "principles of egalitarian justice" are more far-reaching. There are two of them:

1. Each person is to have an equal right to the most extensive total system of equal basic liberties and opportunities (including equal opportunities for meaningful work, self-determination, and political and economic participation) compatible with a similar treatment of all.

2. After provisions have been made for common social (community) values, for capital overhead to preserve the society's productive capacity, allowances made for differing unmanipulated needs and preferences, and due weight given to the just entitlements of individuals, the income and wealth (the common stock of means) is to be so divided that each person will have a right to an equal share. The necessary burdens requisite to enhance human well-being are also to be equally shared, subject, of course, to limitations by differing abilities and differing situations.[7]

These principles are, obviously, full of qualifications. Nielsen concedes that there may be good reasons for occasional departures from perfect equality, even in the best of circumstances. So he allows a limited place for considerations of desert and individual entitlements.

The problem of desert is a familiar stumbling block for egalitarians. Few moralists—Rawls is a prominent exception[8]—are willing to exclude considerations of desert altogether. But once they are admitted, there is trouble for any view that espouses even a rough equality of material possessions. If some people are willing to work harder than others, and therefore make greater contributions to the production of goods, and if this gives them a valid claim to a larger share of those goods, then the demand for anything like "equal distribution" is undercut. How is this point to be accommodated within a theory of equality? One way is to emphasize equality of opportunity as the basic value and to accept the rightness of unequal distributions so long as no one is excluded from earning a larger share. Although he agrees that equality of opportunity will be part of a just social system, Nielsen prefers a different solution. Desert, he says, does have a legitimate role to play in determining the distribution of goods. Today it plays a large role. But in an egalitarian society that role will be diminished.

Why will desert play a lesser role? Nielsen's answer is connected with a certain utopianism in his thinking. An egalitarian society will be a society of abundance in which goods are plentiful. In such circumstances there will be no need to appeal to desert to determine whose basic needs are to be satisfied—there will be enough for all. Nielsen takes it as obvious that the first concern of justice, in such a situation, will be to satisfy everyone's basic needs. After this has been done, considerations of desert may come into play to divide the rest. Desert may be thought of "as a device for dividing the surplus, after basic needs have been met" and for awarding scarce "extras" such as jobs that not everybody can have—he mentions as an example the job of a television commentator.[9] The fact that the talents and traits of character that enable some to contribute more to the social product are not themselves earned counts as a reason against giving desert a more central place.

Nielsen's utopianism also figures prominently in his solution to another of the familiar problems for socialism. There is an obvious problem with the requirement that, in an egalitarian society, the burdens as well as the benefits are to be equally shared. The burdens, of course, include work. The wealth that "is to be so divided that each person will have a right to an equal share" does not grow on trees; labor is required to produce it, and everyone is expected to share in the labor as well as the wealth. It's a pretty picture, and so long as we imagine everyone doing his part in the work, there is little trouble with the idea of each one receiving his share of the wealth in return. The rub comes when we consider that some might not be willing to do their part of the work. (Some might even dislike the whole system and reject its demands.) So how is the provision requiring equal work to be enforced? Are people to be compelled to labor against their wills? One way around this difficulty is to make working a precondition for receiving one's share of the product. Then people will be motivated to work by the realization that otherwise there will be no pay.[10] But that move is, of course, unavailable to a thinker of Nielsen's stripe. It leads straight to a form of meritocracy that he rejects.

Nielsen's solution is to say, in effect, that in an egalitarian society this problem will not arise, or if it does arise, it will arise so infrequently as to present no serious difficulty. When the forms of social life are changed, people are changed as well. In a radically egalitarian society, people will think about their lives and duties in different terms. Patterns of thought and motivation will be different. And so the lazy, unproductive behavior that leads to problems in a nonegalitarian society will largely disappear. Nielsen says:

> A society in which radical egalitarianism could flourish would be an advanced socialist society under conditions of considerable abundance. People would not have a market orientation. They would not be accumulators or possessive individualists, and the aim of their economic organization would not be profit maximization but the satisfaction of the human needs of everyone. The more pressing problems of scarcity would have been overcome. Everyone would have a secure life, their basic needs would be met, and their level of education, and hence their critical consciousness, would be much higher than it is now. . . . In fine, the institutions of the society and the motivations of people would be very different. . . . People would be their own masters with a psychology that thinks in terms of "we" and not just, and most fundamentally, in terms of "I". . . . People would not, in such a secure situation, have such a possessive hankering to acquire things or pass them on. Such acquisitiveness would no longer be a major feature of our psychologies.[11]

This is not, on Nielsen's view, just a fairy tale. It is a kind of society that we could actually achieve if we only had the will to do it. And to worry about people clutching after the benefits while trying to avoid sharing the burdens only betrays that we do not yet grasp what life in the new society would be like.

If all of this sounds a little old-fashioned, that is because it is. It is a Marxist vision of the sort that has gone rapidly out of fashion as the Soviet Union and its client states in Eastern Europe have begun to move away from their socialist commitments. The transformation of those totalitarian regimes is not to be regretted; yet it will be unfortunate if the more humane aspects of Marxist theory are lost as well. The position that Nielsen articulates should remain a major alternative in moral philosophy, and he has given that alternative its most detailed and sophisticated defense.

The Aristotelian Principle

Now I want to consider in a some detail a point that many egalitarian thinkers believe has only minor significance. Philosophical discussions of equality often begin by distinguishing equality as a formal principle from equality as a substantive theory. (In *Equality and Liberty* Nielsen follows this well-worn tradition.) The formal principle was first articulated by

Aristotle, who said that like cases must be treated alike and different cases differently.[12] Interpreting Aristotle's dictum in an obvious way, we may take this to mean that *individuals are to be treated in the same way unless there is a relevant difference between them.* For convenience we may call this the Aristotelian Principle.

The Aristotelian Principle is modest enough, and at first glance it seems obviously correct. Suppose the admissions committee of a law school accepts some applicants and rejects others. Members must be able to point to a relevant difference between individuals in the two groups—they must be able to show that the ones who are accepted are better qualified—otherwise, their decisions are unacceptably arbitrary. Again, suppose a physician prescribes different treatments for two patients. She may justify this by pointing out that their medical problems are different and so require different treatments—one had an infection treatable with penicillin, for example, while the other did not. If their problems were comparable, however, their treatments should be comparable as well. These are simple examples of the Aristotelian Principle at work. More interesting examples might involve giving equal pay for equal work or providing equal social benefits for those of equal need, but the formal point would be the same. "Equal treatment" does not require sameness of treatment in every case, but it does require sameness of treatment in the absence of relevant differences.

As I said, this is a familiar principle that appears near the beginning of most philosophical discussions of equality. But after having formulated this principle, most egalitarian philosophers brush it aside fairly quickly. The problem is not that they doubt its truth. On the contrary, as Richard Wasserstrom once remarked, it seems to be a principle of "rationality itself."[13] The problem, as W. T. Blackstone put it, is that "the equality principle in this form is so general it is almost vacuous."[14] David A. J. Richards adds that the principle is, for this reason, "philosophically uncontroversial."[15] Nielsen quotes Richards with approval.[16] The idea seems to be that the formal principle can be accepted by everyone, regardless of his moral position, because it is empty of any real content. It is compatible with virtually all moral views, egalitarian and nonegalitarian alike. Therefore, more substantive principles are needed to specify the egalitarian ideal. And so the discussions proceed to consider those further principles.

But we should pause here. I do not doubt that further principles are needed for a fully developed theory. However, the Aristotelian Principle is not quite so empty as it first appears. It is not obviously a principle of "rationality itself," and it certainly is not vacuous. On the contrary, the principle has implications that many people will find utterly implausible. Some simple examples will illustrate this.

Suppose I have a book that I don't need and I give it to you. But there is another person who would also like the book, and I don't give it to him. Must I be able to point to a relevant difference between the two of you to justify giving it to you? Am I acting wrongly if there is no such difference? Or suppose I pick up a hitchhiker. Must I also pick up other hitchhikers if there is no relevant difference? In both cases, common sense says that I am entitled to treat people differently, even if there is no relevant difference between them.

Once the basic idea of these examples is seen, it is easy to think of others like them. I have two proposals of marriage—may I not accept whichever I please? In each case, something is *mine*—my book, my transportation, my life—and despite the Aristotelian Principle, apparently I have the right to share it, or not share it, as I choose. A principle that says otherwise can hardly be "philosophically uncontroversial."

There are two possible reactions to such examples. First, we might take them as counterexamples that refute the principle, at least in the form given above. We might then try to interpret Aristotle's dictum in some other way that would not be vulnerable to the counterexamples. Or, alternatively, we might retain the principle in its present form and argue that "common sense" is mistaken. I believe that the second option is best. But before explaining why, let me say something about the first option.

Can we formulate a better version of the principle that will avoid the counterexamples? We may begin with a puzzle. In some cases, such as those involving the physician and the law school admissions committee, it seems that we must treat people similarly if there is no relevant difference between them. But in other cases, such as those involving the book and the hitchhiker, there seems to be no such obligation. The problem is to explain why the cases are different (assuming that they *are* different).

The best explanation that I can think of goes like this. In the medical case, we think that the person with the infection *ought* to be given penicillin. We think this without even considering anyone else with whom the patient might be compared. It is because we make this assumption that we are led to the conclusion that others suffering from the same condition should be given the same treatment—if they have the same problem, then they should be given penicillin also, for the same reason that the first patient should be given it. On the other hand, in the case of the book, we do not start with the assumption that I ought to give it to you. It is permissible for me to give it to you, but I have no obligation in the matter. I am free to give it to you or not, as I please. That is why it does not follow that if I choose to give it to you, I must do likewise for others.

The same explanation holds for the other cases. Because we assume the law school committee *ought* to admit the well-qualified applicant—it would be wrong not to do so—we are committed to thinking that other well-qualified applicants should be admitted as well. And because we assume that we are not obligated to pick up hitchhikers, we do not think that picking up one requires us to do the same for others. In sum, the hypothesis is that we owe equal treatment to all, absent relevant differences, if and only if we start with the belief that we ought to treat the first individual in the specified way.

The hypothesis is confirmed when we make different starting assumptions in the various cases. Suppose that, coming upon a lonely hitchhiker, you think you ought to give him a ride, perhaps because you think you ought to help others whenever you can. Then you should conclude on other occasions that you should pick up other hitchhikers—that is, you should treat them in the same way. After all, they too are people you can help.

We are now in a position to state the formal principle in a somewhat different way than before. The modified principle will not say, simply, that individuals are to be treated similarly unless there is a relevant difference between them. It will be more complicated than that. It will be in the form of a conditional, saying that *if* someone *ought* to be treated in a certain way, and there is no relevant difference between him or her and someone else, then that other individual ought to be treated in that way too. Notice, however, that the same general point applies not only to the concept of obligation but to other moral concepts as well. The same can be said about what it is permissible to do, about what rights people have, and so on. Therefore, the full statement of what I am calling the Modified Principle will be:

> For any individuals X and Y, if X ought to be treated in a certain way (or if it is permissible to treat X in that way, or if X has a right to be treated in that way), and there is no relevant difference between X and Y, then Y ought to be treated in that way (or it is permissible to treat Y in that way, or Y has a right to be treated in that way) also.

Now the cases of the book and the hitchhiker, which were troublesome, can be handled very easily. They are not counterexamples to the Modified Principle, nor are they outside its scope. They fall neatly within it. It is permissible to give someone a book or a ride; therefore, if there is no relevant difference between him or her and another person, then it is permissible to give the other a gift as well. That is all that follows. It does not follow that one *ought* to give the other a book or a ride.

I believe that when philosophers say that the formal principle of equality is a principle of "rationality itself" or that it is "philosophically uncontroversial," it is something like the Modified Principle that they have in mind. The Modified Principle is a principle of reason, in the sense that no one could reject it without falling into self-contradiction. This can be shown by considering the way moral judgments are supported by reasons.

Moral judgments are true only if there are good reasons in support of them. If you are told that you *ought* to treat someone in a certain way, you may ask why, and if no good reason can be given, you may reject the admonition as arbitrary and unfounded. This is a rule of logic:

Let P be the statement that a certain individual ought to be treated in a certain way, and let Q be the statement that another individual ought to be treated in that way. Then, if there are exactly the same reasons in support of (or against) P as there are in support of (or against) Q, it follows that either P and Q are both true or they are both false.[17]

This rule is one way of expressing the familiar idea that moral judgments are universalizable. Beliefs that violate this rule are inconsistent, for it is self-contradictory to say "X ought to be treated in a certain way, and every single reason for treating X in that way also applies to Y, but Y ought not to be treated like that."

The Modified Principle follows from this general rule of logic, for if there are no relevant differences between two individuals, then there can be no reason that applies in one case but not the other. Thus the Modified Principle is not merely an optional rule that one may accept or reject depending on what moral view one happens to take. The same cannot be said of the Aristotelian Principle, however, because it does not follow from the above rule of logic.

It might seem that our problem has now been solved. The Aristotelian Principle is open to troublesome counterexamples, while the Modified Principle is not. The obvious conclusion is that we should abandon the Aristotelian Principle and adopt the Modified Principle in its place. This looks like a familiar move in philosophy: we start with a plausible-looking principle, discover that it is defective, and then recast it to eliminate the defect, keeping the new version as close to the original as possible. However, the situation here is not so simple. Our two principles may seem closely related, but in reality they are miles apart. One is not just a corrected version of the other. The Aristotelian Principle expresses something that egalitarian philosophers believe is important. The Modified Principle does not. To see the difference, we need only to consider a simple case.

Consider an employer who pays women less than men, or blacks less than whites, for the same work. Why is this offensive? The Modified Principle suggests this analysis: First, we observe that there is a certain appropriate salary that the employer ought to pay for the specified work. He ought to pay white men at this level, and he does. But it follows that in the absence of relevant differences he should also pay blacks and women at that level—but he does not. Thus his conduct may be said to violate the Modified Principle.

But is this explanation adequate to describe the offensiveness of his practice? The explanation depends on beginning with the assumption that the white men are paid as they should be paid. But suppose we make a different starting assumption. Suppose there is no "correct" salary that white males "ought" to be paid; there is only a rough range within which a decent salary must fall. Therefore, the employer pays his white male employees a more or less reasonable amount within that range. It is permissible for him to pay white males this amount, but it would also be permissible for him to pay them somewhat less. He does pay blacks and women a lesser amount—but what he pays them is still within the permissible range. Under this assumption, the Modified Principle would not say that he is acting wrongly in paying blacks and women less. His behavior would be a clear instance of unacceptable unequal treatment, but the Modified Principle would be silent about it.

The point is that the offensiveness of unequal treatment does not depend on any starting assumptions about how individuals, considered in isolation, ought to be treated. It may be that we are under no obligation whatever to treat X in a certain way; but *having treated X in that way,* we may then be under an obligation to treat Y in that way as well. The obligation to treat Y in the specified way is created simply by the fact that we have chosen to treat X in that way. The employer in our example may not have been obligated to pay white men quite so much, but once he has chosen to do so, he should pay blacks and women at that level as well.

Other, similar examples come easily to mind. Suppose a father decides to buy one of his children an ice cream cone, when without any fault he could have decided against it. Then, even though it was not true that he ought to have bought one child the ice cream, it will be true that he ought to do the same for his other children. His duty to treat them equally does not depend on the prior judgment that he should have done something for the first child. He is obligated, in a general way, to treat them equally, and the specifics of how one child is to be treated may depend on his choices concerning the other, *even when the initial choice could have been different.* This point is at the very heart of our subject, and if a principle does not capture this, it cannot express the ideal of equal treatment. This is the point expressed in the Aristotelian Principle that is missing from the Modified Principle.

That is why I think the Aristotelian Principle should be retained. Whether it *may* be retained depends on what we ultimately conclude about the purported counterexamples. Perhaps, on closer inspection, it will turn out that they are not so troublesome as it first appeared. Let us look at them again.

I give you a book. Now it might be said that the book was mine, and so I had the right to dispose of it as I pleased. There is something to this. But surely, in deciding to whom to give it, there are considerations I should take into account. If you could benefit from it more than anyone else, or if you deserve it in a way that others do not, I should give it to you. Suppose, though, that there is someone else who could also benefit from it and who is equally deserving. Could not that person rightly feel that some sort of injustice has been done? You got the book and he did not, although he also needed it, or deserved it, just as much. Perhaps it is an injustice for which no one is responsible—I may have had only one book to give. Nevertheless, it is a valid point that he, too, merited the gift. The Aristotelian Principle would imply that something regrettable has happened, and it has. Therefore, this example is not a clear refutation of that principle.

The same can be said for the case of the hitchhikers. Both need a ride, and assuming the equality of their need and deservingness, isn't there an injustice in one getting it and one not? Maybe the one who didn't get the ride was just unlucky; but undeserved bad luck is itself unfair, even if it is "cosmic" unfairness for which no one is responsible. The point is arguable. But at the very least, so long as there is *some* point in noticing the unlucky person's plight, and regretting it, this case does not provide a decisive reason to abandon our original principle. On the contrary, the fact that the Aristotelian Principle captures this point may be counted as one of its virtues rather than one of its vices.

Supplementary Principles: Benefit and Desert

As we have already noted, the formal principle, however it is interpreted, is not enough; additional, more substantive principles must be added to make a complete theory of equality. Nielsen's account of the additional principles incorporates a number of points that any adequate theory must accommodate. But his overall view also includes elements that are more questionable. His two-tiered view, with different moral conceptions operating in different social settings, is puzzling. Why should equality be considered a right only in "situations of plenty where this is possible"? Even in situations of scarcity people could still be equal; they could be equally poor. More generally, one might wonder whether an adequate theory of equality really requires, as an integral part of it, a commitment to through-and-through socialist institutions. And even if one finds Nielsen's utopian vision attractive, one might still wonder whether the achievement of a just degree of equality really *depends on* the possibility of a society that is so radically different from our own that human beings will become different kinds of creatures.

With these thoughts in mind, I want to ask whether there is not a more modest account of the ideal of equality that does not rely on such claims but that is nevertheless adequate for what we want to say about that ideal. Such an account might begin with the Aristotelian Principle (individuals are to be treated in the same way unless there is a relevant difference between them) and the supplementary principles may then be interpreted as specifying criteria of relevant differences. There are two such additional principles that come immediately to mind: one has to do with ability to benefit; the other, with desert.

A difference between individuals justifies differential treatment if it is correlated with a difference in their abilities to benefit from that treatment. This principle, I think, really is "philosophically uncontroversial." If one person can benefit from being treated in a certain way, while another cannot, or if the other person will benefit less, that is surely a good reason for treating them differently. This principle accounts for our judgments in almost all the cases I cited in the previous section. The patient with the infection can benefit from penicillin, while the patient with no such infection cannot benefit from the same treatment; the student with the poor record is less likely to benefit from law school admission than the student with the good record; whites and blacks benefit equally from having jobs; the hitchhikers all need rides; the children will all enjoy ice cream; and so on. These cases, which at first seem so different, are united by this principle.

Desert looks like an independent matter. Nielsen is impressed by the following sort of case. An employer must choose which of two employees to promote (only one promotion is available). The first candidate has worked hard, has willingly put in a lot of overtime, and generally has done everything she could to help the company. The second has never done more than the minimum required of her. Plainly, the first candidate deserves the promotion. Justice seems to require giving it to her, and it is not merely a matter of her needing the promotion more or being able to benefit from it more. She deserves the promotion because she has earned it.

This is compatible with the Rawlsian point (with which Nielsen agrees) that no one deserves native endowments. Much of what makes us the individuals we are—our intelligence and many of our talents and abilities—is the result of a "natural lottery" over which we have no control. Because we did nothing to merit these traits, we do not deserve them, nor do we deserve to receive any benefits because of them. Yet there are some things we *do* control: we control at least some of our actions. I can choose whether to work hard at my job or slack off. Thus, the woman who deserves the promotion does not deserve it because she is smarter or more talented; she deserves it because she has worked for it. One deserves things because of one's past actions. We may think of deservingness, in this sense, as a matter of "doing the best you can with the talents and abilities you have."[18]

Nielsen concedes that desert, in this sense, should play a role in determining the distribution of life's goods. But he says that the role played by desert will be different in different sorts of social settings. (It will play only a marginal role in the future egalitarian society of abundance that he envisions.) Is this so? It will depend, in part, on why one thinks desert is important in the first place. One might, for example, think that the employee in our example deserves the promotion simply by having worked harder for it—work *in itself* merits reward. If one takes this view, then it is hard to see why things would change if social structures were altered. In any social setting, there will still be people who work harder than others. There will still be people who are more helpful and people who are more willing to do the unpleasant things that need doing. Why wouldn't they remain more deserving?

There is, however, a deeper reason for thinking that desert is important. The general practice of treating people as they deserve is a way of granting to people a certain power to control their own destinies. Because we live together in societies, how each of us fares is affected by how other people respond to us. Thus, if I am to control how I fare, I must be able to control, at least to some extent, how I am treated by others. The social practice of acknowledging desert enables each of us to do that. It says to each person: if you behave in such-and-such ways, you will be treated in such-and-such ways in return. Thus, if you aspire to be promoted, there is a way you can go about staking your claim. The recognition of deserts is, in this way, an invaluable part of the social arrangement.

Why should such an arrangement be any less valuable in the transformed society that Nielsen advocates? There seem to be two lines of thought in his discussion. The first is that, in a situation of abundance, the first concern of justice will be the satisfaction of everyone's basic needs.

This, he says, will take priority over considerations of desert. There is surely something to this, although it is not clear whether this should be considered a matter of justice or of simple beneficence. Is there anything about abundance per se that implies that unequal distributions are unjust? Suppose the abundant goods were produced by some people who work hard to produce them, while others choose to stand by. Would it be *unjust* for the free riders to receive less? It seems to me that arguments of desert are no less effective in such a situation. This is compatible, of course, with the idea that we would have a moral duty to provide for the basic needs of all on other grounds—an idea that, in my view as well as Nielsen's, is probably correct.

Nielsen's second line of thought speaks directly to the problem of the free rider. In a truly egalitarian society, he says, there would in fact be few such slackers. People's patterns of motivation would be different, and most people would be contributing to the best of their abilities. We would not, therefore, have reason to distinguish among people so frequently on grounds of their deservingness, and so desert would become a relatively minor consideration. This view of human perfectibility is, of course, common among Marxists; others have their doubts. But whatever one thinks of this, it has only marginal relevance to the theoretical point about the role to be played by the principle of desert. Even if Nielsen is right, it would not mean that in the altered situation the principle of desert would have a different weight. It would only mean that the great mass of people would turn out to be equally deserving; and they would be seen to be equally deserving by reference to the very same principle that we have sketched. That principle, and the weight given to it, would not have changed.

To have a convenient name for it, let us call this the Modest Theory. The Modest Theory takes the Aristotelian Principle as its starting point and supplements that principle with principles of ability to benefit and desert. It has a good bit in common with Nielsen's view, but it is simpler than Nielsen's theory—it is, I think, what we end up with if we accept large parts of Nielsen's view but avoid some of his view's more controversial claims. The Modest Theory does not require his utopianism, and it does not require different principles for societies of greater and lesser abundance. Neither does it require assumptions about the perfectibility of human nature. Nor is it so obviously committed to a socialist perspective.

Nielsen himself might think that the Modest Theory is inadequate to do what a theory of equality needs to do, because it would tolerate greater disparities among people's situations than he thinks should be tolerated. That is partly true; the theory does not by itself absolutely mandate the level of human equality that Nielsen thinks is morally required.

Nevertheless, the Modest Theory comes closer to justifying a Nielsen-style egalitarianism than one might suppose. For if we couple the theory with some of Nielsen's other assumptions—if we accept the Modest Theory and then go on to imagine that we may achieve a situation of abundance to which everyone contributes to the best of his abilities—then the resulting distribution would turn out to be much as he desires. Because I take the Modest Theory to be a conservative minimum, I take this result to be a confirmation of much that Nielsen says about our subject.

The Problem of the Disadvantaged Child

As we noted at the outset, Nielsen begins his discussion with the problem of the disadvantaged child. It is unjust that some children, for no other reason than the circumstances of their births, will have worse lives than others. An adequate theory of justice must give expression to this, and such a theory must not endorse moral conceptions that say otherwise. Nor should an adequate theory imply the acceptance of social arrangements in which this problem persists. Nielsen returns to this point, which he regards as "bedrock," again and again. In his discussion of John Rawls's theory, for example, he takes it as a sufficient refutation of Rawls's principles that they imply

> that justice, and indeed a commitment to morality, would require the acceptance as just and as through and through morally acceptable, a not inconsiderable disparity in the total life prospects of the children of entrepreneurs and the children of unskilled laborers, even when those children are equally talented, equally energetic, and so on.[19]

He adds, "For me, however, the witting acceptance of such disparities, where something could be done about them, particularly when that something would not undermine our basic civil and political liberties, just seems evil." Of course, Nielsen does not limit his discussion of Rawls to this point. He goes on to argue with Rawls in a more conventional theoretical way in some detail. But the problem of the disadvantaged child sets the moral tone of the subsequent discussion: a theory that accepts *this sort of injustice* cannot be right.

I do not know whether Rawls's theory really has this implication—it is a difficult issue—but it does seem to me that Nielsen's general point is an important one. The problem of the disadvantaged child is fundamental, and it should not be relegated to a footnote in any theory of justice. It should be front and center. It is one of the critical issues that motivate interest in the whole subject. Nielsen is surely right to give it a central place in his thinking.

It would seem that the Modest Theory is inadequate to handle this problem. Suppose people are treated in accordance with its principles and as a result X is worse off than Y. There may be nothing wrong with this, according to the Modest Theory, because their different positions reflect their deserts. However, their children will also be affected by how they fare: X's children will now suffer the disadvantage of having less affluent parents. Because children are affected by how their parents fare, we cannot assure equal life prospects for them by assuring justice for their parents, at least not if we think that justice permits treating the parents as they deserve.

This point may be expressed as a general argument against any theory that countenances seriously unequal distributions:

1. Suppose we say that, for whatever reason—desert, perhaps—it can be just for some adults to have a great deal less than others.

2. So long as we retain anything like the traditional family, the welfare of children will inevitably be affected by the fortunes of their parents. Children of less affluent parents will have inferior life prospects. And the children themselves will have done nothing to deserve this.

3. It is unjust for some children, through no fault of their own, to have inferior life prospects.

4. Therefore, a system that permits seriously unequal distributions of goods among adults, coupled with the traditional family structure, inevitably leads to injustice for children.

5. Therefore, it is unacceptable to permit seriously unequal distributions of goods among adults, even if they deserve it, so long as we retain anything like the traditional family structure.

6. The traditional family structure should be retained.

7. Therefore, a theory that permits seriously unequal distributions of goods among adults is unacceptable.

It appears, then, that if the Modest Theory is to have any chance of avoiding this problem, it must be expanded to include at least one additional principle. We may call it the Equal Start Principle: Social institutions are to be arranged so that all children have an equal chance at a good life.

If this principle were made a part of the Modest Theory, it would not be merely an ad hoc addition designed to handle a particular problem. On the contrary, it would be a natural supplement to the theory, because it deals with how people are to be treated prior to their reaching the age of competency. (It is a familiar point that in moral philosophy we always need special provisions for dealing with children and other incompetents who are not able to care for themselves or make autonomous decisions about their own lives.) It is not clear, however, that the Equal Start Principle really needs to be added to the theory as a separate provision. The theory may imply it already. After all, we may take it as given that all children are equally deserving—because they are only children, they have not yet reached an age at which they could make the autonomous decisions that would make them *less* deserving. But if their needs and deserts are substantially the same, then the Modest Theory would say that they should be treated similarly because there is no relevant difference between them. Thus, the life prospects that are available to some should be available to all.

The moral argument for socialism becomes clear when we consider what this would mean in practice. If the traditional family is retained, we cannot realistically hope to provide equal opportunities for children without making the circumstances of their parents substantially equal, regardless of the adults' individual merits. There is a real tension between the Equal Start Principle and the principle of desert. Treating adults according to the latter principle would, it seems, inevitably compromise the former.

The major alternative to socialism, among doctrines that take this problem seriously, is welfare liberalism, with its familiar programs of family assistance and compulsory education. Welfare liberalism attempts to solve our problem by providing enough assistance to families so that even the children of the poor have a decent chance, while accepting, at the same time, justified disparities among the positions of the adults. Yet liberalism's record of achievement in this regard is spotty at best, and one may well doubt whether it is possible within its limits to provide the equal life prospects for children that justice demands.

Nevertheless, it is important to keep the question of *what the principles of justice are* separate from claims about *what sort of social system is required for their implementation*. It is one thing to say that only in socialist institutions could the principles of justice be satisfied—to say, for example, that only in a socialist society can the problem of the disadvantaged child be eliminated. It is another thing to incorporate the requirement of socialism into the principles themselves. Nielsen seems to do this: the language he uses in framing his "principles of egalitarian justice" seems to make it a part of the principles themselves that only socialist institutions will do. Perhaps that will turn out to be so. But there is nothing inherently socialist about the idea of equality as such. The overall merits of socialism versus welfare liberalism remains a separate issue.

I, for one, do not find the socialist vision altogether attractive, if only because I am not sure I would want to live in a community that had so many committee meetings. (I do not mean this just as a flippant remark; the forms of social life that would go with large numbers of people having joint control over so many detailed things seem quite unappealing.) Social theorists have, of course, raised much more serious objections to the various socialist proposals, some having to do with such mundane but nevertheless important matters as efficiency. But one undeniably attractive thing about such a community is that within it the problem of the disadvantaged child would be solved. Could that problem be solved apart from instituting a society such as Nielsen envisions? We should hope that it can. But if it cannot, then that society might turn out to be the best we can aspire to, committee meetings and all.

Notes

1. Kai Nielsen, *Equality and Liberty: A Defense of Radical Egalitarianism* (Totowa, N.J.: Rowman & Allenheld, 1985), 7–8.
2. Nielsen, *Equality and Liberty*, 8.
3. Robert Nozick, *Anarchy, State, and Utopia* (New York: Basic Books, 1974).
4. Nielsen, *Equality and Liberty*, 9.
5. Nielsen, *Equality and Liberty*, 9.
6. Nielsen, *Equality and Liberty*, 14.
7. Nielsen, *Equality and Liberty*, 48.
8. John Rawls, *A Theory of Justice* (Cambridge: Harvard University Press, 1971), 103–4.
9. Nielsen, *Equality and Liberty*, 129.
10. An interesting twist is suggested by John Rawls in "The Priority of Right and Ideas of the Good," *Philosophy and Public Affairs* 17 (1988): 251–76. Rawls suggests that leisure time might be included on the list of basic goods. Thus those who choose not to work can be regarded as already having been compensated with an increased supply of that good, and so they do not need to be supported in other ways, such as by being fed. But for criticism of this proposal, see Philippe Van Parijs, "Why Surfers Should Be Fed: The Liberal Case for an Unconditional Basic Income," *Philosophy and Public Affairs* 20 (1991): 101–31.
11. Nielsen, *Equality and Liberty*, 65–66.
12. Aristotle, *Nichomachean Ethics* 1131a.
13. Richard Wasserstrom, "Rights, Human Rights, and Racial Discrimination," in *Moral Problems*, ed. James Rachels (New York: Harper & Row, 1971), 117.

Originally published in *Journal of Philosophy* 61 (1964).

14. W. T. Blackstone, "On the Meaning and Justification of the Equality Principle," in *The Concept of Equality*, ed. W. T. Blackstone (Minneapolis: Burgess, 1969), 116.

15. David A. J. Richards, "Justice and Equality," in *And Justice for All*, ed. Tom Regan and Donald VanDeVeer (Totowa, N.J.: Rowman & Littlefield, 1982), 242.

16. Nielsen, *Equality and Liberty*, 4.

17. For simplicity, I omit reference to permissibility and rights, but they should be understood here as before.

18. See chap. 12.

19. Nielsen, *Equality and Liberty*, 82–83.

12

What People Deserve

In 1811 Johann Gottlieb Fichte was named rector of the newly created University of Berlin. Like many other university administrators, the famous philosopher made the mistake of thinking he could control the students. He lasted less than a year in the job.

Fichte was appalled by the violence that was a common part of university life in Europe. Shortly after taking office, he gave a speech denouncing such "traditional customs" as dueling, affairs of honor, compulsory drinking, and fighting. He wanted these put aside with the old order that had come to an end when Prussia was defeated by Napoleon. But his speech had little effect. Within a few weeks such fierce fighting had broken out between student associations that the army had to be called in to stop it. A little later, a student named Brogi complained to Fichte that he had been publicly beaten by another student for refusing to accept a challenge to duel. The matter was referred to the Court of Honor (a body composed of faculty and students), and the court punished both men, finding Brogi's cowardice as offensive as his attacker's blows. Fichte protested, but to no avail. The last straw came when the hapless Brogi was attacked once again, this time by the son of a prominent government official who dared him to complain. Brogi did, and again the Court of Honor punished him for it. This time Fichte quit in disgust.[1]

In the controversy that surrounded these events, Fichte's opponents, chief of whom was the celebrated scholar Friedrich Schleiermacher, insisted that the violence that so disturbed the rector was nothing more than the natural exuberance of youth. But what caused Fichte to resign was not the fighting, exuberant or otherwise. Fichte was incensed not so much because Brogi had been beaten as because the Court of Honor had punished him for complaining about it. Brogi was an innocent victim who had done nothing to deserve the court's rough treatment. His attackers may have deserved punishment, but he did not.

Desert is a puzzling notion. It connects with some of our most power-ful moral feelings: when people are treated contrary to their deserts, we may, like Fichte, become indignant and see it as an intolerable violation of justice. At the same time, it is not clear just what desert is or why it is important. What makes one person more or less deserving than another? In Brogi's case, desert is connected with guilt—he did not deserve pun-ishment because he had committed no offense. But the notion has a wider application. People may deserve economic success, the loyalty of their friends, a good reputation, and a thousand other things. What accounts for these deserts? Social position? Talent? Virtue? Contributions to soci-ety? And wouldn't any answer we give merely betray our ideological bias? It is not surprising that many philosophers have been skeptical about the whole idea of desert. Wouldn't it be better, they ask, if we for-got about trying to treat people as they deserve and concentrated instead on trying to treat people decently? Moreover, they say, it is not even clear that there is any such thing as desert. Perhaps desert is just a prescientif-ic notion that will disappear when we have attained a properly sophisti-cated understanding of human character and conduct. We may find then that no one really deserves anything, good or ill, because in the final analysis no one is really responsible for what he or she does.

With these thoughts in mind, the theory of desert may be approached with some trepidation. A theory of desert should, of course, tell us what desert is, and it should specify the principles that determine when some-one deserves something. Most important, it should provide an account of the *basis* of desert—the reasons people deserve things. But it is not enough for the theory's principles to encapsulate what we already happen to believe. The theory should provide a justification for whatever principles are espoused. It should explain why the principles are important, what values they express, and why a reasonable person should accept them. In doing this, the theory may provide the resources needed to allay the skep-tical doubts about desert, if indeed that can be done.

Desert and Past Actions

What people deserve always depends on what they have done in the past. The familiar lament, "What have I done to deserve this?" is not just an idle remark; when desert is at issue, it asks exactly the right question. Consider this case:

The two candidates for promotion. The owner of a small business must decide which of two employees to promote. The first is a man who has been a loyal and hardworking member of the staff for many years. He has frequently taken on extra work without complaint, and in the company's early days, when its future was in doubt, he would put in overtime without demanding extra pay. His efforts are one reason that the company survived and prospered. The other candidate is a man who has always done the least he could get by with, avoiding extra duties and quitting early whenever he could. We may call them Worker and Slacker. Which should the owner promote?

Clearly, Worker deserves the promotion. He has earned it and Slacker has not.

Deserving the promotion is not the same as needing it or wanting it. Both Worker and Slacker might benefit from the promotion; perhaps both could use the extra money and status it would bring. But this has nothing to do with desert. Although Slacker might benefit just as much from being promoted, he does not have the same claim to it as Worker because he has not earned it in the same way.

Nor is the question of desert the same as the question of who would perform better in the new position. Obviously, there is reason to think Worker would do better, because he has shown himself to be more diligent. But again, that is not the basis of Worker's claim. Even if we knew that Slacker would reform and do just as well in the new position—the promotion may be just the prod he needs—Worker would still have an independent claim on the promotion, based simply on his past performance.

Of course, desert is not the only consideration that must be taken into account: none of this is to say that, despite Worker's greater efforts, the employer might not have sufficient reason to promote Slacker instead. He might promote Slacker because he thinks, for some reason, that this will do the most good for everyone in the long run. But in that case the promotion will be granted on grounds other than desert—Worker deserved the promotion more, but Slacker got it anyway, for other reasons. The situation is not unlike that of the owner of a family business promoting her son or daughter ahead of other workers. She may have the right to do so, and in some sense it may even be the right thing for her to do, but the decision has nothing to do with desert and indeed goes against it.

These thoughts suggest a certain hypothesis, namely:

The Past Actions Claim: What people deserve depends on their own pastbehavior and only on their own past behavior. More specifically, it depends on their voluntary past behavior, on things they have done by their own uncoerced choice.

I believe this is true, and the theory of desert I defend will incorporate this idea. The first question that arises, then, is whether there are bases of desert other than one's past behavior. If so, what are they? And if not, why not?

In a seminal essay, Joel Feinberg contends that a person's *characteristics* can supply the basis of desert. "If a person is deserving of some sort of treatment," Feinberg writes, "he must, necessarily, be so in virtue of some possessed characteristic or prior activity."[2] Among these characteristics Feinberg includes abilities, skills, and physical attributes. In a tennis game, for example, the most skillful player deserves to win, and in a beauty contest the prettiest or most handsome deserves to win.

Is this so? Does the most skillful player deserve to win an athletic competition? It seems a natural enough thing to say. But suppose the less skilled player has worked hard to prepare for the match. She has practiced every day, left off drink, and kept to a strict regimen. Meanwhile her opponent, who is a "natural athlete," has partied, drunk a lot, and done little in the way of training. But she is still the most skilled and as a result can probably win anyway. But does she *deserve* to win, simply because she is better endowed by nature? (And does she deserve the acclaim and benefits that go with winning?) Of course, skills are themselves often the product of past efforts. People must work to sharpen and develop their natural abilities; therefore, when we think of the more skillful as the more deserving, it may be because we think of them as having worked harder. Ted Williams practiced batting more than anyone else on the Red Sox, and so he deserved his success. But he deserved it for his work and not merely for his natural endowments.

Again, do the prettiest and most handsome deserve to win beauty contests? No doubt it is *correct* for the judges to award the prize to the best-looking. But this may have little to do with the contestants' deserts. Suppose a judge in the Miss America Pageant were to base her decision on desert; we might imagine her reasoning: "Miss Montana isn't the prettiest, but after all, it's not her fault, and she's done her best with what nature provided. She's studied the art of makeup, had her teeth and nose fixed, and spent hours practicing walking down runways in high-heeled shoes. That dazzling smile didn't just happen; she had to learn it by spending hours before a mirror. Miss Alabama, on the other hand, is prettier, but she just entered the contest on a lark—walked in, put on a costume, and here she is, looking great." If all this seems ridiculous, it is because the point of such contests is not to separate the more deserving from the less deserving. (And maybe it is also because beauty contests are just ridiculous, period.) The criterion is beauty, not desert, and the two have little to do with one another. The same goes for athletic contests: the systems of scorekeeping are not designed to identify the most deserving competitors.

But this is a point that many philosophers today will concede. The idea, once commonplace, that superior native endowments make one more deserving is no longer so popular, at least among those who systematically study the subject. It has fallen into disrepute since the publication of John Rawls's *A Theory of Justice*. Rawls writes:

> Perhaps some will think that the person with greater natural endowments deserves those assets and the superior character that made their development possible. Because he is more worthy in this sense, he deserves the greater advantages that he could achieve with them. This view, however, is surely incorrect. It seems to be one of the fixed points of our considered judgments that no one deserves his place in the distribution of native endowments, any more than one deserves one's initial starting place in society.[3]

Rawls refers to "our considered judgments," but there is something more here than an appeal to our intuitions. There is also an implicit argument, namely, that native endowments are not deserved because no one *does anything* to deserve them; they are a result of a "natural lottery" over which we have no control. If you are naturally smart, or pretty, and I am not, then you are just luckier; and you do not deserve better merely on that account. This fits well with the hypothesis we are considering, that people deserve things only because of their past actions.

What else might plausibly be thought to provide a basis for desert? It has sometimes been suggested that *achievements* are pertinent. Thus it may be argued that Slacker could deserve the promotion, despite Worker's greater effort, if Slacker had succeeded in contributing more to the company. (If he were smarter and more talented than Worker, for example, Slacker's efforts might have produced more despite his having exerted himself less.) But achievements are only the products of native endowments combined with work—often with a good bit of luck thrown in—and if one cannot deserve things because of one's native endowments, neither can one deserve things because of the achievements that those endowments make possible. To see what someone deserves, we have to separate the two components (native endowments and work) and identify the contribution made by each. The maximally deserving man or woman is not simply the one who achieves the most but the one who achieves the most he or she can given the abilities with which he or she is endowed. The key idea, as far as desert is concerned, is "doing the best you can with what you have."

It is not just a brute fact that past actions are the only bases of desert. There is a reason that this is so. A fair amount of our dealings with other people involves holding them responsible, formally or informally, for one thing or another. But it is unfair to hold people responsible for things over which they have no control. People have no control over their native endowments—over how smart, or athletic, or beautiful they naturally are—and so we may not hold them responsible for those things. People are, however, in control of (at least some of) their own actions, and so they may rightly be held responsible for the situations they create, or allow to exist, by their voluntary behavior. But those are the only things for which they may rightly be held responsible, because those are the only things over which they have control. The concept of desert serves to signify the ways of treating people that are appropriate responses to them, given that they are responsible for those actions or states of affairs. That is the role played by desert in our moral vocabulary—and, as ordinary-language philosophers used to say, if we did not already have such a concept, we would need to invent one. Thus the explanation of why past actions are the only bases of desert connects with the fact that if people were never responsible for their own conduct—if strict determinism were true—no one would ever deserve anything, good or bad.

Desert and Responsibility

According to the view we are considering, we may deserve things by working for them but not simply by being naturally intelligent or talented or lucky in some other way. But it may be thought that this view is inconsistent, because whether someone is willing to work is just another matter of luck, in much the same way that intelligence and talent are matters of luck. Rawls suggests this. Why, he asks, do some people strive harder than others? And he answers:

> It seems clear that the effort a person is willing to make is influenced by his natural abilities and skills, and the alternatives open to him. The better endowed are more likely, other things being equal, to strive conscientiously, and there seems to be no way to discount for their greater fortune.[4]

Again,

The assertion that a man deserves the superior character that enables him to make the effort to cultivate his abilities is equally problematic; for his character depends in large part upon fortunate family and social circumstances for which he can claim no credit. The notion of desert seems not to apply to these cases.[5]

So, if a person does not deserve anything on account of intelligence or natural abilities, how can he or she deserve anything on account of industriousness? Isn't willingness to work just another matter of luck?

This points to a deep problem about the legitimacy of the concept of desert. As we have seen, the notion of desert is tied to the notion of individual responsibility: to say that Worker deserves the promotion more than Slacker because he worked harder for it assumes that the two were responsible for their respective levels of effort. But that, it may be argued, is not true. Both men's efforts were the result of forces over which they had no control. Rawls mentions that the better-endowed tend to strive harder, but obviously other factors may also be cited. Perhaps Worker's parents raised him to be hardworking, while Slacker's did not. So how can we say that either man deserves to be treated better, when neither of them is responsible for the factors that determined his performance? Everyone's character and conduct are ultimately shaped by forces he does not control, and so no one merits credit (or blame) for anything he does.

If this is correct, the Past Actions Claim is mistaken, but not because there are bases of desert other than past actions. On the contrary, if this is correct, nothing could justify judgments of desert—not even past actions—because in reality no one ever deserves anything. The whole idea of desert turns out to be spurious.

Nothing short of a complete theory of free will could completely rebut this troubling argument. Absent such a theory, the possibility that determinism is true threatens to undermine any defense of desert. I cannot provide a complete theory of free will, so my defense here must be less than fully adequate. Nevertheless, we may notice a few points that any adequate theory should incorporate. These points may remove some of the argument's sting.

(1) What does it mean to say that someone is responsible for his or her actions? To give the question a pertinent focus, we may ask under what conditions someone is *blameworthy* for having done something. There are three such conditions: he or she must have done the act in question; the act must in some sense have been wrong; and he or she must have no excuse for having done it.[6]

The notion of an excuse is crucial here. Excuses are facts that get you off the hook when you have done something bad: it was an accident, you may say, or you didn't know what you were doing, or you were forced to do it. Excuses are different from justifications. A justification is part of an argument that the apparently wrong action was in fact permissible. When an excuse is offered, however, it is typically admitted that the act was wrong, but it is suggested that, despite this, blame is not a justified response.

It is not possible to give a complete list of morally acceptable excuses. Generally recognized excuses include mistake, accident, insanity, coercion, inexperience, and ignorance. But the list is essentially open ended; there is no way to establish that we have identified all possible excuses, and future experience might turn up others that we have not thought of before. (For example, during the Korean War, American prisoners who cooperated with the Chinese were said to have been "brainwashed" by their captors, and some years later the same was said about Patricia Hearst when she was kidnapped by members of the Symbionese Liberation Army and subsequently joined that group. The attempt to develop a concept of brainwashing was essentially the attempt to establish a new category of excuse.) What most excuses have in common, though, is that they represent the person's actions as involuntary, as not fully or knowingly chosen. And the implicit argument is that, if actions are not so chosen, the actor should not be blamed for them.

The logic of credit is similar to the logic of blame. Someone is praiseworthy for having done something if he or she did it, it was a good thing to do, and there are no conditions present analogous to excuses. It is curious that there is no name for these analogous conditions. We have a word, "excuses," for the conditions that make blame inappropriate; but we have no word for the comparable conditions that make praise inappropriate. Yet clearly similar conditions function in similar ways. If you do something splendid, but you do it by accident, or from ignorance, or you were coerced, you do not merit praise for it as you would if you had done it voluntarily. Perhaps there is no general word for these conditions because people do not ordinarily try to avoid being praised. But the point remains. To make up our own terminology, we might call these "credit-eliminating conditions."

We may, therefore, recast Rawls's argument about industriousness like this: a person's good character "depends in large part upon fortunate family and social circumstances for which he can claim no credit." This includes his willingness to "strive conscientiously." The same goes for those of poor character who are unwilling to strive conscientiously, for laziness is also the result of family and social circumstances over which the individual had no control. Therefore, the fact that someone has had an unfortunate upbringing should count as a morally acceptable excuse for present lack of effort; and similarly, the fact that someone else has had a fortunate upbringing should count as a credit-eliminating condition. Thus Worker gets no credit for his hard work, and Slacker gets no blame for his slacking off. Neither is to be viewed as more deserving than the other.

(2) Should Slacker's background—the various factors that have made him lazier than Worker, whatever they were—count as an excuse for his lack of effort? The first thing to notice is that a person's character is not *entirely* something over which the individual has no control. There are plenty of people who have tried, with some success, to change aspects of their personalities. Examples are not hard to find: an ill-tempered man comes to realize that he would be better off if he behaved more pleasantly, so he deliberately tries to alter his conduct. When he finds himself becoming angry, he makes an effort to stop. At first this is difficult—it goes against the grain for him—but with practice it gets easier, until finally pleasant behavior has become habitual and he isn't an ill-tempered man anymore. This sort of thing does happen, and when it does, it is not true to say that the person's character—or at least, this aspect of it—is the result of forces over which he had no control. On the contrary, it is the result of his own actions.

Among philosophers, Jean-Paul Sartre has made the most of this sort of point. Sartre believes that the standard picture of the relation between character and conduct is mistaken. The standard picture is that people have certain sorts of characters, and as a result they perform certain sorts of actions. But, according to Sartre, this gets things the wrong way around. In reality, he argues, people freely choose their actions, and as a result they come to have their particular kind of character.[7] The ill-tempered man simply *is* the man who chooses to go on behaving in an ill-tempered manner. The standard picture encourages us to think he has an excuse: ill temper is just a feature of his personality fixed by circumstances he does not control. Sartre objects that viewing other people in this way regards them, falsely, as passive objects rather than as subjects possessing the power to choose, while thinking of oneself like this means living in "bad faith," refusing to accept responsibility for one's choices. Indeed, Sartre seems to think that the standard picture is motivated primarily by our desire to evade responsibility. Responsibility, he says, is a frightening thing, and we are inclined to accept any way of understanding our condition that permits us to avoid it.

Sartre takes an extreme view of the matter: he contends that character is *always* a product of free choice, that it is *never* determined by external forces. We are, as he puts it, "condemned to be free."[8] But even though he insists that freedom is terrifying, Sartre's picture of humans as absolutely free is an attractive conception that appeals to our vanity—it is flattering to think of ourselves as special, as set apart from the rest of nature, in this way. To think that we are entirely determined by impersonal forces diminishes us. Nevertheless, on reflection Sartre's view seems as wrongheaded as the opposite one he rejects. The boring fact seems to be that some aspects of people's characters are the results of their choices while many more are not.

Industriousness is a characteristic that may or may not be the result of personal decision. Some people may be industrious because of "fortunate circumstances": they may be hardworking because they are gifted people who from an early age were encouraged to make the most of their talents. Others, however, may be like the ill-tempered man mentioned above: once lazy, they may have decided that they no longer wanted to be that way and took steps to change. This is not impossible, and once again, when it happens, it is not accurate to say that the person's newly gained spirit owes nothing to his choices.

(3) Does everyone who fails to "strive conscientiously" do so because of impoverished talents and training? It does not seem likely that this is always so. We may distinguish different sorts of people in this regard.

On one hand, it may be that some people have been so psychologically devastated by a combination of poor native endowment and unfortunate family and social circumstances that they no longer have the capacity for making anything of their lives. If such a person doesn't work very hard at anything, it's no use blaming him, because, as we would say, he just hasn't got it in him to do any better. On the other hand, though, there are those in whom the capacity for effort has not been extinguished. They have adequate if not ample talents, and their spirits have not been crushed by poverty or anything like that. Among these, some choose to work hard, while others, who could so choose, do not. It is true of everyone in this latter category that he is able, as Rawls puts it, "to strive conscientiously." The explanation of why some strive while others do not has to do with their choices. Thus we have:

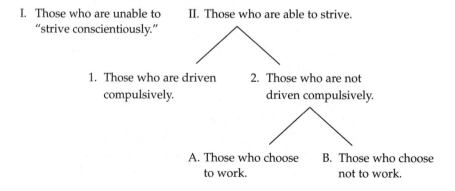

I. Those who are unable to   II. Those who are able to strive.
   "strive conscientiously."

        1. Those who are driven   2. Those who are not
           compulsively.   driven compulsively.

                        A. Those who choose   B. Those who choose
                           to work.   not to work.

The commonsense view is that there are people in each of these categories. This, however, may be denied: it may be said that no one who has the wherewithal to work hard could choose not to do so. But it is not difficult to understand why people might choose to slack off. After all, there are costs associated with working, especially when the work is not something one particularly enjoys, and some people might prefer not to pay those costs. Consider Worker and Slacker again. Worker worked overtime, without extra pay, when Slacker did not. This means Worker has had to give up some of the free time that Slacker has enjoyed. Perhaps Slacker didn't work more because he wanted to do other things instead. It is certainly possible that Worker would also have preferred to do other things, but he made a different choice. Surely we can mark a difference here without lumping Slacker in with the unfortunate people who are just *unable* to "strive conscientiously." Nor need we deny that there are such unfortunate people, as there plainly are. Thus, when we say that those who work hard are more deserving of success, promotions, and so forth, than those who don't, the relevant comparisons may be limited to people in whom the capacity for effort has not been extinguished—in particular, to people in categories II.2.A and II.2.B. This is entirely consistent with a compassionate stance toward those in category I.

(4) Finally, we may note that industriousness is an odd sort of "natural asset," different in kind from the other talents and abilities that one may have from the natural lottery. Industriousness—the willingness to work— is a personal quality that combines with each of one's other abilities, enabling one to use them. Musical talent gets one nowhere until it is combined with work; the same goes for mathematical talent, business acumen, and any other ability one might have. Industriousness therefore seems to be a trait on a different level, a sort of "super asset" that enables one to make something of other assets. Moreover, it is hard to separate industriousness as a character trait from actual choices to work. Industriousness, at least for people of type II.2.B, seems to consist simply in making such choices.

But no matter what sort of character trait industriousness is, our account of desert does not say that people deserve anything for possessing it. People do not deserve things on account of their willingness to work, but only on account of their actually having worked. Worker does not deserve the promotion because he has been willing to work hard in his present job, or because he is willing to work hard in the new position. Rather he deserves the promotion because he actually *has* worked hard. Therefore it is no objection to the view I am defending to say that industriousness is a character trait that one does not merit, even if that is so. For, on this view, the basis of desert is not a character trait of any kind, not even industriousness. The basis of desert is what a person has actually done.

Why the Past Is Important

When we cite a person's deserts as a reason for treating him or her in a certain way, we are appealing to what might be called "backward-looking considerations"—we cite what has happened in the past as a justification for present decisions. But why should the past matter? Philosophers have sometimes suggested that it is irrational to base our decisions on what is over and done with. The past cannot be changed and it is pointless to dwell on it. Rational choice, therefore, is future-oriented: we should focus our attention on creating the best possible future and forget about the past. It is easy to feel the force of this.

Why, then, is the past important? The first thing to notice is that the distinction between past and future, as it is being deployed here, is not quite so straightforward as it first appears to be. Whether we are looking to the past or to the future depends on what point of view we adopt. Of course, when the employer takes Worker's efforts as a reason for promoting him, he is looking to the past. But consider instead Worker's position as he does the things needed to earn the promotion. *He* is looking to the future. He wants certain things to happen in the future—to be promoted—and so, to get what he wants, he does things in the present. He sets in motion a chain of events that will eventually produce the desired outcome. This is forward-looking, goal-directed behavior that is rational on anybody's account.

A problem arises only because the chain of events that links the action and the desired outcome includes someone else's action—between Worker's efforts and his promotion comes the employer's decision. If the connecting events were only impersonal physical occurrences, linked by cause and effect, there would be little that is puzzling. But here, one of the events in the chain is someone else's voluntary action. That is what creates the difficulty.

In order for Worker's forward-looking strategy to be effective, he must be able to count on the employer to accept his work as a reason to promote him. In other words, he must be able to count on the employer to accept a backward-looking reason when the appropriate time comes. But in a way, neither person is acting independently of the other. They are both acting in a context in which the other's actions play a vital part. It is as though they were teammates playing a game with fixed rules. The employer expects Worker to work conscientiously to promote the company's ends, and Worker expects the employer to reward him for doing so. The implicit understanding that the employer will do his part makes it rational for Worker to adopt the strategy of doing as the employer wants. It is an arrangement from which everyone benefits.

This is connected with a more general reason why desert is important. Because we live together with other people in mutually cooperative societies, how each of us fares depends not only on what we do but on what others do as well. If we are to flourish, we need to obtain the good treatment of others. A system of understandings in which desert is acknowledged gives us a way of doing that. Thus, acknowledging deserts is a way of granting people the power to determine their own fates.

Absent this, what are we to do? What are the alternatives? We might imagine a system in which the only way for a person to ensure good treatment by others is somehow to coerce that treatment from them; or we might imagine that good treatment always comes as charity. Thus Worker might try threatening his employer; or he might simply hope the employer will be nice to him. But the practice of acknowledging deserts is different from both of these. The practice of acknowledging deserts gives people control over whether others will treat them well or badly, by saying to them: if you behave well, you will be *entitled* to good treatment from others because you will have earned it. Without this control people would be in an important sense impotent, less able to affect how others will treat them and dependent entirely on their powers of coercion or on the charity of others for any good treatment they might receive.

If this is correct, then even from the employer's point of view the arrangement whereby he promotes the harder-working employee is not merely a convenient deal that furthers his particular ends. It is part of a larger system of understandings that grants to people, including his employees, the power to determine their own fates in social settings in which their welfare depends on how others respond to them. Acknowledging deserts is at least as important as empowering people in this way.

I believe this is the deepest reason that desert is important. But there is one other reason we might notice before going on. That reason is connected with the costs of work that were mentioned above. We noted that in working harder Worker had to forgo benefits that Slacker was able to enjoy: while Worker was spending his time working, Slacker was able to do things that Worker might have liked to do but was unable to do. (This, of course, will be typical of any situation in which one person chooses to expend time and effort on a task that is less enjoyable than what he or she might otherwise be doing, while another person—faced with the same choice—opts for the more enjoyable alternative.) This suggests a simple argument for rewarding the harder worker. Other things being equal, burdens and benefits should be distributed equally. Slacker has had a benefit (more leisure time) that Worker has not had, while Worker has had a burden (more work) that Slacker has not had. Giving Worker a benefit now (the promotion) may therefore be seen as nothing more than righting the balance. Slacker has already had a greater share of life's goods. Contrary to superficial appearances, then, giving Worker the promotion does not make their respective situations less equal; in fact, it alters the situation in the direction of greater equality. So this is a reason egalitarians in particular should favor treating people according to their deserts.

Principles of Desert

Rawls says, "None of the precepts of justice aims at rewarding desert."[9] This may seem an odd thing to say until we remember that Rawls believes no one ever deserves anything. On the view we are considering, however, there are some principles of justice that focus directly on desert.

Sometimes people deserve specific benefits because of what they have done—Worker deserves, specifically, to be promoted. He does not deserve an ice cream cone or a place in the church choir, although we can easily imagine past actions in virtue of which someone might deserve (specifically) those things. There is, of course, a negative side to this idea: someone (Slacker, for example) may deserve *not* to be promoted, or even to be fired, because of past performance. Desert also comes in degrees: someone can be more deserving than someone else, who is deserving to a lesser extent. Moreover, *what* one deserves may vary, even within the same activity-relative context. A person may deserve not to be fired but to be demoted or to be held at the same salary level without a raise. Thus, one principle governing what people deserve is this:

> *Deserving responses to one's performance in special activities:* Where there are particular types of benefits associated with particular types of activities, people deserve the benefits to the extent that they have done as well as they could in the activities.

Those who have done as well as they could in the activities—that is, those who have done the best they could with the talents and abilities they have—deserve the associated benefits. Those who have performed to the very best of their abilities are maximally deserving, while those who have chosen to do less than that are less deserving. Those who have done little deserve few benefits and may even deserve to be excluded from the activity in the future; for example, one may deserve to be demoted or even to be fired from a job. The view that desert depends on past performance explains these variations neatly—it is because there are different possible levels of effort that one may deserve different degrees of outcome.

Our examples so far have not concerned matters that would be regarded as distinctly "moral," even though they have concerned important matters about how people are to be treated. The distinction between moral and nonmoral is notoriously slippery. It isn't clear where the line should be drawn, and it isn't even clear whether it matters where the line is drawn— does it matter, for example, whether one says that the duty to promote the most deserving worker is a moral duty or only a duty of some other kind, say a duty of fair play? Whatever one calls it, it is a significant duty that may be more stringent than other duties, even those that are called "moral."

Perhaps it will be good enough here to draw the distinction this way: moral deserts are deserts that one has, not in virtue of one's performance in a special type of activity (such as working at a job), but in virtue of one's more general way of dealing with other people. A constant feature of everyday life is that we face situations in which what we do may be helpful or harmful to others. In such circumstances how we behave toward others determines what we deserve from them. Consider this example:

> *The ride to work.* Suppose you, Smith, and Jones all work at the same place. One morning your car won't start and you need a ride to work, so you call Smith and ask him to come by for you. But Smith refuses. It is clear that he could do it, but he doesn't want to be bothered, so he makes up some excuse. Then you call Jones, and he gives you the ride you need. A few weeks later, you get a call from Smith. Now he is having car trouble and he asks you for a ride. Should you accommodate him?

Perhaps you will think you should help Smith, despite his own unhelpfulness—after all, it would be little trouble for you, and by helping him you might teach him a lesson in generosity. But if we focus on what he *deserves,* a different answer seems obvious: he deserves to be left to fend for himself. Jones, on the other hand, is an entirely different matter. If Jones should ask you for a ride, you have every reason to give it: not only will it help him, he deserves it. This is especially clear when we consider the case of a forced choice:

The simultaneous requests. Smith calls and asks for a ride. Meanwhile, Jones is on the other line also needing a ride. But they live in opposite directions, so it is impossible for you to help both. Which do you help?

If we did not concede that Jones's past conduct makes him more deserving, we would be hard put to explain why it seems so obvious that helping Jones is the mandatory choice.

Particular people may be especially obligated in this way. If someone has done you a favor, *you* are indebted to her and you specifically owe it to her to return the favor. It is you, and not someone else, who owes Jones the ride. Sometimes this is thought to end the matter: if someone has helped you, it is said, you are indebted to her; otherwise you have no obligation. But it is shortsighted to view things in this way. Anyone at all can justifiably take as a good reason for treating someone well the fact that this person has treated others well. Suppose Jones is habitually helpful to people, while Smith is not; but you personally have never had much interaction with either of them. Now suppose you must choose which to help, and you cannot help both. Surely their respective histories constitute a reason, even for you, to prefer Jones. Thus we have:

The Principle of Desert: People deserve to be treated in the same way that they have (voluntarily) treated others. Those who have treated others well deserve to be treated well in return, while those who have treated others badly deserve to be treated badly in return.

Above we cited some reasons why desert is important. Those reasons apply here equally well. Acknowledging moral desert permits people, who are after all largely dependent for their welfare on what other people do, to control their own fates by allowing them to earn good treatment at the hands of others. They do not have to rely on coercion or charity. Moreover, those who treat others well will have, in the course of doing so, forgone benefits for themselves. (In giving you the ride, Jones was inconvenienced in a way that Smith was not.) So once again reciprocating is a way of making the distribution of burdens and benefits more nearly equal.

To these reasons another may be added. If reciprocity could not be expected, the morality of treating others well would come to occupy a less important place in people's lives. In a system that respects deserts, someone who treats others well may expect to be treated well in return, while someone who treats others badly cannot. If this aspect of moral life were eliminated, morality would have no reward and immorality would have no bad consequences, so there would be less reason for one to be concerned with it. If people were perfectly benevolent, of course, such incentives would not be needed. But for imperfectly benevolent beings such as ourselves, the acknowledgment of deserts provides the reason for being moral that is required for the whole system to be effective.

These principles have both positive and negative sides. Those with a generous temperament may find the former appealing but recoil from the latter: they may like the idea that some people deserve good treatment but dislike the companion idea that others deserve bad treatment. After all, to say that someone deserves to be treated badly seems, on the face of it, mean-spirited and unsympathetic. But perhaps this feeling may be diminished if we remember that, on the account we are considering, desert is only one factor among others that should be taken into account in an overall assessment of how someone should be treated. Desert is a reason that counts against Smith, but it is not the only reason that may apply. As we noted above, there may be good reasons for giving him the ride despite his deserts: he needs the ride, and helping him might teach him generosity. Perhaps you should, all things considered, help him. The principle of moral desert only says that, in doing so, you would be helping him despite a consideration that weighs against it.

Forgiveness

Sometimes when people have behaved badly, it is wise not to treat them badly in return; it is better to forgive them and let bygones be bygones. In such instances we might continue to recognize that they deserve worse; yet at the same time we choose to set this consideration aside. Some philosophers have found this paradoxical. How, they ask, can we say that someone deserves ill treatment and at the same time endorse forgiveness? If we ought to treat people as they deserve, and someone deserves to be treated badly, then forgiving him (and forgoing the bad treatment) necessarily involves failing to do what we ought to do. It would follow, then, that we ought never to forgive people. Thus, the argument goes, we cannot both acknowledge deserts and countenance forgiveness. The two are not compatible.[10]

It would be strange if this reasoning were correct, because the concept of forgiveness appears to make sense only when it is *combined* with some notion of ill desert. In order to properly forgive someone, he or she must have done something that needs forgiving—something that would normally elicit a negative response, which we forgo when we forgive. Thus the concept of forgiveness seems not only compatible with the notion of ill desert; it seems to require it. But of course the reasoning is not correct. A theory of desert does not have to hold that we should always treat people as they deserve. It need only say, more modestly, that desert is one consideration alongside others in determining what on the whole should be done.

We may distinguish three general attitudes regarding forgiveness. The first is that repaying deserts is a strict duty that may not be brushed aside; thus, "forgiveness" (of a sort) is permissible only after debts have been paid and justice has been done. This view is commonly attributed to Kant, although I do not know that he ever said as much outright. A less harsh view is that sometimes we should forgive people's transgressions (forgoing the repayment of deserts) and sometimes not. That is the view of common sense. Humane people might, however, think that even this is too harsh. Bishop Butler apparently thought so: he argued that one should *always* forgive wrongdoing.

Butler believed that retaliation is never right. Although resentment and the desire for revenge are in a sense natural feelings, he says, they should never be indulged—they are not associated with morally acceptable reasons for action. Rather than returning evil for evil, we should in every instance forgive the offender and strive to do what is best for him (or what is best for everyone on the whole). In the sermon "Upon Forgiveness of Injuries" he wrote:

> It is not man's being a social creature, much less his being a moral agent, from whence *alone* our obligations to good-will towards him arise. There is an obligation to it prior to either of these, arising from his being a sensible creature; that is, capable of happiness or misery. Now this obligation cannot be superseded by his moral character.[11]

Oddly, in the same paragraph in which these words appear, Butler endorses public executions. But what justifies this, he says, is not "the guilt or demerit of the criminal." Rather, it is that "his life is inconsistent with the quiet and happiness of the world: that is, a general and more enlarged obligation necessarily destroys a particular and more confined one of the same kind, inconsistent with it." Butler makes this observation to underscore his general view that "Guilt or injury does not dispense with or supersede the duty of love and good-will."

Butler gives two general reasons for holding that forgiveness is always the best policy. First, if we return evil for evil, we only make things worse: we resent the offender's harming us; and now he will resent us harming him; so in the future he will be even less likely to treat us well. One evil leads to the next, without end. Thus, he says, resentment is "a passion which, if generally indulged, would propagate itself so as almost to lay waste the world."[12]

Second, Butler points out that all of us sometimes need to be forgiven; but if we do not forgive others, how can we expect others to forgive us? He cites the story in St. Matthew's gospel about the man who owed money to a king. The man could not pay and begged the king to forgive him. The king took pity on him and forgave the debt. But then this same man encountered someone who owed him money, and who could not pay, but he had no pity and had the debtor thrown into prison. Later, the king heard what had happened and was outraged; so the king ordered this man to be "delivered unto the tormentors," as was his due.[13] The moral is clear: if we wish others to forgive us our debts, then we had better forgive them.

Butler believed that we should always forgive people's transgressions. But his arguments do not support such a sweeping conclusion. We might agree with him that sometimes forgiveness is right, for the very reasons he cites, and yet keep to the commonsense view that sometimes it is not called for. To determine which attitude is correct, we need to inquire more generally into the role of forgiveness in moral life.

Why should we sometimes—perhaps even usually—forgive people's offenses, rather than ruthlessly holding them accountable? What value does the practice of forgiving have for us? The key idea, I think, is that *forgiving people is a way of establishing or restoring desirable relationships with them.* The practice of forgiving must be understood in the context of two general facts about human life. The first is that we are social creatures: we live among other people—family, friends, neighbors, fellow workers—and we have a wide variety of relationships with them. We cannot fare well in life apart from these relationships. We need to have loving relations with some people and mutually cooperative interactions with a great many others. The second fact is that we are imperfect: we sometimes behave offensively, and when we do, our misconduct may prevent us from forming beneficial relationships with other people or it may disrupt relationships we already have. Therefore, when this happens, we need to be able to remedy things. This is where forgiveness comes in. Forgiving people enables us to create and preserve good relations with them when bad behavior threatens to drive us apart.

Consider Smith again, who would not do you a favor but who now asks that you help him. If you refuse, you join with him in creating a hostile situation in which neither of you is ever likely to help the other. Of course, you can always say it's his fault; but the hostility on both sides will remain. (This is the point of Butler's first argument.) On the other hand, if you help him, you may establish a different sort of situation, one in which friendly relations become possible.

A lot depends, of course, on whether the other person can be expected to follow suit, and this explains why being *asked* for forgiveness is important. Someone who asks forgiveness admits that he was wrong and implicitly offers to do better in the future. An apology is an overture to healing a relationship or to creating a better one; to reject it shows not merely a lack of generosity but an unwillingness to enter into an improved situation. At the same time, if he does not ask forgiveness, you may rightly wonder whether ignoring his past misconduct would do any good. He may just be taking advantage of you. If he shows no remorse, then perhaps treating him as he has treated others would be a better lesson than forgiving him.

Forgiveness can be especially important in restoring a relationship that has gone bad. Forgiving a friend who has wronged you can heal the friendship, while not forgiving her may mean its end. The more intimate the relationship, the more important this sort of consideration becomes: not forgiving a stranger is one thing; not forgiving one's spouse is another. Holding a grudge may be (barely) compatible with a distant and formal sort of relationship, even a mutually cooperative one, but grudges will spoil a friendship or a marriage, so renouncing grudges has the same importance as maintaining such ties. The practice of forgiveness enables imperfect human beings to live together, sustaining cooperative, friendly, and even loving relations with one another, despite their flaws.

The connection between forgiveness and fostering improved relationships also explains another important feature of the concept: it explains why only the person who has been wronged can forgive that wrong. If you have offended your mother, only she can forgive you. Others cannot. The reason is that your relationship with *her* is healed only when *she* accepts your apology. Of course there is a sense in which third parties can forgive: seeing that you are sincerely repentant, I can decide not to hold your mistreatment of your mother against you, even if she turns her back on you. But that is less than full-blown forgiveness. It repairs your relation with me, but not with her.

This may seem wrongheaded to religious people who believe that ultimately forgiveness must come from God. Is it not God, and only God, who has the power to forgive us our sins? If the answer is yes, it is for a peculiar reason. The concept of sin is different from the concept of wrongdoing. Wrongs may be committed against specific people—your mother, your neighbor, your friend—and they are the ones who need to forgive you if your relations with them are to be repaired. Sins, however, are offenses against God, and because they are offenses against him, he must forgive you if your relation with him is to be made right. In the Christian tradition it is sometimes said that all wrongdoing is sinful; thus every wrong is seen as an offense against God, requiring his forgiveness. Even if one adopts this outlook, however, the wrong done to your mother is still a wrong against her as well, and it still requires her forgiveness if your good relationship with her is to be restored.

But religious thinkers have sometimes gone a step further by treating the concept of sin as a *replacement* for the ordinary notion of wrongdoing. This, however, leads to a impoverished understanding of moral life, for we are deprived of the vocabulary needed for expressing our moral relations to one another. If we can only sin, we can only wrong God. We cannot wrong one another. And we can be forgiven by God, but we cannot forgive one another.

Therefore, there is nothing in the concept of forgiveness, or in the explanation of why it is a desirable practice, that is incompatible with the acknowledgment that sometimes people deserve to be treated badly. On the contrary, the two notions go together. In forgiving people, we choose—for good reason—to ignore their deserts, to put them out of mind and forget about them. But forgetting something does not mean it ceases to exist: to forgive someone is to treat him well despite his deserts. Still we might ask whether, in the spirit of generosity, it would be better simply to forgo this kind of thinking. Why not refrain altogether from harsh judgments and resolve instead simply to treat people as generously and as well as we can? This was Butler's proposal. As a prescription for living, there may be much to recommend it. But in moral theory we want the unvarnished truth, and jettisoning the idea of ill desert would leave our theory deficient in several respects.

First, if we jettison the idea of negative desert, we will have to jettison the idea of positive desert along with it. Superficially it may appear that we could keep one while eliminating the other: we could *say* that some people deserve good treatment but that no one ever deserves ill, and if nothing more is said, this might seem consistent. But the inconsistency would emerge when we tried to provide a rationale for this combination of beliefs. What reasoning could justify holding that good performance merits a positive response that would not also imply that bad performance merits a negative response? The answer, so far as I can tell, is none. And, as we have already seen, if we deny that anyone can merit good treatment, we deny people the power to control their own fates by earning good treatment at the hands of others.

Second, even if we resolve always to treat people as generously as possible, the notion of ill desert must be retained as a tiebreaker. Suppose Jones has done you many favors in the past, while Smith has always treated you badly, and now both need your help in circumstances in which you can help only one. You might want to forgive Smith, but still it would be unfair to Jones simply to treat them equally. In a situation of forced choice, the difference in their past actions cannot with justice be ignored.

And finally, there is another complication that connects forgiveness with desert—both good and ill—in a different way. If others are not perfect, then neither are you; and so, as Butler observed, there will be occasions on which you will need to be forgiven. If you have forgiven others, then you will deserve similar consideration from them. This is, in fact, just a special application of the principle of moral desert: you deserve to be treated as well as you treat others; so if you have forgiven others, you will deserve to be forgiven yourself, whereas if you have not been forgiving in the past, you will deserve less consideration now. This is the valid point behind Butler's second argument. The point is not just that you cannot *expect* to be forgiven if you do not forgive others; the point is that if you refuse to forgive others, you do not *deserve* to be forgiven yourself. It is a point of moral logic and not, as Butler seems to think, just a brute fact about human psychology. Thus, even the activity of forgiving comes within the scope of the principle of desert. To be forgiven is one of the many things that one may merit by one's past behavior.

Notes

1. This story is recounted in Rudiger Safranski, *Schopenhauer and the Wild Years of Philosophy,* trans. Ewald Osers (Cambridge: Harvard University Press, 1989), 122–23.

2. Joel Feinberg, "Justice and Personal Desert," in *Doing and Deserving* (Princeton: Princeton University Press, 1970), 58. Emphasis mine.

3. John Rawls, *A Theory of Justice* (Cambridge: Harvard University Press, 1971), 103–4.

4. Rawls, *Theory of Justice,* 312.

5. Rawls, *Theory of Justice,* 104.

6. I am ignoring some complications that would be important in a more detailed analysis; for example, that one may be blameworthy for omissions as well as for actions. But these complications are not important for the present discussion.

7. Jean-Paul Sartre, *Being and Nothingness,* trans. Hazel E. Barnes (New York: Philosophical Library, 1956), pt. 4.

8. Sartre, *Being and Nothingness,* 439.

9. Rawls, *Theory of Justice,* 311.

10. Jeffrie Murphy points out that this sort of argument is at least as old as St.

Anselm. See Jeffrie G. Murphy and Jean Hampton, *Forgiveness and Mercy* (Cambridge: Cambridge University Press, 1988), 168–69.

11. *The Works of Joseph Butler*, ed. W. E. Gladstone (Oxford: Clarendon Press, 1896), 2:159.

12. *Works of Joseph Butler*, 2:161.

13. Matt. 18:34 AV.

13

Coping with Prejudice

"Good sense," said Descartes, "is of all things in the world the most equally distributed, for everybody thinks himself so abundantly provided with it, that even those most difficult to please in all other matters do not commonly desire more of it than they already possess."1 Much the same might be said about prejudice: everyone believes himself or herself to be objective and free of bias. We recognize that other people may be prejudiced, but we imagine that we ourselves see things as they really are.

But of course this is a mistake. We feel that we are unprejudiced only because we are unaware of our biases and how they work. This is true not only of bigots but of relatively open-minded people as well. It is a mistake for any of us to think that we are free of bias. Even when we are striving hardest to be objective, prejudices of all sorts can creep into our thinking without our noticing it.

To illustrate this, we may consider a type of example that does not often occur to us. We are familiar enough with prejudice based on race or gender. But those are not the only ways in which we discriminate. There is an impressive body of evidence that we are also prejudiced against people because of their height. I do not mean abnormally short or tall people—dwarfs or giants. That sort of prejudice is familiar enough. The less widely-recognized form of prejudice is against shorter people whose height falls within the normal range. Let me briefly mention some of the investigations that show this.2

In one study, 140 job-placement officers were asked to choose between two applicants with exactly the same qualifications, but one was described, parenthetically, as being 6'1" while the other candidate was listed as 5'5". One hundred two of the recruiters judged the taller candidate to be better qualified, while only one preferred the shorter candidate. The rest of them—a mere 27 percent—recognized that the two were equally qualified.

Other studies have shown that a person's earning potential is affected more by height than by, say, educational performance. One study compared the starting salaries of male librarians between 6'1" and 6'3" with the starting salaries of male librarians less than 6'. The same comparison was then made between those who had been in the top half of their classes academically and those in the bottom half. The average difference in starting salary between the taller and shorter graduates was found to be more than three times greater than the difference between the salaries of the more and less academically gifted. Another study using a sample of over five thousand men found that after twenty-five years of pursuing their varied careers, those who were 5'6" or 5'7" were earning on average $2,500 per year less than those who were 6'0" or 6'1".

The moral seems to be: if you could choose between being tall and being smart, from a crass economic standpoint, it's better to be tall.

The same sort of prejudice influences the way we vote. Of all U.S. presidents, only two—James Madison and Benjamin Harrison—were shorter than the average height for American males at the time of their election. And since 1904, the taller candidate has emerged victorious in 80 percent of presidential elections. Another moral might be drawn: if you are trying to predict the outcome of such an election, forget the other factors and put your money on the taller man.

Prejudice against short people seems importantly different from racist or sexist prejudice, because the latter sorts of prejudice seem to be motivated, at least in part, by the fact that members of the dominant group derive advantages from the discriminatory practices. These advantages are often economic. However, this seems much less plausible where height is concerned. It seems more likely that prejudice regarding height has some other, deeper psychological source. John S. Gillis, a psychologist who has written at length about this, has speculated that the source of our association of height with ability is to be found in childhood experiences:

> All of us experience a real association between height and power throughout our childhood. Adults tower over us physically as children, and they are the ones who control every single important thing in our lives. This may be the fountainhead of heightism. Each of us begins life with a dozen years or so of learning that the bigger person is more powerful and intelligent. This learning takes place not so much on an intellectual level but, more importantly, on the emotional level. Our attitudes and feelings are shaped in ways of which we are unaware.[3]

Whatever the source of these feelings, it is clear that they have deep and long-lasting effects.

The facts about "heightism" are quite remarkable. They suggest a number of points that should be of interest to anyone who is thinking about the philosophical problem of equality, especially as it relates to the formulation and assessment of social policies. First, the studies I have cited show that prejudice can have its influence quite unconsciously. No one—or so nearly no one as makes no difference—realizes that he thinks less well of shorter people. Yet the available evidence shows that this prejudice exists, and that it is widespread. The people who are affected by it are simply unaware of it.

Second, this evidence also suggests that people are very good at rationalizing their prejudiced judgments. The men and women whose actions were studied in these investigations—those who hired, promoted, and gave pay raises to the taller candidates—were, no doubt, reasonable people who could "explain" each decision by reference to the lucky employee's objective qualifications. No one believed that he was simply rewarding height. Yet the evidence shows that this is what was happening much of the time. The behavior induced by prejudice includes, importantly, the verbal behavior that "justifies" the prejudiced judgments.

These points, taken together, have a discouraging implication. They suggest that it is difficult even for people of good will to prevent such prejudice from influencing their deliberations. If I am prejudiced in ways that I do not fully realize and I am skilled at coming up with reasons to "justify" the decisions that prejudice leads me to make, then my good intention to "think objectively"—no matter how sincerely I want to do this—may be depressingly ineffective.

The Justification of Quotas

People ought to be treated fairly. Yet we know that our assessments of people are often corrupted by prejudice. Does this make any difference in the sorts of policies that should be adopted?

Choosing Widgets

Suppose you are the president of a manufacturing company and each year in the course of your business you need a supply of widgets. Widgets vary greatly in quality, and from among the hundreds available you need to get the ten best you can find. You are not able to devote much of your own time to this task, but luckily you have an assistant who is one of the most astute widget evaluators in the land. "Examine all the available widgets," you tell her, "and bring me the ten best."

In the fullness of time your assistant brings you ten good widgets, and all seems well. But then you notice that all ten were made at the Buffalo Widget Works. This is odd, because you know that the Albany Widget Works makes an equally good product; and moreover, you know that the pool from which your assistant made her selection contained equal numbers of Albany widgets and Buffalo widgets. So why should the ten best all come from Buffalo? One would expect that, on average, five would come from Buffalo and five from Albany. But perhaps this was just a statistical fluke, and it will all average out over time.

The next year, however, much the same thing happens. You need ten widgets; you assign your assistant to identify the best; and she brings you nine made in Buffalo and only one made in Albany. "Why?" you ask, and in response she assures you that, even though the Albany company does make excellent widgets, most of the best ones available this year happened to be from Buffalo. To prove the point she gives you quite an intelligent and persuasive analysis of the merits of the widgets in this year's pool. You are so impressed that you name her Vice President for Widget Procurement (VPWP).

In subsequent years the story is repeated again and again, with only slight variations. Each year you are told that almost all the best available widgets are from Buffalo. You begin to feel sure that something peculiar is going on. Briefly, you wonder whether your VPWP is accepting bribes from the Buffalo company, but you reject that hypothesis. She is an honest woman, and you cannot help but believe that she is using her best judgment. Then you consider whether, in fact, the Buffalo widgets are simply better than the Albany widgets. But you reject this possibility also; other experts testify that they are equally good.

Finally, you make a discovery that explains everything. It turns out that your vice president was raised in Buffalo, where there is a strong sense of civic pride, and an even stronger sense of rivalry with Albany. Children in Buffalo, it seems, have it drilled into them that everything about Buffalo is better than anything about Albany. Moreover, before coming to work for you, your VPWP worked for the Buffalo Chamber of Commerce and was in charge of promoting Buffalo products. Obviously, then, she is prejudiced, and that explains why she almost always judges Buffalo widgets to be superior.

What are you to do? You could forget about it; after all, the widgets you are getting from Buffalo are pretty good. But you don't want to do that; it is important to you to have the very best widgets you can get. So you talk to your VPWP, you confront her with your suspicion that she is prejudiced, and you stress the importance of getting the best widgets regardless of whether they are from Buffalo or Albany. She is a bit offended by this because she is a good woman and she believes herself to be impartial. Again, she assures you that she is selecting the best widgets available, and if they happen to be from Buffalo, she can't help it. And as time passes, nothing changes; she continues to select mostly Buffalo widgets.

Now what? You are certain she is prejudiced, but because the prejudice is entirely unconscious, your VPWP seems unable to overcome it or even to recognize it. You could get a new VPWP. But you don't want to do that, because this woman is an excellent judge of widgets, except for this one problem. Then an obvious solution occurs to you. You could simply change your instructions. Instead of saying, each year, "Bring me the ten best widgets," you could say, "Bring me the five best Buffalo widgets and the five best Albany widgets." She might not like that—she might take it as an insult to her ability to judge widgets impartially—but, if it is true that Albany widgets are equally as good as Buffalo widgets, this would result in your getting a better overall quality of widget, on average, year in and year out.

(Although the proof of this may be obvious, perhaps it is worthwhile to spell it out. If we assume that Albany widgets are, on average, as good as Buffalo widgets, we are assuming something like this: The best Albany widget is likely to be as good as the best Buffalo widget. The next-best Albany widget, although it is not as good as the best Albany widget, is likely to be as good as the next-best Buffalo widget, although that Buffalo widget is not as good as the best Buffalo widget. The third-best Albany widget is likely to be as good as the third-best Buffalo widget. And so on. Therefore, a group that includes Buffalo widgets one through eight and Albany widgets one and two will not be as good as the group that includes the five best from each source. Of course, our assumption—that Albany widgets are on average as good as Buffalo widgets—does not guarantee this sort of one-to-one correlation. But if we are assuming that quality is randomly distributed in the two groups, rather than, say, that one group dominates in the upper half of the pool, then one-to-one correlation is a reasonable approximation of the distribution.)

The VPWP might, however, offer an interesting objection. She might point out that, in carrying out your new instructions, she would sometimes have to include in the total of ten an Albany widget that is inferior to a Buffalo widget that was also available. You will have to admit that this is so. But your problem is a practical one. You can trust the VPWP to judge which are the best Albany widgets, and you can trust her to judge which are the best Buffalo widgets. But you cannot trust her to compare objectively the relative merits of a widget from one city with a widget from the other city. In these circumstances, your new instructions give you a better chance of ending up with the best overall supply. Or to put it another way: you want the best-qualified widgets to get the jobs, and the quota system you have established will see to that more effectively than the alternative method of simply allowing your VPWP to exercise her judgment.

Hiring People

In the workplace, people ought to be treated equally, but often they are not. Among the important reasons is prejudice; after all, somebody has to decide who is to be hired, or promoted, or given a pay raise, and those who get to make such decisions are only human and might be prejudiced. Social policies ought to be devised with this in mind. Such policies should contain provisions to ensure that people are given equal treatment, insofar as this is possible, despite the fact that those policies must be administered by imperfect human beings.

Of all the kinds of policies that have been devised to combat discrimination, quotas are the most despised. Almost no one has a good word to say about them. Yet the widget example suggests that, under certain circumstances, quotas can be defensible. Can a similar argument be constructed, not for choosing widgets, but for hiring people?

Suppose you are the dean of a college, and you are concerned that only the best-qualified scholars are hired for your faculty. You notice, however, that your philosophy department never hires any women. (They did hire one woman, years ago, so they have a token female. But that's as far as it has gone.) So you investigate. You discover that there are, indeed, lots of women philosophers looking for jobs each year. And you have no reason to think that these women are, on average, any less capable than their male colleagues. So you talk to the (male) chairperson of the department and you urge him to be careful to give full and fair consideration to the female applicants. Being a good liberal fellow, he finds this agreeable enough—although he may be a little offended by the suggestion that he is not already giving the women due consideration. But the talk has little apparent effect. Whenever candidates are being considered, he continues to report, with evident sincerity, that in the particular group under review a male has emerged as the best qualified. And so, he says each year, if we want to hire the best-qualified applicant we have to hire the male, at least this time.

This is repeated annually, with minor variations. One variation is that the best female philosopher in the pool may be listed as the department's top choice. But when, predictably enough, she turns out to be unavailable (having been snapped up by a more prestigious university), no women in the second tier are considered to be good alternatives. Here you notice a disturbing asymmetry: although the very best males are also going to other universities, the males in the second tier are considered good alternatives. Momentarily, then, you consider whether the problem could be that philosophical talent is distributed in a funny way: while the very best women are equal to the very best men, at the next level down, the men suddenly dominate. But that seems unlikely.

After further efforts have been made along these lines, without result, you might eventually conclude that there is an unconscious prejudice at work. Your department, despite its good intentions and its one female member, is biased. It isn't hard to understand why this could be so. In addition to the usual sources of prejudice against women—the stereotypes, the picture of women as less rational than men, and so forth—an all-male or mostly male group enjoys a kind of camaraderie that might seem impossible if females were significantly included. In choosing a new colleague, the matter of how someone would "fit in" with the existing group will always have some influence. This will work against females, no matter their talents as teachers and scholars.

Finally, then, you may conclude that the existing prejudice cannot be countered by any measure short of issuing a new instruction, and you tell the philosophy department that it must hire some additional women, in numbers at least in proportion to the number of women in the applicant pool. The reply, of course, will be that this policy could result in hiring a less qualified woman over a better qualified man. But the answer is the same as in the example about the widgets. You are not trying to give women a special break, any more than you were trying to give Albany widgets a special break. Nor are you trying to redress the injustices that women have suffered in the past; nor are you trying to provide "role models" for female students. You may be pleased if your policy has these effects, but the purpose of your policy is not to achieve them. Your only purpose is to get the best-qualified scholars for your faculty, regardless of their gender. The fact of unconscious prejudice makes the usual system of simply allowing your experts—the philosophy department—to exercise their judgment an imperfect system for accomplishing that purpose. Allowing them to exercise their judgment within the limits of a quota system, on the other hand, may be more effective, because it reduces the influence of unconscious prejudice.

It is sure to be objected that people are not widgets, and so the two cases are not analogous. But they do seem to be analogous in the relevant respects. The features of the widget example that justified imposing a quota were: (1) There was a selection process that involved human judgment. (2) The result of the process was that individuals from a certain group were regularly rated higher than members of another group. (3) There was no reason to think that the members of the former group were in fact better than the members of the latter group. (4) There was reason to think that the human beings who were judging these individuals might have been prejudiced against members of the latter group. The case of hiring women faculty also has these four features. That is what permits the construction of a similar argument.

This argument takes into account a feature of the selection process that is often ignored when quotas (or "affirmative action," or "reverse discrimination") are discussed. Often, the question is put like this: assuming that X is better qualified than Y, is it justifiable to adopt a policy that would permit hiring or promoting Y rather than X? Then various reasons are produced that might justify this, such as that a preferential policy redresses wrongs, or that it helps to combat racism or sexism. The debate then focuses on whether such reasons are sufficient. But when the issue is approached in this way, a critical point is overlooked. People do not come prelabeled as better or worse qualified. Before we can say that X is better qualified than Y, someone has to have made that judgment. And this is where prejudice is most likely to enter the picture. A male philosopher, judging other philosophers, might very well rate women lower, without even realizing he is doing so. The argument we are considering is intended to address this problem, which arises before the terms of the conventional discussion are even set.

Of course, this argument does not purport to show that any system of quotas, applied in any circumstances, is fair. The argument is only a defense of quotas used in a certain way in certain circumstances. But the circumstances I have described are not uncommon. Actual quota systems, of the sort that have been established and tested in the courts during the past three decades, often have just this character: they are instituted to counter the prejudice, conscious or otherwise, that corrupts judgments of merit. Here is a real case that illustrates this.

In 1972 there were no blacks in the Alabama State Police. In the 37-year history of the force, there had never been any. Then the NAACP brought suit to end this vestige of segregation. They won their case in the trial court when federal district Judge Frank Johnson condemned what he termed a "blatant and continuous pattern and practice of discrimination." Judge Johnson did not, however, simply order the Alabama authorities to stop discriminating and start making their decisions impartially. He knew that such an order would be treated with amused contempt; the authorities would have been only too happy to continue as before, "impartially" finding that no blacks were qualified. So in order to prevent this and to ensure that the Alabamians could not avoid hiring qualified blacks, Johnson ordered that the state hire and promote one qualified black for every white trooper hired or promoted, until 25 percent of the force was black.

Judge Johnson's order was appealed to the Eleventh Circuit Court, where it was upheld. Time went by while the state was supposed to be carrying out his instructions. In 1984, twelve years later, the district court reviewed the situation to see what progress had been made. Forced by the court to do so, the department had hired some blacks. But virtually none had been promoted. The court found that, among the six majors on the force, none was black. Of the 25 captains, none was black. Of the 35 lieutenants, none was black. Of the 65 sergeants, none was black. Of the 66 corporals, however, there were four blacks. The court declared: "This is intolerable and must not continue."

The state of Alabama's last hope was the U.S. Supreme Court, which heard the case and rendered its decision in 1987. By a five-to-four vote, the Supreme Court upheld Judge Johnson's orders, and the *Birmingham News* ran a front-page story describing the "bitter feelings" of the white troopers, who viewed the ruling as a "setback." A spokesman for the Alabama Department of Public Safety assured the newspaper, "The department will comply with this ruling." It was clear enough from the official statements, however, that "complying with the ruling" would force the department to take steps—actually promoting blacks—that it would never take voluntarily.[4]

The Circumstances in Which Quotas Are Justified

The imposition of a quota may be justified as a way of countering the effects of prejudice. As I have said, this argument does not justify just any old quota. Our argument envisions the imposition of a quota as a corrective to a "normal" decision-making process that has gone wrong. For present purposes we may define a normal process as follows: (1) The goal of the process is to identify the best-qualified individuals for the purpose at hand. (2) The nature of the qualifications is specified. (3) A pool of candidates is assembled. (4) The qualifications of the individuals in the pool are assessed, using the specified criteria, and the individuals are ranked from best to worst. (5) The jobs, promotions, or whatever are awarded to the best-qualified individuals.

This process may go wrong in any number of ways, of course, some of them not involving prejudice. We are not concerned here with all the ways in which things can go wrong. We are concerned only with the following set of circumstances: First, we notice that, as the selection process is carried out, individuals from a certain group are regularly rated higher than members of another group. Second, we can find no reason to think that the members of the former group are in fact better than the members of the latter group; on the contrary, there is reason to think the members of the two groups are, on average, equally well qualified. And third, there is reason to think that the people performing the assessments are prejudiced against members of the latter group. These are the circumstances in which our argument says the imposition of a quota may be justified.

Even in these circumstances, however, the use of a quota does not eliminate human judgment, and so it does not guarantee that prejudice will disappear from the equation. Prejudice is eliminated from one part of the process, but it may reappear at a different point.

Consider again the male philosophy professors who always recommended the hiring of other males. In our example, the dean concluded that the male philosophers were prejudiced. In order to reach this conclusion, however, the dean had to make the judgment that female philosophers are equally as talented as males. (Otherwise, there would have been no grounds for thinking that the philosophy department's preference for hiring males was the result of bias.) An analogous judgment had to be made by Judge Johnson. He had to assume that black people were as qualified as whites for employment and promotion in the Alabama State Patrol. But prejudice can infect these general assessments just as it can influence the specific judgments that were being made by the philosophy professors and the highway patrol officials.

Therefore, our argument seems to require the assumption that some people—the hypothetical dean and, more to the point, actual federal court judges—are less prejudiced than others.

This assumption, however, seems correct. Some people are in fact less prejudiced than others; that is why prejudiced decisions can sometimes be successfully appealed. In general, people who are a step removed from a decision-making process are in a better position to be unbiased, or at least to recognize their biases and act to correct them, than those who are close to the "front lines." Part of the reason is that they have less at stake personally. The dean does not have to live in the philosophy department, and the judge does not have to work in the highway patrol. Another part of the reason is that in many instances the officials who impose the quotas are better educated and are more practiced in dealing with prejudice than those on whom the quotas are imposed. Judge Johnson was one of the most distinguished southern jurists with long experience in handling civil rights cases. The argument that I have presented does indeed assume that he was more capable of thinking objectively about what was going on, as well as about the likely qualifications of blacks, than the officials of the Alabama highway patrol. If that assumption is false, then our argument in defense of his action collapses. But I do not think that assumption is false.

Our argument has one other limitation that should be mentioned. It does not apply in the case of decisions made solely on the basis of "objective" criteria—test scores and the like—assuming, of course, that the tests really are objective and do not contain hidden bias. We can imagine procedures that, by using only such objective criteria, leave no room for the operation of prejudice. So in such cases the "normal" procedure will work well enough. The best-qualified will win out, and quotas will be unnecessary.

But such cases will be rare. Consider the range of cases that must be dealt with in the real world. Is there any decision procedure that a rational person would adopt for hiring teachers that would not disclose that an applicant for a teaching job was female? Should we be willing to hire teachers without an interview? Is there any imaginable multiple-choice test that one would be willing to use as the sole criterion for promotion in a police department? Would we want to eliminate the use of the assessments of those who have observed the officer's performance?

Moreover, it should also be remembered that so-called objective criteria often involve the use of tainted evidence. Suppose, in order to be perfectly impartial, I resolve to make a hiring decision using only objective criteria such as college grades. In this way I prevent any prejudices that I might have from coming into play. So far, so good. But the grades themselves were handed out by teachers whose prejudices could have come into play during the grading process.

Objections and Replies

The quota policy mandated by Judge Johnson continues to cause controversy. Newspaper columnist James J. Kilpatrick summed up the case against the judge's order succinctly. In the process of complying with the judge's ruling, he wrote, "white troopers with higher test scores and objectively better qualifications lost out. They themselves had engaged in no discrimination. They were the innocent victims of a remedial process addressed to blacks as a group. Were those whites denied equal protection of the law?"[5] These familiar objections are often taken to vitiate the whole idea of quotas as such. Do they undercut the argument presented here? In the time-honored way, we may consider these objections one by one.

Objection: People ought to be hired or promoted on the basis of their qualifications, and not on the basis of their race or sex. To give preference to a black merely because he is black, or to a woman merely because she is a woman, is no more defensible than to prefer a white man because he is white or male.

Reply: The whole point of the argument is that quotas may be justified as part of a plan to make sure that people are hired or promoted on the basis of their qualifications. The sort of policy that I have discussed does not involve hiring or promoting on the basis of race or gender, but only on the basis of qualifications. Quota policies are being defended, in some circumstances, because they are the most effective policies for achieving that goal.

Objection: The white male who is passed over is not responsible for the injustices that were done to blacks in the past; therefore it is unfair to make him pay the price for it. As Kilpatrick pointed out, the Alabama state troopers who were not promoted were not responsible for the injustices that were done to blacks, so why should they now be penalized?

Reply: Again, this misses the point. The argument does not envision the use of quotas as a response to past discrimination, but as a way of preventing, or at least minimizing, *present* discrimination. Sometimes people who defend the use of quotas or other such policies defend them as only temporary measures to be used reluctantly until racism and sexism have been eliminated. It may be agreed that if racist and sexist prejudice were eliminated, there would be no need for race- or gender-based quotas. But unfortunately, despite the progress that has been made, there is little reason to expect this to happen anytime soon.

Objection: To repeat the most obvious objection: Wouldn't there be some instances of injustice (that is, instances in which a less well qualified individual is preferred to a better-qualified individual) under a policy of quotas that otherwise wouldn't occur? And isn't this inherently unfair?

Reply: Of course this will inevitably happen. But the question is whether there would be fewer injustices under this policy than under the alternative of "hiring strictly according to qualifications," which means, in practice, hiring according to assessments of qualifications made by biased judges. Some philosophers have also urged that it is not acceptable to treat someone unjustly for the purpose of preventing other injustices, but that point, even if it is correct, doesn't apply here. The choice here is between two policies neither of which is perfect and each of which would inevitably involve some injustices. The relevant question is, which policy would involve more?

Objection: Finally, there is an objection that will surely have occurred to many readers. If our argument were accepted, wouldn't it lead to all sorts of quotas—not only to quotas favoring blacks and women, but also to quotas favoring short people, for example? After all, as has been pointed out here, short people are also the victims of bias.

Reply: If it were possible to devise practical policies that would ensure fair treatment for short people, I can see no reason to object. However, I do not know whether there are particular circumstances in which quotas would be practicable and effective, so I do not know whether such a policy would be defensible. The problem is that prejudice against short people has never been perceived as a serious social issue; consequently it has received little study, and it is less well understood and its effects are less well documented than, say, racist or sexist prejudice. But I know of no reason to rule out in advance the adoption of policies that would counter this sort of bias.

This admission might be taken to be a reductio ad absurdum of our argument. The very idea of quotas in favor of short people may seem so silly that if the argument leads to this, then the argument may be thought absurd. But why? One might well fear the intrusion of the heavy hand of government in still another area. Yet, if in fact short people are being treated unfairly—if they are singled out for unfavorable treatment because of an irrelevant characteristic—this seems, on its face, just as objectionable as any other form of discrimination and just as good a cause for corrective action. "Heightism" is not now a social issue. But it could become one.

In the meantime, those who have studied the subject have made some modest suggestions. John S. Gillis, the psychologist I quoted above, has made this form of prejudice his special concern. Here are a few of the things he proposes we do:[6] Employers should become aware of height bias and try to ensure that it does not influence personnel decisions. (The effects of such individual efforts might be small and imperfect, but they are better than nothing.) To help break the psychological connection between height and worth, we should avoid using the word "stature" to refer to status, caliber, and prestige. Teachers should stop the common practice of lining up schoolchildren according to height, which suggests to the children that this correlates with something important. Gillis also urges that metric measurements be used to indicate height. This, he says, would help to break "the mystique of the six-footer"—being 6 feet tall is perceived as a grand thing for a man, but being 183 centimeters tall doesn't have the same ring. These are all modest and reasonable proposals. The imposition of quotas in hiring and the like would be a much more drastic measure, which probably would not be wise until such time as heightism is established as a more pressing social concern.

Notes

1. Elizabeth S. Haldane and G. R. T. Ross, *The Philosophical Works of Descartes* (New York: Dover Books, 1955), 1:81.

2. The following information is drawn from John S. Gillis, *Too Tall, Too Small* (Champaign, Ill: Institute for Personality and Ability Testing, 1982).

3. Gillis, *Too Tall*, 125.

4. *Birmingham News*, 26 February 1987, sec. A, p.1.

5. James J. Kilpatrick, "Reverse Discrimination Is Still Discrimination," *Birmingham News*, 5 November 1986, sec. A, p. 9.

6. Gillis, *Too Tall*, chap. 7.

14

Morality, Parents, and Children

At about the time Socrates was being put to death for corrupting the youth of Athens, the great Chinese sage Mo Tzu was also antagonizing his community. Unlike the Confucianists, who were the social conservatives of the day, Mo and his followers were sharply critical of traditional institutions and practices. One of Mo's controversial teachings was that human relationships should be governed by an "all-embracing love" that makes no distinctions between friends, family, and humanity at large. "Partiality," he said, "is to be replaced by universality."[1] To his followers, these were the words of a moral visionary. To the Confucianists, however, they were the words of a man out of touch with reality. In particular, Mo's doctrine was said to subvert the family, for it was taken as implying that one should have as much regard for strangers as for one's own kin. Meng Tzu summed up the complaint when he wrote that "Mo Tzu, by preaching universal love, has repudiated the family."[2] Mo did not deny it. Instead, he argued that universal love is a higher ideal than family loyalty and that obligations within families should be understood only as particular instances of obligations to all mankind.

The conflicting thoughts that motivated this ancient dispute have lost none of their power, and so the debate continues today. The idea that morality requires us to be impartial, clearly articulated by Mo Tzu, is a recurring theme of Western moral philosophy. Perhaps the most famous expression of this idea was Bentham's formula, "Each to count for one and none for more than one."[3] But this is not just a utilitarian idea; it is common ground to a wide range of theories and thinkers. Not only utilitarians, but Kantians, Christians, socialists, and contractarians have held the view, in one form or another, that morality and impartiality go hand in hand.[4]

Meanwhile, critics of these theories continue to argue, as did Meng Tzu, that they "repudiate the family." The basic idea of morality as impartiality is that no one's interests counts for more than anyone else's. But what about one's children? Don't parents have special obligations to their own children that they do not have to other children or to children in general? Isn't it all right to be partial where one's own family is concerned?

Our instincts are with the Confucianists. Surely, we think, parents do have special obligations to care for their own. Parents must love and protect their children; they must feed and clothe them; they must see to their medical needs, their educations, and a thousand other things. Who could deny it? At the same time, we do not believe that we have such duties toward strangers. Perhaps we have a general duty of beneficence, but that duty is not nearly so extensive or specific as the duties we have toward our own young sons and daughters.

The problem is not merely that we have special *duties* to our children, although we do. Duty is a cold and impersonal thing. A good parent's concern for her children is not motivated by duty but by love, and love is utterly incompatible with regarding someone as just another individual whose interests are to be weighed against the interests of everyone else. As John Cottingham puts it, "A parent who leaves his child to burn, on the ground that the building contains someone else whose future contribution to the general welfare promises to be greater, is not a hero; he is (rightly) an object of moral contempt, a moral leper."[5]

The problem may be given a deeper and more general form. What has been said about parents and children may also be said, with appropriate emendations, about our relations with other family members, with friends, and with anyone else whom we love. All these relationships seem to include special obligations as part of their very nature. Friends, husbands, and wives are not just members of the great crowd of humanity. They are all special, at least to those who love them. The problem is that the conception of morality as impartiality seems to conflict with any kind of loving personal relationship. Mo Tzu notwithstanding, it seems to conflict with love itself.[6] I will discuss parents and children, but it should be kept in mind that the deeper issue has to do with personal relationships in general.

The Problem of Luck

The ideal of impartiality says that we may not draw circles around individuals or groups and declare that they are to be treated as "special" when moral decisions are made. This seems plausible when we think of obnoxious doctrines such as racism and anti-Semitism. But surely, we think, such a circle can be drawn around one's own family. If the idea of impartiality says otherwise, then that idea must be rejected. This is the conclusion reached by some philosophers, who believe that although the conception of morality as impartiality may seem plausible when stated abstractly, it is refuted by such counterexamples as parental obligation.[7] Their thought is that we should reject this conception and look for a new, "partialist" theory of morality, one that would acknowledge from the outset that personal relationships can be the source of special obligations.

Rejecting the idea of impartiality has a certain appeal, for it is always exciting to learn that some popular philosophical view is no good and that there is interesting work to be done in formulating an alternative. However, we should not be too quick here. It is no accident that the conception of morality as impartiality has been so widely accepted. It seems to express something deeply important. It explains why racism and sexism are morally odious; and if we abandon this conception, we lose our most natural and persuasive means of combating those doctrines. If for no other reason than this, it seems desirable to retain the notion of impartiality, at least in some form.

But there is another, equally important reason that we should not simply abandon the ideal of impartiality in the face of such counterexamples as parents and children. A counterexample refutes a theory only if there is absolutely no doubt about the validity of the counterexample. If it is possible that the counterexample is flawed, the theory need not be immediately discarded. Before that is done, further investigation may be required. The present case is like this. No matter how powerful it may be, the feeling that our children have a special claim on us is not absolutely beyond doubt. There is at least one reason for doubting that our instincts here are correct. The reason has to do with luck.

The point about luck can be brought out like this: Suppose a parent believes that when faced with a choice between feeding his own children and feeding starving orphans, he should give preference to his own. This is natural enough. But the orphans need the food just as much, and they are no less deserving. It is only their bad luck that they were not born to affluent parents; and why should luck count, from a moral point of view? Why should we think that a moral view is correct if it implies that some children should be fed while others starve, for no better reason than that some were unfortunate in the circumstances of their birth? This seems to be an extremely important matter—important enough, perhaps, that we should take seriously the possibility that a child's being one's own does not have the moral importance that we usually assume it has. At the very least, we should not simply assume that a correct moral theory must incorporate a bias in favor of the lucky.

Thus, while the abandonment of impartialism might be a way of avoiding one problem (about personal relationships), it saddles us with another problem (about luck) that is equally embarrassing. These are twin problems, each as troubling as the other. This is why, even when we are considering our duties toward children, partialism should not be assumed to be superior on its face to impartialism. We should not just assume that one view is correct and the other is incorrect. Instead we should be deeply puzzled about how we might avoid both problems, if that is possible.

Why Should It Matter That a Child is One's Own?

Can we find some way of keeping both ideas—morality as impartiality and special parental obligations? Can we understand them in a way that makes them compatible with one another?

As it turns out, this is not difficult. We can say that impartiality requires us to treat people in the same way *only when there are no relevant differences between them.* This qualification is obviously needed, quite apart from any considerations about parents and children. For example, it is not a failure of impartiality to imprison a convicted criminal while innocent citizens go free, because there is a relevant difference between them (one has committed a crime; the others have not) to which we can appeal to justify the difference in treatment. Other examples come easily to mind. But once we have admitted this qualification, we can make use of it to solve our problem about parental obligations. The fact that a child is one's own can be taken as providing the "relevant difference" that justifies treating it differently.

But we are not free to call just any old difference "relevant." If it were claimed that there is a relevant difference between blacks and whites that justifies treating whites better—the difference being that they are members of different races—we would think this mere bluster and demand to know why *that* difference should count for anything. Similarly, it may be only hand-waving to say that there is a relevant difference between one's own children and others that justifies treating one's own better—the difference being that they are one's own. In the same spirit, we need to ask why that difference matters. Why does it matter that a child is one's own?

It is easy to explain why children in general have a special claim on our attention. They are especially vulnerable to harm because they are not as capable as adults of protecting themselves from danger. They are also relatively helpless to provide for their needs, so they have no choice but to depend on others. Moreover, as has often been remarked, children are *innocent;* because they are too immature to be responsible for their own actions, they will have done others no culpable harm. These facts justify a policy of looking out for children in a way that we do not normally look out for other adults.

But this does not address the question of why one's own children should be regarded as special. One's own children are no different, in vulnerability or innocence, from others. So what makes them special? The idea that our own children have a superior claim to our care may be defended in various ways. The following arguments seem most important.

The Appeal to Intuition

The appeal to intuition is not exactly an argument, but I mention it first because it seems to lurk somewhere in the background of most partialist discussions. It may seem so obvious to untutored common sense that parents should be especially concerned with their own children's welfare that arguing the point may appear pedantic and unnecessary. When common sense is so clear, how can we possibly go against it?

But neither intuitions nor the deliverances of "common sense" are, in general, reliable guides to truth. They may be nothing more than manifestations of social conditioning, prejudice, and self-interest. At one time people's common sense told them that some races are superior to others and that women should be subordinate to men. Many people today are intuitively certain that homosexuals are sinister, devious people. This alone should be enough to discredit appeals to intuition in any morally serious discussion. Still, one might think, the intuition about parents and children is different. It is much more fundamental and seems much more unassailable than the others.

It is, indeed, fundamental, at least in the sense that it springs from a very deep source. Thanks to the theory of kin selection, we now understand why our feelings about our children are so powerful. The theory of kin selection explains the natural concern that parents have for protecting their own as a product of the evolutionary process. Evolution works through natural selection, and the effect of natural selection is to preserve and transmit to future generations genes associated with characteristics that confer advantages in what Darwin called "the struggle for life." Protectiveness toward one's offspring is such a characteristic.

To see how this works, consider two animals—call them Loving Mother and Indifferent Mother—one of whom has genes that dispose her to be protective of her offspring while the other does not. (You may think of them as humans, monkeys, baboons, or even insects. It doesn't matter.) Thus, Loving Mother will try to ensure her offspring's welfare, while Indifferent Mother will have no special concern for her own. The outcome

will be that Loving Mother's offspring will have an advantage over
Indifferent Mother's, for they will have a helper, and so they will have a
better chance of surviving and eventually having offspring themselves. It
follows that Loving Mother's genes are more likely to be represented in
future generations, because the bearers of those genes, her offspring, are
more likely to survive and reproduce. And as the process is repeated, generation after generation, the genes associated with protective behavior
will become widespread throughout the population, while the genes associated with indifference will tend to disappear.

Humans, no less than other animals, are the products of natural selection, and that is why we have such a powerful tendency to favor our own
children's interests over the interests of other children. This explains why
our protective feelings toward them seem so natural and so inescapable.
The feeling that impels us to treat our own children as special is among
the deepest instincts we have, and considering its evolutionary origins,
that is not surprising.

It is tempting to find in this a vindication of partialism. We might say
that, because the instinct to protect our own is built into our very genes,
there is little point in arguing against it. We may as well just accept it and
tailor our moral theories accordingly. But the temptation should be resist-
ed. Explaining the origin of a feeling is not the same as morally justifying
it, and so the moral question remains. Our own children's welfare *does*
matter more, to most of us, than the welfare of other children; but *should*
it matter more, from a moral point of view? Even if there were no possibility of changing human behavior, the latter question would still have
some interest. Some sociobiologists have also argued that male domi-
nance is built into our genes.[8] Even if this were true, it would not follow
that it is a good thing. From a moral point of view, learning this might be
like learning that people are inescapably vulnerable to a certain disease:
we can't change the fact of the disease, but we can regret it and do what
we can to make life as bearable as possible for its victims.

The Argument from Social Roles

But partialists have more to go on than mere intuitions. There are a
number of plausible arguments that may be invoked in defense of their
view. The first line of reasoning begins with some observations about
social roles. It is not possible for an isolated individual to have anything
resembling a normal human life. For that, a social setting is required. The
social setting provides roles for us to fill—thus, in the context of society,
we are able to be citizens, friends, husbands and wives, hospital patients,

construction workers, scientists, teachers, customers, sports fans, and all the rest. None of us (with rare heroic exceptions) creates the roles he plays. They have evolved over generations of human life, and we encounter them simply as given, as the raw materials out of which we may fashion our individual lives.

These roles define, in large measure, our relations with other people. They specify how we should behave toward others. A teacher must wisely guide his students, a friend must be loyal, a husband should be faithful, and so on. To the extent that you fail in these respects, you will be an inferior teacher, a bad friend, and a poor husband. You can avoid these obligations by declining to enter into these roles: not everyone will be a teacher, not everyone will marry, and some unfortunate people will not even have friends. But you can hardly avoid all social roles, and you cannot fill a social role without at the same time acknowledging the special responsibilities that go with it.

Parenthood is a social role, and like other such roles, it includes special duties as part of its very nature. You can choose not to have children, or having had a child, you may give it up for adoption. But if you are a parent, you are stuck with the responsibilities that go with the role. A parent who doesn't see to his children's needs is a bad parent, just as a disloyal friend is a bad friend and an unfaithful husband is a poor husband. And that is why (according to this argument) we have obligations to our own children that we do not have to other children.

The Argument from Social Roles is plausible, but how far should we be persuaded by it? The argument has several weaknesses.

First, we need to distinguish two claims: that a mother's obligations to her own children *have a different basis* from her obligations to other children; and that a mother's obligations to her own children *are stronger than* (take precedence over) her obligations to other children. If successful, the Argument from Social Roles would show only that our obligations to our own children are based on different considerations than are our obligations to other children. (We have a social relationship with our own children that is the basis of our obligation to them, while our obligations to other children are based on a general duty of beneficence.) But the argument would not show that the former obligations are stronger or that they take precedence over the latter—and that is what we were tying to demonstrate.

The second point is related to the first. The Argument from Social Roles trades on the notion of what it means to be a "bad father" or a "bad mother." Now suppose we admit that a man who ignores the needs of his own children is a bad father. It may also be observed that a man who ignores the cries of orphans, when he could help, is a bad man—a man lacking a proper regard for the needs of others. While it is undesirable to be a bad father (or mother), it is also undesirable to be a bad man (or woman). So, once again, the Argument from Social Roles does nothing to show that our obligations to other children are weaker.

Third, there is the point about luck. The system of social roles acknowledged in our society makes special provision for children lucky enough to live in homes with parents. This system favors even more those lucky enough to have affluent parents who can provide more for them than less affluent parents are able to provide. So even while granting that social roles involve special obligations, we can still ask: is this a morally decent system? The system itself can be an object of criticism.

We do not have to look far to find an obvious objection to the system. The system does well enough in providing for some children, but it does miserably where others are concerned. There is no social role comparable to the parent-child relationship that targets the interests of orphans or the interests of children whose parents are unable (or unwilling) to provide for them. Thus this system may be found wanting because luck plays an unacceptably important part in it.

Fourth, and finally, students of social history might find the Argument from Social Roles to be more than a little naïve. The argument draws much of its strength from the fact that contemporary American and European ideals favor families bound together by love. Anyone who is likely to read these words will have been influenced by that ideal—consider how the reader will have passed over the fourth paragraph of this essay, with its easy talk of parents loving and protecting their children, without a pause. Yet the cozy nuclear family, nourished by affectionate relationships, is a relatively recent development. The norm throughout most of Western history has been very different.

In *The Family, Sex, and Marriage in England, 1500–1800,* Lawrence Stone points out that as recently as the seventeenth century affectionate relations between husbands and wives were so rare as to be virtually nonexistent and certainly were not expected within "normal" marriages. Among the upper classes, husbands and wives occupied separate stations within large households and rarely saw one another in private. Children were sent away immediately after birth to be looked after by wet nurses for twelve to eighteen months; then, returning home, they were raised largely by nurses, governesses, and tutors. Finally they were sent away to boarding school when they were between seven and thirteen, with ten the most common age.[9] The children of the poor were, of course, worse off. They left home at an equally early age, often to work in the houses of the rich. Stone writes:

About all that can be said with confidence on the matter of emotional relations within the sixteenth- and early seventeenth-century family at all social levels is that there was a general psychological atmosphere of distance, manipulation, and deference. . . . Family relationships were characterized by interchangeability, so that substitution of another wife or another child was easy. . . . It was a structure held together not by affective bonds but by mutual economic interests.[10]

And what of parental duties? Of course there has always been a recognition of some special parental duties, but in earlier times these were much more restricted and were not associated with bonds of affection. Until sometime in the eighteenth century, it seems, the emphasis in European morals was almost entirely on the duties owed by children to parents, rather than the other way around. Children were commonly said to owe their parents absolute obedience, in gratitude for having been given life. The French historian Jean Flandrin notes that "in Brittany the son remained subject to the authority of his father until the age of sixty, but marriage contracted with the father's consent emancipated him."[11] Pity the man whose father lived to a ripe old age and refused consent for marriage—his only emancipation would be to flee. Both Stone and Flandrin make it clear that while parental *rights* is an old idea, the idea of extensive parental *obligations* is a notion of much more recent vintage. (The debate between Mo Tzu and the Confucianists was also conducted in such terms; for them, the primary issue was whether children had special duties to their fathers, not the other way around.)

These observations about social history should be approached with caution. Of course they do not refute the idea of special parental obligations. However, they do go some way toward undermining our easy confidence that present-day social arrangements only institutionalize our natural duties. That is the only moral to be drawn from them, but it is an important one. In this area, as in so many others, what forms of social life seem "natural" depends on the conventions of one's society.

The Argument from Proximity

A second argument in support of special parental obligations goes like this. It is reasonable to accept a social arrangement in which parents are assigned special responsibility for their own children because parents are *better situated* to look after their own. Granted, all children need help and protection. But other children are remote, and their needs are less clear, while a parent's own children live in the same house and the parent is (or ought to be) intimately familiar with their needs. Other things being

equal, it makes sense to think that A has a greater responsibility for helping B than for helping C if A is better situated to help B. This is true in the
case of helping one's own children versus helping other children; therefore, one's obligation in the first instance is greater.

This argument is plausible if we concentrate on certain kinds of aid.
Children wake up sick in the middle of the night; someone must attend to
them, and that "someone" is usually Mother or Father. The parents are in
a position to do so, and (most of the time) no one else is. The complaint
"You nursed those children, but you didn't help the other children who
woke up sick elsewhere in the world" is obviously misguided. The same
goes for countless other ways that parents assist their children, by making
them take their medicine, by stopping them from playing in the roadway,
by bundling them up against the cold, and so on. These are all matters of
what we might call *day-to-day care*.

Day-to-day care involves a kind of personal attention that a parent
could not provide for many others because it would be physically impossible. The importance of proximity is that it makes these kinds of caring
behaviors possible; the impossibility of doing the same for other children
is just the impossibility of being in two places at once. So, if there is partiality here, it is a partiality that we need not worry about, because it cannot be avoided.

This type of argument is less plausible, however, when we consider
more general, fundamental needs, such as food. Is a parent in a better
position to feed his own children than to provide for others? At one time
this might have been the case. Before the advent of modern communica-
tions and transportation, and before the creation of efficient relief agencies, people might have been able to say that while they could feed their
own, they were unable to do much about the plight of children elsewhere.
But that is no longer true. Today, with relief agencies ready to take our
assistance all over the world, needing only sufficient resources to do so, it
is almost as easy to provide food for a child in Africa as to provide for
one's own. The same goes for providing basic medical care: international
relief agencies carry medical assistance around the world on the same
basis.

Therefore, the Argument from Proximity is, at best, only partly successful. Some forms of assistance do require proximity (getting up in the
middle of the night to attend sick children) but others do not (providing
food). The argument might show that where day-to-day care is concerned, parents have special duties. But the same cannot be said for the
provision of other fundamental needs.

The Argument from Personal Goods

A third argument hinges on the idea that loving relationships are personal goods of great importance. To love other people, and be loved in return, is part of what is involved in having a rich and satisfying human life. A loving relationship with one's children is, for many parents, a source of such happiness that they would sacrifice almost anything else to preserve it. But as we have already observed, love necessarily involves having a special concern for the well-being of the loved one, and so it is not impartial. An ethic that required absolute impartiality would, therefore, require forgoing a great personal good.

The intuitive idea behind this argument may seem plain enough. Nevertheless, it is difficult to formulate the argument with any precision. Why, exactly, is a loving relationship with another person such a great good? Part of the answer may be that we all fare better if there are others around willing to help us when we need it. If A and B have a loving relationship, then A can count on B's assistance, and vice versa, so they are both better off. Of course, pacts of mutual assistance could be made between people who are not joined by bonds of affection, but affection makes the arrangement more dependable. People who love one another are more apt to remain faithful when the going is hard.

But this is not the whole story. Bonds of affection are more than just instrumentally good. To be loved is to have one's own value affirmed; thus it is a source of self-esteem. This is important for all of us, but especially for children, who are more helpless and vulnerable than adults. Moreover, there is, at a deep level, a connection between love and the meaning of life (another murky but undoubtedly important notion). We question whether our lives have meaning when no one values us and we ourselves find nothing worth valuing, when it seems to us that "all is vanity." Loving relationships provide individuals with things to value and with a sense of being valued, and so their lives are given this kind of meaning.

These are important points, but they do not prove as much as they are sometimes taken to prove. In the first place, there is a lot about parental love that is consistent with a large measure of impartiality. Loving someone is not only a matter of preferring their interests. Love involves, among other things, intimacy and the sharing of experiences. A parent shows his love by listening to the child's jokes, by talking, by being a considerate companion, by praising, and even by scolding when that is needed. Of course these kinds of behaviors also show partiality, since the parent does not do these things for all children. But these are only further instances of day-to-day interactions that require proximity; again, if this is partiality, it is partiality that cannot be avoided. And there is another difference between these kinds of support and such things as providing food, medical care, and so forth. The companionship, the listening, the talking, the praising and scolding are what make personal relationships personal. That is why the psychic benefits that accompany such relationships are more closely associated with the companionship, the listening, and so on, than with such relatively impersonal things as providing food.

Finally, it is not necessary, in order to have a loving relationship with one's children and to derive from it the benefits that the Argument from Personal Goods envisions, to regard their interests as always having priority, especially when the interests in question are not comparable. One could have a loving relationship that involves all the intimacies of day-to-day care and the provision of life's necessities while acknowledging, at the same time, that when it comes to choosing between luxuries for these children and food for orphans, the orphans' needs should prevail. At the very least, there is nothing in the Argument from Personal Goods that rules out such an approach.

The Argument from the Need to Be Treated as Special

Our discussion has brought us to a promising juncture. In examining the preceding arguments, we have seen that, even from an impartial point of view, something very close to the "normal" way that parents relate to children might be justified. We can approve of parents' living with their children, providing day-to-day care, sharing intimate moments and pleasures, and loving them, all without making the assumption that the child's being their own confers on it any special moral status. So it is beginning to appear that the gap between prevailing social values and the requirements of impartiality is not so great as we first supposed.

However, in a challenging essay James Lindeman Nelson has argued that this is only an illusion. The kind of relationship between parents and children that could be justified from an impartialist perspective, he says, would involve only a sort of counterfeit parental love, not the real thing. The "demand that we especially prize the interests of our children" is not satisfied by "the happenstance of day-to-day care"; to think it is "misses the seriousness of parental regard."[12] Moreover, he urges, the kind of watered-down love that an impartialist perspective would permit could not be sufficiently constant to provide for children's emotional needs, for *children need to be regarded as special* in just the way that the impartialist view forbids. Following his discussion of a case in which a father has donated an organ to save his child's life, Nelson writes:

> But we have needs other than for organs, and a chief point of the ethical enterprise is to respond to them. The mainstream model [that is, the impartialist model] is in principle unable to respond to one of these needs: the need for partiality itself, which might also be called the need for intimacy, or for love. Young children in particular, but people in general, it seems, have a need to be special, to be singled out, to be more to someone than simply one end-in-herself among others. Institutions of intimacy, such as various types of friendship, marriage, and family, are among the ways we have of responding to this need, and their ubiquity in our lives testifies to the importance of the need they serve.
>
> But the response has to be real, which is why no attitude fully compatible with mainstream impartialism will meet the case. The need for partiality can't be met by a commitment to the loved one's interests that is so weak it always gives way whenever it conflicts with impartial moral considerations. Nor need it be so strong that it always trumps those considerations. But at least "at the margin"—in situations where the verdict of impartial regard pulls at least slightly in a different direction than does the impulse of parental affection—if a parent doesn't respond to her children's needs preferentially, any claim she might make to love her children seems otiose.[13]

There is a lot here that seems correct, and if it is correct, it is important—these are matters that no adequate moral theory can ignore. So let us assume that what Nelson says about the need of children to be regarded as special is true: that children (and even perhaps adults) cannot flourish unless they see themselves "singled out" by some others as objects of special care. And let us further assume that this sense of being singled out requires that their interests be given preference "at the margin." Can we acknowledge this need, and permit its satisfaction, within an impartialist framework? Maybe we can.

Impartiality requires that, absent relevant differences, people be treated alike. There are, generally speaking, no relevant differences between children in these respects; all children need to be regarded as special in the way Nelson describes. Why should we not say, then, that from the impartial point of view, social life should be arranged so that this need, which all children have, is provided equally to all? How could this be done? As Nelson observes, we already have social institutions that do precisely this for most people: "Institutions of intimacy, such as various types of friendship, marriage, and family, are among the ways we have of responding to this need." If such institutions do the job so well, then a moral approach that emphasized impartial concern for the needs of all children would not require that those institutions be abolished. On the contrary, it would want the benefits of such institutions be made available to all children and not just the lucky ones. And to the extent that these benefits are not in fact available to all children, the impartialist view would say that things are not as they should be.

It may be objected that in adopting such an approach, we would really be abandoning the impartialist perspective—we would, after all, be countenancing in individual parents attitudes and styles of decision making that are contrary to what impartiality would require. But a moral theory may legitimately distinguish between (a) the reasons for action internal to institutional practices, together with the associated attitudes and motivations of people operating within the framework of the institution; and (b) the justification of the institution itself. It may seem paradoxical but it is nevertheless true that sometimes the larger purpose served by an institution can be advanced by encouraging those acting within it to adopt attitudes and styles of decision making that seem opposed to that purpose. Thus a moral theory concerned with the equal satisfaction of everyone's needs could regard the institutions of the family and friendship as desirable because there are human needs that cannot be satisfied apart from such institutions, while at the same time recognizing that people functioning within those institutions will not themselves be concerned at all with the "equal satisfaction of needs."

When the matter is viewed from this perspective, then, it turns out that the partialist and the impartialist are not necessarily making conflicting claims. The partialist point concerns the nature of the attitudes and motivations of people occupying particular roles within social institutions. The impartialist point concerns the justification of those institutions as a whole. Therefore each may, in its own way, be correct. But if this is how the matter should be viewed, it is more a victory for impartialism, because it is the impartialist principles that turn out to be more fundamental.

There is one other respect in which impartialism emerges as the better overall view. As was noted, the impartialist must regard the total social system as morally lacking if *all* children, not just the lucky ones, are not provided the benefits of such institutions. This follows straightaway from the impartialist perspective. But could the partialist also insist on this? On what grounds? Unsupplemented partialism is the view that one may— indeed should—regard the interests of one's own children as fundamentally more important. If one's own children's needs are met, therefore, the most important thing is accomplished, and while one might have some degree of regret if the needs of other children are not also met, it seems that this would have to be a secondary, less important matter. Our discussion began when we noticed that partialists accuse impartialism of having wildly implausible implications about parental regard. But now it seems to be the implications of partialism, with its lack of sufficient regard for all children, that are implausible.

The Moral Point of Utopian Thinking

We began with a problem—the apparent incompatibility of special parental obligations with the ideal of impartiality—and we have now found a possible solution. This solution rejects the idea that the interests of any child, including one's own, are more important than any other child's interests. But it nevertheless regards the social institution of the family, within which people are deeply partial, as morally justifiable, on the grounds not only that it is an effective way of providing for the rearing of children but also because this institution and its associated practices meet deep human needs that otherwise could not be satisfied. The remaining point, on which the impartialist would insist, is that the social system is morally deficient if the benefits of such institutions are not available to all.

This insistence is apt to seem inescapably utopian, for in the real world it is hardly attainable. But utopian thinking has its point, especially in moral philosophy. Thinking about what things would be like in a better world is a useful way of identifying the values that are worth espousing. In this sort of imaginative exercise, it is not necessary to pretend that conditions are perfect. But it is necessary to imagine that human beings are better, that they behave in a more responsible and humane manner. In such a world, would partialist or impartialist values prevail? What would relations between adults and children be like in Utopia?

Here is one plausible picture of such a world. In it, children with living parents able to provide for them would be raised by their parents, who would give them all the love and care they need. Parents who through no fault of their own were unable to provide for their children would be given whatever assistance they need. Orphans would be taken in by families who would raise and love them as their own, and the burdens involved in such adoptions would be willingly shared by all.

It is fair to say that, in this sort of world, the ideal of impartiality is realized. In this world people do not act as if any child is more important than any other. One way or another, equal provision is made for the needs of all. Moreover, luck plays no part in how children will fare. The orphan's needs are satisfied too. When it is said by the Mohists that "love is universal" or by their modern counterparts the utilitarians that we should "promote the interests of everyone alike," this might be the point: in the morally best world, no one's interests would be given priority over anyone else's.

The idea of special obligations nevertheless has a limited place even in Utopia. In the world I have sketched, some special obligations are acknowledged, because particular adults (most often parents) are assigned special responsibility for looking after particular children. However, the reason for this arrangement is consistent with the idea of impartiality and inconsistent with the thought that one's own children somehow merit more. The reason is that this is the best way to see that the needs of all children are satisfied. Moreover, the recognition of some special obligations might be welcomed, even in Utopia; it need not be merely something that is grudgingly admitted. The arguments we have already considered suggest that there are special benefits to be derived from a social system in which particular adults are assigned responsibility for particular children—the benefits that go with loving personal relationships. This gives us reason to think that such an assignment would be part of the best social system—a system that would, at the same time, make adequate provision for all.

Of course we do not live in Utopia, and it might be objected that in the real world we inhabit, it would be silly or disastrous to start telling parents to stop favoring their own children—silly, because no one would listen, or disastrous, because if some did, their children would suffer greatly. (There might be a coordination problem: it might not be wise for some to adopt the "best" policy unless all do.) So what is the point of thinking about Utopia? A picture of Utopia gives us an idea, not only of what we should strive for, but of what is (in one sense) objectively right and wrong. Conditions may exist in our own world that make it wrong to act as though we lived in Utopia. But that is only because in our world human behavior is flawed. It may nevertheless be true that, in a deep sense, utopian behavior is morally best.

Let me try to make this suggestion clearer by considering a different sort of example. It has been argued by many thinkers that there is nothing immoral in mercy killing when it is requested by a dying person as a humane alternative to a slow, painful death. Others have objected that if mercy killing were permitted it would lead to further killings that we would not want—we might begin by killing people at their own request to put them out of misery, but then we would begin to pressure sick people into making such requests, and that would lead to killing old people who have not requested it, and then we would go on to killing the feeble-minded, and so on. I do not believe these things would happen.[14] But suppose they would. What would follow? It would not follow that mercy killing is immoral in the original case. The objection would show, paradoxically, that there are good reasons why we should not perform actions that are moral and humane. Those reasons would have to do with the imperfections of human beings—the claim is that people are so flawed that they would slide down the slippery slope from the (moral) practice of euthanasia to the additional (immoral) practices described.

This suggests that moral philosophy might be idealistic in a way that "applied ethics" is not. Moral philosophy describes the ideals that motivate perfect conduct, the conduct of people in Utopia.[15] In Utopia, as Thomas More observed in his book of that name, euthanasia would be accepted[16] and the slippery-slope argument would be irrelevant, because people in Utopia do not abuse humane practices. Applied ethics, however, takes into account the messy details of the real world, including the prejudices, faults, and vices of real human beings, and recommends how we should behave considering all that as well as the ideals of perfect conduct.

What does this mean for the question of special parental obligations? It means that there is a point to the philosophical insistence that "all children are equal," even if in the real world it would be unwise to urge particular parents to stop providing preferential care for their own. The practical question is, therefore, how nearly we can expect to approach the ideal system in the real world and what specific recommendations should be made, in light of this, to real parents.

Practical Implications

How should parents, living not in Utopia but in our society, who are concerned to do what is morally best, conceive of the relation between their obligations to their own children and their obligations to other children? We may begin by setting out three contrasting views. All are implausible, but for different reasons.

Extreme Bias. On this view, parents have obligations to provide for their own children but have no obligations at all to other children. Anything done for other children is, at best, supererogatory—good and praiseworthy if one chooses to do it, but in no way morally mandatory. On this view, parents may choose to provide not only necessities but also luxuries for their own children while other children starve, and yet be immune from moral criticism.

Extreme Bias is not plausible, because it makes no provision whatever for a duty of general beneficence. It is impossible to believe that we do not have some obligation to be concerned with the plight of the starving, whoever they are, even if that obligation is much less extensive than our obligations to our own kin. Thus it will not be surprising if this view turns out to be unacceptable.

Complete Equality. The opposite view is assumed by its opponents to be implied by the idea of morality as impartiality—the view that there is no difference at all between one's moral obligations toward one's own children and one's moral obligations toward other children. This view denies that there are any good moral grounds for preferring to feed one's own child rather than an orphan in a foreign country. In our society anyone who accepted and acted on such a view would seem to his neighbors to be morally deranged, for doing so would seem to involve a rejection of one's children—a refusal to treat them with the love that is appropriate to the parent-child relationship.

The Most Common View. What, in fact, do people in our society seem to believe? Most people seem to believe that one has an obligation to provide the necessities of life for other children only after one has already provided a great range of luxuries for one's own. On this view, it is permissible to provide one's own children with virtually everything they need in order to have a good start in life—not only food and clothing but, if possible, a good education, opportunities for travel, opportunities for enjoyable leisure, and so on. In the United States the children of affluent parents have TV sets, stereos, and computers all laid out in their own rooms. They drive their own cars to high school. Few people seem to think there is anything wrong with this. Parents who are unable to provide their children with such luxuries nevertheless aspire to do so.

The Most Common View imposes some duty regarding other children, but not much. In practical terms, it imposes a duty only on the rich who have resources left over even after they have provided ample luxuries for their own offspring. The rest of us, who have nothing left after doing as much as we can for our own, are off the hook. But it requires only a little refection to see that this view is also implausible. How can it be right to spend money on luxuries for some children, even one's own (buying them the latest trendy toys, for example), while others do not have enough to eat? Perhaps, when confronted with this, many people might come to doubt whether the Most Common View is correct. But certainly most affluent people act as if it were correct.

Is there a better alternative? Is there a view that escapes the difficulties of Extreme Bias, Complete Equality, and the Most Common View and that is consistent with the other points that have been made in our discussion? I suggest the following.

Partial Bias. We might say that while we do have a substantial obligation to be concerned about the welfare of all children, our own nevertheless come first. This vague thought needs to be sharpened. One way of making it more precise is this. When considering similar needs, you may permissibly prefer—perhaps you even ought—to provide for the needs of your own sons and daughters. For example, if you were faced with a choice between feeding your own children and contributing the money to provide food for other children, you could rightly choose to feed your own. You may even prefer the interests of your own children "at the margin," as Nelson puts it, when the choice is between some benefit for your own child and a slightly greater benefit for some other child. But if the choice is between some relatively trivial thing for one's own and necessities for other children, preference should be given to helping the others. Thus if the choice is between providing trendy toys for your own (already well-fed) children and feeding the starving, you should feed the starving.

This view will turn out to be more or less demanding, depending on what one counts as a "relatively trivial thing." We might agree that it is indefensible to buy trendy toys for some children (even for one's own) while other children starve. But what about buying them nice clothes? Or college educations? Are we justified in sending our children to expensive colleges? Clearly, the line between the trivial and the important can be drawn at different places. Nevertheless, the intuitive idea is plain enough. On this view, a parent may provide the necessities for his own children first, but he is not justified in providing them luxuries while other children still lack the necessities. Even in a fairly weak form, this view would require much greater concern for others than the view that is most common in our society.

From the point of view of the various arguments we have considered, Partial Bias stands out as the superior view. It is closer to the utopian ideal than either Extreme Bias or the Most Common View; it is morally superior in that it makes greater provision for children who have no loving parents; it is consistent with the arguments we have considered concerning the benefits to be derived from loving relationships; and it is perhaps as much as we can expect from people in the real world.

What would the adoption of Partial Bias mean for actual families? It would mean that parents could continue to provide loving, day-to-day care for their own children, with all that this involves, while giving them preferential treatment in the provision of life's necessities. But it would also mean preferring to provide the necessities for needier children rather than luxuries for their own. Children in such families would be worse off, in an obvious sense, than the children of affluent parents who continued to live according to the dictates of Extreme Bias or the Most Common View. However, we might hope that they would not regard themselves as "deprived," for they might learn the moral value of giving up luxuries so that other children do not starve. They might even come to see their parents as morally admirable people. That hope is itself utopian enough.

Notes

1. Fung Yu-lan, *A Short History of Chinese Philosophy* (New York: Macmillan, 1960), 92

2 Vitaly A. Rubin, *Individual and State in Ancient China* (New York: Columbia University Press, 1976), 36.

3. Mill's formulation was less memorable but no less emphatic: he urged that, when weighing the interests of different people, we should be "as strictly impartial as a disinterested and benevolent spectator." John Stuart Mill, *Utilitarianism* (Indianapolis: Bobbs-Merrill, 1957), 22. Originally published in 1861.

4. In a valuable discussion, R. M. Hare argues that virtually all the major moral theories incorporate a requirement of impartiality and adds that his own "universal prescriptivism" is no exception. R. M. Hare, "Rules of War and Moral Reasoning," *Philosophy and Public Affairs* 1 (1972): 167–71.

5. John Cottingham, "Partialism, Favouritism, and Morality," *Philosophical Quarterly* 36 (1986): 357.

6. The point is a familiar one that pops up in all sorts of surprising contexts. For example, in *On the Plurality of Worlds* David Lewis discusses an ethical objection to his thesis that all possible worlds are equally real, a thesis he calls "modal realism." The objection is that, if modal realism is true, our actions will have no effect whatever on the total amount of good or evil that exists. (If we prevented an evil from occurring in this world, it would still exist in some other world. As Lewis puts it, "The sum total of good throughout the plurality of worlds is non-contingently fixed and depends not at all on what we do.") Thus we might as well forget about trying to maximize the good. Lewis comments, "But if modal realism subverts only a 'truly universalistic ethics', I cannot see that as a damaging objection. What collapses is a philosophers' invention, no less remote from common sense than modal realism itself. An ethics of our own world is quite universalistic enough. Indeed, I dare say that it is already far too universalistic; it is a betrayal of our particular affections." David Lewis, *On the Plurality of Worlds* (Oxford: Basil Blackwell, 1986), 128.

7. See, for example, Cottingham, "Partialism, Favouritism, and Morality"; and James Lindeman Nelson, "Partialism and Parenthood," *Journal of Social Philosophy* 21 (1990): 107–18.

8. See, among others, E. O. Wilson, *Sociobiology: The New Synthesis* (Cambridge: Belnap Press of Harvard University, 1975), 553.

9. Lawrence Stone, *The Family, Sex, and Marriage in England, 1500–1800* (New York: Harper & Row, 1979), 83–84.

10. Stone, *Family, Sex, and Marriage*, 88.

11. Jean Flandrin, *Families in Former Times*, trans. Richard Southern (Cambridge: Cambridge University Press, 1979), 130.

12. Nelson, "Partialism and Parenthood," 114.

13. Nelson, "Partialism and Parenthood," 114. Nelson cites Ira Gordon's *Human Development: A Transactional Analysis* (New York: Harper & Row, 1975) in support of this assessment. Gordon writes: "The child begins to develop his sense of competence, his sense of self-worth, from the way he is treated and evaluated by other members of his family. We have seen that it is not techniques alone that convey to him the attitudes and beliefs his parents hold about him. The presence of love and his perception of being loved is important."

14. For a discussion see James Rachels, *The End of Life* (Oxford: Oxford University Press, 1986), chap. 10.

15. On this point I am following Richard Brandt, although he does not put it in just this way. Brandt writes: "What I mean by 'is objectively wrong' or 'is morally unjustified' is 'would be prohibited by the set of moral rules which a rational person would prefer to have current or subscribed to in the consciences of persons in the society in which he expected to live a whole life, as compared with any other set of moral rules or none at all.'" "The Morality and Rationality of Suicide," in *Moral Problems*, ed. James Rachels, 2d ed. (New York: Harper & Row, 1975), 367. Clearly, this would be a set of rules appropriate for Utopia, where it is assumed that people will actually live according to the rules. In the real world, we can make no such assumption, and sometimes this will mean that we should do things that, according to this definition, would be objectively wrong.

16. Thomas More, *Utopia*, trans. Paul Turner (Harmondsworth, England: Penguin Books, 1965), 102. Originally published in 1516.

15

When Philosophers Shoot from the Hip

These days moral philosophers often find themselves in the heady position of being called upon by newspapers to comment on the latest public controversies. Being treated as quotable experts by the media may be old stuff for economists and a few other academic types, but it is a new experience for philosophers, a visible result of the applied ethics movement that began twenty years ago. Sometimes the newspapers want columns of commentary. The op-ed page, pioneered by the *New York Times*, has now become a regular feature of most large metropolitan dailies. Op-ed columns aren't much like articles in *Bioethics*, but for the general public they are a good substitute. They allow enough space, and writing them allows one enough time, for serious reflection.

Sometimes, however, the newspapers want something different. The telephone rings, and a reporter rattles off a few "facts" about something somebody is supposed to have done. Ethical issues are involved—something alarming is said to have taken place—and so the "ethicist" is asked for a comment to be included in the next day's story, which may be the first report the public will have seen about the events in question.

When this happens, the reporters usually aren't interested in detailed analysis or lengthy qualifications—a short, pithy quote is what's wanted. Nor are the reporters eager to hear reassurances that the alarming events really aren't alarming. That doesn't make good copy. What makes good copy is the idea that a new development is morally troubling, or worse. And frequently philosophers are available to provide just such comments. The story then appears, with a pronounced moral slant: "Such-and-such has happened, and the ethicists say it's bad." More often than not, this combination of reporters' interests and philosophers' snap judgments has a conservative effect. The new developments are viewed as troubling against the background, not of careful analysis, but of accepted wisdom.

In March 1990 a story appeared in the newspapers about a Los Angeles couple who had decided to have another child in the hope that the baby's bone marrow cells could be used to save the life of their teenaged daughter. Abe and Mary Ayala, who are in their forties, had not intended to have an additional child; in fact, Abe Ayala had had a vasectomy. But their seventeen-year-old daughter, Anissa, was dying of leukemia, and a bone marrow transplant was her only hope. After two years of searching in vain for a suitable donor, they decided to have another child because there was a one-in-four chance that the new family member would be a "match." So Abe Ayala had his vasectomy reversed and Mary Ayala became pregnant. The baby, a girl named Marissa, was born on 6 April, and she is indeed a compatible donor. The transplant procedure, which will be performed sometime in the fall, will involve little risk for the baby, and Anissa's chances of surviving will rise from zero to between 70 and 80 percent.

The Ayalas were understandably elated to learn that Anissa's life might be saved. However, the newspaper stories prominently featured quotations from medical ethicists who labeled their decision "troublesome" and even "outrageous." "The ideal reason for having a child," said a well-known figure in the field, "is associated with that child's own welfare—to bring a child into being and to nurture it. One of the fundamental precepts of ethics is that each person is an end in himself or herself, and is never to be used solely as a means to another person's ends without the agreement of the person being used." The Ayalas' baby "is not seen as an end in itself, but as a means to another end. The fact that the other end is laudable doesn't change that." Another expert was quoted as saying that the Ayalas' decision means "we're willing to treat people like objects"—and, he added, "I don't think we ought to do that."[1]

The Ayalas are real people, not characters in a made-up classroom example, and they didn't much care for the ethicists' comments. Mrs. Ayala said that the ethicists ought to be worrying more about the shortage of marrow donors and less about their decision. Anissa herself was asked what she thought about all this, and she said that she was "sort of troubled" by the criticism but added, "We're going to love our baby."

If Anissa were trained in philosophy, she might find the criticisms less troubling. She might observe that people have always had babies for all sorts of reasons other than the "ideal" one. Real life rarely lives up to philosophers' expectations. People have children so that the children can share in the family's work, to please the grandparents, or just because it's expected of them. They sometimes have second children because they don't want the first to be an "only child." None of this is strange or unusual; it's just the way life is. What is important is, as Anissa insists, that once born, the children are loved and nurtured within good families. Anissa might also point out that her mother, in fact, had wanted another baby anyway—it was only her father's wish to have no more children. And finally, she might express some appropriate skepticism about the idea that an individual "is never to be used solely as a means to another person's end without the agreement of the person being used." Does this mean that, if Anissa already had a baby sister, the baby could not be used as a donor because the baby was not old enough to give permission? Should Anissa herself be left to die for the sake of respecting this principle? Perhaps the ethicist quoted in the *New York Times* thinks so; he was quoted as saying, "It's outrageous that people would go to this length."

Curiously, there is an argument, proceeding from principles endorsed by the most conservative pro-life advocates, that supports the Ayalas' decision. This argument invokes the idea that we are conferring a benefit on someone by bringing them into existence. The new baby, not Anissa, seems the really big winner here: after all, if her parents had not decided to have her, the baby would not have gotten to exist. Those who oppose abortion sometimes ask: Aren't you glad your mother didn't have an abortion? The answer, of course, is that most of us are happy that our mothers didn't do that; otherwise we wouldn't be here now. The people who ask this question think that something follows about the morality of abortion, although it isn't clear what, but they usually fail to notice that we could just as well ask: Aren't you glad that your parents didn't practice birth control? (Orthodox Catholics, at least, are consistent on this point.) We should be equally happy that contraceptives were not used by our parents, and for the same reason: otherwise, we wouldn't be here now. Similarly, Anissa's little sister might someday be asked: Aren't you glad that your parents decided to have you? Aren't you fortunate that Anissa needed those stem cells? Perhaps this means that conservatives who take a pro-life view ought to be happy with the Ayalas' decision rather than critical of it.

It might be doubted, however, that this is a sound argument. The idea that we are conferring a benefit on someone by bringing him into existence is easily disputed. A different sort of reasoning might be more effective. First we may consider two separate questions:

1. Suppose a couple, before having any children, is trying to decide whether to have one child or two. They slightly prefer having only one. But they are told that if they have only one child, it will die when it is a teenager. However, if they have two, both will probably live full lives. Would it be wrong for the couple to decide, for this reason, to have two children?

2. Suppose a couple already has two children, one a teenager dying of leukemia and the other an infant who is the only available bone-marrow donor. The infant cannot give its permission, of course, but then again it would not be harmed by the procedure. Would it be wrong, under these circumstances, to use some of the infant's stem cells to save the teenager's life?

It would be easy enough to argue that the answer to both these questions is no. Then the inference to the permissibility of the Ayalas' decision would be obvious.

But this is a peripheral point. Our subject here is the performance of philosophers—"ethicists"—as commentators on public events. Sometimes they do what we might think philosophers ought to do: challenge the prevailing orthodoxy, calling into question the assumptions that people unthinkingly make. But just as often they function as orthodoxy's most sophisticated defenders, assuming that the existing social consensus must be right and articulating its theoretical "justification." And when all else fails, there is a familiar argument that can be relied upon: the slippery slope. Any departure from business as usual can be pronounced "troubling" because of what it might lead to. The Ayalas' decision was also criticized on this ground. It was said that it might lead to "fetus farming" or to abortions so that the aborted fetus can be used for lifesaving purposes.

Of course we don't know exactly what will happen to the Ayala family, or to social values, in consequence of decisions such as theirs. But two comments seem relevant. First, there is nothing new about their sort of decision. In the publicity surrounding the Ayala case, it was revealed that other families had been making similar decisions for quite some time. Dr. Robertson Parkman, head of the division of research immunology and marrow transplantation at Los Angeles Children's Hospital, told a reporter that he personally knows of cases going back to 1974 in which families have had additional children to obtain marrow transplants. But until now there has been little publicity about it. The new publicity also revealed that, in earlier cases, medical ethicists have been able to do much more than complain about such decisions after the fact. In 1986 a California woman, Phyliss Baker, who had had a tubal ligation, asked a physician to reconnect her Fallopian tubes so that she could have another child. The physician, knowing that Mrs. Baker was trying to save the life of her three-year-old son, who needed a marrow transplant, consulted a bioethicist and then refused to do the operation. The physician's and the bioethicist's moral scruples were preserved, and Travis, the three-year-old, died.[2]

Second, the recent history of medical ethics is dotted with episodes in which ethicists have reacted with alarm to new developments, predicting dire consequences that never occurred. In *Classic Cases in Medical Ethics,* Gregory E. Pence recounts several such episodes.[3] A review of these cases suggests caution, lest our quick-and-easy comments today look silly tomorrow. In 1978, for example, Louise Brown was the first baby to be born as a result of in vitro fertilization. This important event prompted alarmed and highly critical responses from physicians, theologians, and philosophers that are embarrassing to look back upon today. Pence reminds us of a whole series of exaggerated statements and predictions: terrible consequences were sure to follow for the parents, the child, and society. But today Louise is a normal, happy, rambunctious child, and so are many others like her.

What will happen to the Ayalas? One plausible scenario is that Anissa will be saved, the new baby will grow up happy—or at least with the same mixture of happiness and unhappiness as the rest of us—and the Ayalas, like the Browns, will forever after think that ethicists are jerks. If terrible consequences transpire, then of course it might turn out that they were wrong. But in their particular circumstances, I do not see how they could have been wrong to weigh their daughter's life more heavily than the philosophers' vague fears.

Postscript

The preceding was written in 1990, after the birth of Marissa but before the transplant was performed. The transplant was successful, and five years later Anissa was in remission, working as a recruiter for the Costa Mesa Red Cross.

Notes

1. *New York Times,* 17 February 1990, sec. A, p. 1.
2. *Birmingham News,* 16 April 1990, sec. D, p. 4.
3. Gregory E. Pence, *Classic Cases in Medical Ethics* (New York: McGraw-Hill, 1990).

Index

About the Author

James Rachels is University Professor of Philosophy at the University of Alabama at Birmingham. He has also taught at New York University, the University of Miami, Duke University, and the University of Richmond. His other books include *The End of Life: Euthanasia and Morality* (1986), *The Elements of Moral Philosophy* (1986), and *Created from Animals: The Moral Implications of Darwinism* (1990).